Praise for this book

'The great value of this book comes from seeing aid as profoundly political, that is, the new poverty reduction consensus is not dismissed as pure rhetoric, nor endorsed as an unquestionable good, but instead analysed in terms of its actual impact and reconfiguration of domestic political arenas. Most revealingly perhaps, the book shows how partnerships can undermine democratic accountability, promoting a distinctively technocratic approach to development. For anyone seeking to understand the contemporary aid relationship, this is both crucial and exciting reading.'

– *Rita Abrahamsen, author of* Disciplining Democracy: Development Discourse and Good Governance in Africa

'A fascinating ground-level exploration of the current development mantras "civil society participation" and "country ownership". The case studies pull no punches in arguing that international institutions, including some international NGOs, have entrenched their places at the policy-making table and helped marginalize independent national civil society formations and indigenous institutions. The analysis shows the dangers of a new generation of one-size-fits-all thinking, but also the importance of national political circumstances in determining outcomes.'

– *Alex Wilks, Coordinator, European Network on Debt and Development*

About this book

Poverty Reduction Strategies (PRSs) are the new buzzwords in development aid. Some seventy developing countries have already elaborated them in response to the International Monetary Fund, the World Bank and bilateral aid agencies requiring them as a precondition for rolling over past debts or obtaining new assistance. While it may be premature to reach conclusions as to their economic and social impacts, the implications for local policy making and political processes, as this book explains, are already becoming clear. The authors of this study have conducted detailed, field-level research in three representative countries – one African (Tanzania), one Asian (Vietnam) and one Latin American (Honduras). They have studied the changing relations between the governments of these countries, donor agencies, and civic organizations (both local NGOs and Western private development agencies) that have participated in formulating the new generation of PRSs.

PRSs, as with the Structural Adjustment policies that they have ostensibly replaced, run up against, the authors conclude, a central paradox: in vesting decisive policymaking powers in external agencies, the very process of drawing up development strategies to prioritize reducing poverty can gravely undermine the consolidation of democratic forces, structures and ideas in developing countries. While the nuanced conclusions of these field studies show how variegated is the political terrain, and so the specific impacts of PRSs, in different countries, serious questions do arise about the long-term political consequences of this new generation of contemporary development practices.

Already the Tanzania study in this book has been discussed by the Development Assistance Committee (DAC) of the OECD countries, and at a very high level in the World Bank. The wider range of cases published for the first time in this book is likely to command attention in aid agency circles generally, and Development Studies as a field of study, and will be seen as critically relevant to Comparative Politics if the forces impacting on domestic political processes are to be properly understood.

JEREMY GOULD | editor

The new conditionality

The politics of poverty reduction strategies

Zed Books
LONDON | NEW YORK

The new conditionality: The politics of poverty reduction strategies, was first published by Zed Books Ltd, 7 Cynthia Street, London N1 9JF, UK and Room 400, 175 Fifth Avenue, New York, NY 10010, USA in 2005

www.zedbooks.co.uk

Cover designed by Andrew Corbett
Set in Arnhem and Futura Bold by Ewan Smith, London
Printed and bound in China

Distributed in the USA exclusively by Palgrave Macmillan, a division of St Martin's Press, LLC, 175 Fifth Avenue, New York, NY 10010.

A catalogue record for this book is available from the British Library.
US CIP data are available from the Library of Congress.

ISBN 1 84277 522 7 hb
ISBN 1 84277 523 5 pb

Contents

Figures, tables, box | vii Acronyms and abbreviations | viii Preface | x

1 Poverty, politics and states of partnership 1

JEREMY GOULD

The poverty reduction consensus | 1 Approach | 4 The pro-poor policy process as a political arena | 8 Case studies | 13

2 Tanzania: merging in the circle 17

JEREMY GOULD AND JULIA OJANEN

The state–donor partnership in Tanzania | 17 Changing political opportunities of non-state actors | 24 The Poverty Monitoring System: extending the partnership | 31 Discipline and empower: transnational actors and civil society | 38 Representative democracy and the politics of policy implementation | 52 Poverty reduction and democratic politics | 60

3 Vietnam: dealing with donors 66

IRENE NØRLUND, TRAN NGOC CA AND NGUYEN DINH TUYEN

Historical context | 68 The context of the CPRGS | 73 The process leading to the CPRGS | 84 Partner agendas | 96 Broader perspectives on the process | 101

4 Honduras: transforming the concessional state? 104

MAARIA SEPPÄNEN

Country context | 104 The organization of aid relationships | 109 The dynamics of civic activism in Honduras | 116 Political implications of the Honduran PRS process | 127

5 **Conclusion: the politics of consultation** 135

JEREMY GOULD

New conditionalities and state formation | 136 Strategic incentives in aid relations | 139 Crosscutting trends in post-developmental politics | 141 Political implications of the new conditionality | 146 A glimmer of sanity? | 149

Notes | 152 About the contributors | 161
Bibliography | 163 Index | 174

Figures, tables, box

Figures

1.1 The public policy arena 5
2.1 Model of CSO involvement in influencing national policy planning in Tanzania 41

Tables

1.1 Socio-economic indicators for the three case studies, 2003 13
2.1 Principles of aid harmonization in Tanzania 20
3.1 FDI inflows and ODA, Vietnam 74
3.2 Vietnam's external debt and debt service, 1998–2002 83
5.1 Indicators of aid dependence for Honduras, Tanzania and Vietnam 144

Box

2.1 PRSP Process in Tanzania 30

Acronyms and abbreviations

ADB	Asian Development Bank
ASONOG	Association of Non-governmental Organizations (Honduras)
BWIs	Bretton Woods Institutions
CABEI/BCAIE	Central American Bank of Economic Integration
CAS	Country Assistance Strategy
CBO	Community-based Organization
CCM	Chama Cha Mapinduzi (Tanzanian ruling party)
CDF	Comprehensive Development Framework
CG	Consultative Group
CPRGS	Comprehensive Poverty Reduction and Growth Strategy (Vietnam)
CSO	Civil Society Organization
DAC	Development Aid Committee (OECD)
DfID	Department for International Development (UK)
DSA	'Dissemination, Sensitization and Advocacy' (Poverty Monitoring System Technical Working Group, Tanzania)
ESAF	Enhanced Structural Adjustment Facility (IMF)
FAO	Food and Agriculture Organization (UN)
FDI	Foreign Direct Investment
FOSDEH	Foro social de la deuda externa de Honduras (Social Forum for Foreign Debt, Honduras)
GNI	Gross National Income
GoT	Government of Tanzania
GSO	General Statistical Office (Vietnam)
GTS	Grupo técnico de seguimiento (Technical Follow-up Group, Honduras)
GTZ	Deutsche Gesellschaft für Technische Zusammenarbeit (Germany)
HEPR	Nationally Targeted Programme for Hunger Eradication and Poverty Reduction (Vietnam)
HIPC	Highly Indebted Poor Countries
IDB	Inter-American Development Bank
IMF	International Monetary Fund
INGO	International Non-governmental Organization
I-PRSP	Interim Poverty Reduction Strategy

JBIC	Japan Bank for International Cooperation
JSA	Joint Staff Assessment (WB/IMF)
LERES	Centre for Legal Research and Services (Vietnam)
LGRP	Local Government Reform Programme (Tanzania)
LNGO	Local NGO
MoLISA	Ministry of Labour, Invalids and Social Affairs (Vietnam)
MPI	Ministry of Planning and Investment (Vietnam)
MTEF	Medium-term Expenditure Framework
NEC	National Executive Committee (CCM)
NGO	Non-governmental Organization
ODA	Official Development Aid
PACCOM	People's Aid Coordinating Committee (Vietnam)
PAR	Public Administration Reform (Vietnam)
PER	Public Expenditure Review
PMRT	Plan maestro de reconstrucción y transformación (Master Plan for Reconstruction and Transformation, Honduras)
PMS	Poverty Monitoring System
PPA	Participatory Poverty Assessment
PRBS	Poverty Reduction Budget Support
PRGF	Poverty Reduction and Growth Facility (IMF)
PRS	Poverty Reduction Strategy
PRSC	Poverty Reduction Support Credit (WB)
PRSP	Poverty Reduction Strategy Paper
PTF	Poverty Task Force (Vietnam)
PWG	Poverty Working Group
R&A	'Research and Analysis' (Poverty Monitoring System Technical Working Group, Tanzania)
SAP	Structural Adjustment Programme
Sida	Swedish International Development Agency
SOE	State-owned Enterprise
SWG	Sector Working Group
TCDD	Tanzania Coalition of Debt and Development
TPAA	Transnational Private Aid Agency
UNDP	United Nations Development Programme
URT	United Republic of Tanzania
VHLSS	Vietnam Household Living Standard Survey
VPO	Vice President's Office (Tanzania)
WB	World Bank
WTO	World Trade Organization

Preface

This book's original impetus came, somewhat improbably, from a commissioned evaluation of the United Nations Development Programme's work in Tanzania. United Nations country programmes must be reviewed every five years, and in 2001 I was asked to take part in an assessment of the UNDP's achievements in Tanzania since 1997. At the outset I knew only a little about Tanzania, much less about the UNDP, but in the course of thirty days of meetings and interviews in Dar es Salaam and Mwanza our team experienced an epiphany of sorts concerning radical changes underway in the world of development aid. We learned among other things how, during the previous five years, the United Nations' important role as a countervailing force to the neo-liberal dictates of the Bretton Woods institutions (the IMF and the World Bank) had evaporated. The UN – in which poor, indebted states like Tanzania have statutory representation on a vote per country basis – had been marginalized along with its development agency, the UNDP, while the World Bank and the IMF – over which Tanzania had virtually no influence – had acceded to a position from which they could dictate the parameters of domestic development policy.

A number of factors have contributed to the demise of the United Nations system as an alternative source of development funding and policy advice. Foremost among these is the failure of the United States to make good its financial commitments to the UN. By the time of our country review mission in Tanzania, the UNDP had ceased to be a funding agency and was subsequently reduced to 'facilitating' the 'harmonization' of donor activities in Tanzania; in effect, firming up the hegemonic role of the World Bank and the IMF in the realm of development policy and finance.

I am indebted to the staff of the UNDP's Tanzania country office, above all to Sally Fegan-Wyles, Inyang Ebong-Harstrup and Arthur van Diesen, for their candour and patience in instructing us about the realities of aid in the new millennium. Our many discussions opened my eyes to, among other things, the importance of the Highly Indebted Poor Countries (HIPC) debt relief initiative and the concomitant Poverty

Reduction Strategy Paper (PRSP) formulation process in reconfiguring the relationship between recipient governments and donors.

I left Tanzania wondering whether the configurations of power I had observed there were occurring in other places in a similar fashion. This curiosity begat a proposal for a comparative study of how poverty reduction strategies were being formulated in six indebted countries around the world. Eventually, the governments of Finland and Sweden provided funding to carry out fieldwork in Honduras, Tanzania and Malawi for the case studies included here. Special thanks are due Reeta Alanko and Timo Voipio of the Finnish Foreign Ministry, as well as Karl-Anders Larsson, James Donovan and Helene Bjuremalm of the Swedish International Development Authority. We are especially grateful to these agencies for providing not only financial resources, but also full autonomy to pursue the research on our own terms.

Researchers from the Ch. Michelsen Institute (Bergen) participated in the original research project with studies on Malawi (by Arne Tostensen and Maxton Tsoka) and Zambia (by Edgar Bwalya, Lise Rakner and Lars Svåsand). Their report can be consulted at <www.cmi.no/publications/>. Their critical comments on the study framework and interpretation of the data were very helpful in polishing our analyses. Discussions with David Booth of the Overseas Development Institute (London) in the formative stages of the study were also of great benefit. Needless to say, none of our colleagues at UNDP, the Finnish Foreign Ministry, Sida, CMI or ODI is in any way responsible for the conclusions and interpretations elaborated in the ensuing chapters.

A great many people were generous with their time and knowledge in the course of writing this book. Many of them are acknowledged in connection with the individual case studies. More than anyone, Julia Ojanen must be singled out for her decisive contribution to this book as telepathic co-author, incisive reader, penetrating critic and keeper of the faith.

Jeremy Gould
Lusaka and Helsinki

1 | Poverty, politics and states of partnership

JEREMY GOULD

The poverty reduction consensus

Looking back on the final decade of the twentieth century, it is evident that many highly indebted post-colonial nations of the South have entered a new phase of state formation. This new phase is signalled by a reconfiguration of the social forces commanding action in the name of the state, by changes in the means available to states for regulating citizens and markets, as well as by shifts in the political culture of governing. The main impetus for these shifts undoubtedly comes from changes in the way post-colonial Southern states are subsumed by regional and global economic structures. At the same time, changes in external links have also had transformative implications for social relations of governance within post-colonial societies – for the relationships between rulers and ruled that define the nature of 'stateness' at any given moment.[1]

This volume documents and explores emerging forms of post-colonial stateness by interrogating a pivotal instance of the ways external and domestic political processes intersect. The example at hand is the 'poverty reduction consensus' – a campaign of the self-styled 'international donor community' to transform relationships between creditor agencies and debtor governments of the South. What were, until recently, uneasy modes of bondage based on harshly imposed borrowing conditions are now portrayed as 'partnerships' based on mutuality and trust. Such a transformation implies significant changes in the procedures and modalities of aid, and in the relationships between the actors involved in the negotiation and disbursement of foreign grants and credits. Most of all, it implies a leap of faith, a reconsideration of the way people think and talk about aid and the social relations that the deployment of aid engenders.

The essays in this volume proceed from the premise that such transformations are indeed taking place, and that they are likely to have important implications for the way politics is played out. The mainstream view within the aid industry is to celebrate the new partnership modality as a revolutionary breakthrough in the global development effort. The authors of this volume take a more introspective view. Our aim is to map out the implications of the new aid modalities for the configuration of domestic political domains and, consequently, for the way the state is being reconstituted. In operational terms, this study looks at how the formulation of Poverty Reduction Strategy Papers (PRSPs) – a new form of 'processual' conditionality built into the 'partnership' concept – has affected relations between creditor, state and civic (non-state) actors.

The formulation of a PRSP is a condition for eligibility for debt relief under the Highly Indebted Poor Countries (HIPC) programme initiated by the Bretton Woods institutions (the World Bank and the International Monetary Fund – henceforth the BWIs).[2] As formulated by the BWIs (e.g. IMF 2004), PRSP processes are to be

- country-driven, involving broad-based participation
- results-oriented and focused on outcomes that benefit the poor
- comprehensive in recognizing the multidimensional nature of poverty and in the proposed policy response
- partnership-oriented involving coordinated participation of development partners
- Based on a long-term perspective for poverty reduction

Completing a PRSP has become fashionable whether or not a country is eligible for HIPC debt relief (Vietnam, for example, is not). It signals the client state's readiness to enter into a partnership with the BWIs and thus qualify for concessional lending in the future. Under the terms of these partnerships, the donor community promises governments not only cheap credits, but also greater 'ownership' of social policies. For elected leaderships, often struggling with contracting public economies, the increased leeway for political manoeuvre that the (partial) relief of foreign debt and/or concessional financing can provide is an important incentive. In return, recipient governments are required to commit themselves to a multi-tethered programme of state reform.

The core of the reform agenda comprises a radical renovation of the mechanics of public financial management. Among pivotal components, recipient governments must, first, tie their budgets to a

Medium-term Expenditure Framework (MTEF) that conforms to criteria defined by the IMF; second, public accounts are to be available for routine audits by donor representatives under the auspices of a Public Expenditure Review (PER); and third, the bulk of budget expenditures must be targeted to the over-riding goal of poverty reduction as defined in a Poverty Reduction Strategy (PRS) endorsed by the boards of both the World Bank (WB) and the International Monetary Fund (IMF). Since the early 1990s, the focus of the World Bank's policy-based lending has expanded strongly towards the social sectors and public sector reform.[3] Underpinning these arrangements is not only the promise of debt relief, but also the eventuality of accessing new credits under the Poverty Reduction and Growth Facility (PRGF) of the IMF – successor to the now-defunct Enhanced Structural Adjustment Facility – or the World Bank's parallel Poverty Reduction Support Credits (PRSCs). While these loans have new names, their key macro-economic policy conditionalities remain intact; the policy prescription has not been adjusted to suit the overall goals of poverty reduction.

By September 2003, PRSPs had been endorsed by the boards of the BWIs in fifty-four countries, and many more were still in the pipeline.[4] The donor community's global campaign to recast post-colonial governance through the HIPC/PRSP initiative has confronted very different social, economic and political contexts. Like the preceeding BWI policy formula, the Structural Adjustment Programmes (SAPs), the PRS approach seems to be a one-size-fits-all recipe. Yet, there is broad agreement among scholars concerning the 'overwhelming importance of context' for the outcomes of a poverty reduction strategy (Piron and Evans 2004: 34). Following this line of thought, a central aim of the present study is to document how the standard partnership template has been 'localized' in very diverse conditions, and to understand better the different kinds of social relations of governance that emerge from the confrontation between the 'new conditionalities' and local politics.

At the same time, the study is equally concerned with deepening the understanding of the contours of the global donor initiative, to comprehend what social forces and interests underpin the shift in strategy from Structural Adjustment to Pro-Poverty Partnerships. One cannot be so naïve as to accept the players' own explanations about the need for 'partnership' at face value. Obviously, the policies of the

BWIs are not hermetically isolated from the foreign policy concerns of the powerful transnational players – above all the United States, Europe and Japan – that control their decisions. Neither, on the other hand, need one be so cynical as to believe that the current rhetorical commitment to humanitarian goals, such as halving abject poverty by 2015, is simply a smokescreen to conceal the aims of a sinister fraternity of neo-imperialist powers. Reality lies, no doubt, somewhere between naïveté and cynicism, and to capture the truth requires both care and transparency in devising the analytical tools needed to dissect the empirical evidence.

Approach

Given the complexity of a comparative analysis such as this, considerable attention must be paid to methodological issues. Such issues fall into two broad categories. One concerns the theorization of the empirical field in which the various players interact and where the social relations of governance are forged, maintained and contested. The other relates to the concepts and analytical strategy which would allow for accurate description and understanding of the processes at hand.

The empirical field The three case studies presented below employed a common approach. This was necessary to ensure the comparability of individual case findings, but also because there were no ready-made methodologies to fall back on in the study of how lending conditionalities affect the social relations of governance in post-colonial contexts. Conceptual tools and analytical strategies needed to be worked out before data collection could proceed. The nature of the research design arrived at was predicated on the importance of grounding analysis in first-hand empirical material as far as possible. It was felt that too much of what Moore (2001) has termed 'authoritative knowledge' about PRS processes was based on second-hand accounts recycled from one 'rapid assessment' to the next. It was decided from the outset to privilege first-hand accounts whenever possible.

Research teams focused on mapping the interaction of players in the political space created by what might be termed the 'consultative imperative'. That is, we studied as concretely as possible the factors affecting the opportunities of players to improve their leverage on

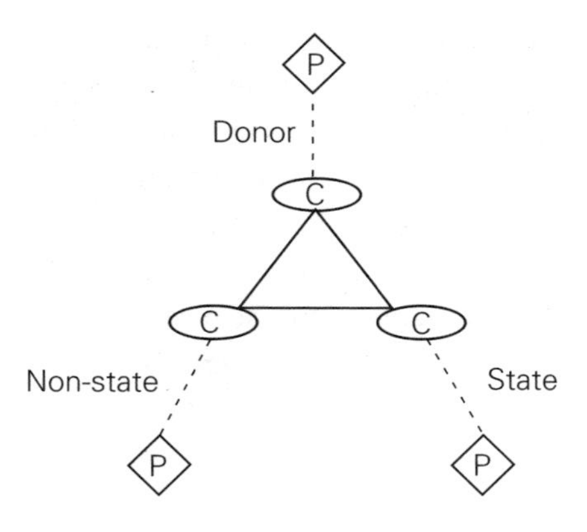

FIGURE 1.1 The public policy arena

public policy as a result of the requirement that the PRS be formulated 'in consultation with key stakeholders'. A notion of *the public policy process* was thus the pivotal element in our empirical orientation. PRSPs are outcomes of public policy processes, and are formulated in what political anthropologists have long termed an *arena* or *field* defined by a constellation of influential players (e.g. Swartz 1968). Their relations with one another – of alliance, disregard or overt competition – constitute the social relations of governance through which struggles over influence and outcomes are played out. The constellation of players in this field might be visualized with the aid of the 'molecule' sketched in Figure 1.1.

The figure depicts three groups, or sectors, of actors relevant to the public policy process: donors, the state and non-state actors. Within each sector is a group of 'core' actors (represented by the ovals marked 'C') in direct control of policy formulation. A hypothetical coalition of these core players is situated in the centre of the molecule. Other players within each sector have less leverage on policy formulation. These more peripheral players are portrayed by the rectangles marked 'P'.

Historically, post-colonial policy elites have derived their power from an exclusive, dyadic link between state and donors. Preliminary analysis suggested that PRS processes should be seen in terms of an 'iron triangle'. The notion of an 'iron triangle', the configuration of players at the core of the 'molecule', is often used in policy studies to characterize a coalition of public and private interests that has captured or dominates a policy process. Empirical analyses of iron triangles identify groupings of politicians, bureaucrats and private actors (e.g. business or civic lobbies) whose coordinated action blocks or advances a specific policy agenda.[5] Undeniably, this image of a state/donor/civil society coalition corresponds closely to the observable congregation of actors around the formulation of Poverty Reduction Strategies. These are precisely the players that populate the pivotal sites of the PRS policy process: consultative workshops, inter-agency task forces, thematic committees, participatory poverty assessment teams and so on.

On the basis of this conceptualization, the following issues attracted our interest:

1. *Reconfiguration of relations between core players.* Did any new actors gain access to the policy elite and thus increase their policy leverage? Were any traditional players excluded? How did the presumed incorporation of non-state actors affect the dynamic of the iron triangle, and the relationship between the donors and the state?
2. *Changing relations among actors within the three sectors.* How did the consolidation of a core triangle of actors affect relations between core and periphery? Of particular interest was the relationship between 'core' actors in the non-state sector and those not included in the process.
3. *Empowerment v. marginalization of policy ideas and agendas.* Which development concepts and goals gained currency as the new coalition of core players emerged?

Conceptualizing 'partnership'

> **partnership** 1. The fact or condition of being a partner; association or participation. Now esp. of relationships in industry and politics: [...] **1933** *Planning 25 Apr. 2* It aims at giving labour effective *partnership* in industry and at creating a new attitude of mind to replace sterile hostilities; **1941** *Ann. Reg. 1940 140* The attainment by India of free and equal *partnership* in the British Commonwealth; **1959** *Times Lit. Suppl. 31 July 449/2* It has been a cardinal principle in Rhodesia that the way should be open not for *apartheid* but for *partnership*, and that the new State will avoid the racial impasse of the Union [of South Africa].[6]

The new poverty reduction partnerships are based on consensus and the idea of mutual interest among state and donor actors. The partnership idea is far from new, nor is it politically neutral. Indeed, the above citations provide historical evidence that 'partnership' is commonly invoked when the more powerful party to an asymmetrical relationship feels threatened by impending hostilities and confrontation.

Under the emerging partnership modality of aid management, the administration of public finances is based on intimate working relations between donor and government technocrats on a day-to-day basis, and on a diverse array of institutional arrangements (task forces, working groups, ad hoc committees, workshops) through which state and donor actors allegedly share responsibility for policy choices and the analysis of their implications. A new, and we will argue, definitive feature of the emerging partnerships is an attempt to draw a select class of 'constructive' non-state actors – policy advocates and self-styled representatives of 'the poor'– into the circle of consensus and intimacy which cements the partnership.

By defining the reduction of poverty as the over-riding normative framework for all public policy and expenditure, and by seeking to extend the policy consensus to include 'civil society', the push for state–donor partnership reveals itself as neo-liberalism reconstituted in a populist mode – 'structural adjustment in the name of the poor' (to cite Malaluan and Guttal 2002). At the rhetorical level, poverty reduction strategies identify growth as a primary objective; at the level of regulatory instruments and budgetary allocations, these frameworks translate almost exclusively into expanded social sector spending. This in turn necessitates substantial new lending from international financial agencies – lending based on strict macro-economic policy conditionalities.

The populist element is unmistakably evident in the political mechanisms prescribed to enhance the legitimacy of the new partnerships. The cornerstone of the populist strategy is the accentuated emphasis on a vaguely defined and amorphous notion of 'the poor' as the primary source of political legitimation – 'adjustment with a human mask' to quote the prescient phrase coined by UNRISD in 1990 (Thérien 2002: 250). In practice, it means extending membership within the iron triangle to select members of middle-class professionalized groups (largely national and transnational private agencies). The consultative imperative that has been one of the criteria for a Bretton Woods assessment of any PRS is thus a hallmark of the emerging trend towards *populist neo-liberalism*.

Weyland's (1999) comparison of Latin America with Eastern Europe in the 1990s identifies a number of points of commonality between neo-liberal and populist politics. Both neo-liberals and populists tend to be hostile to the institutions of constitutional democracy; both act in a political universe populated by self-interested individuals rather than organized, corporate groups. Both populists and neo-liberals tend to fuse their alliance at the apex of the state apparatus. Both perceive prolonged economic crisis as an opportunity to consolidate power.

These features also pertain to emerging partnerships between heavily indebted client states and their external financial patrons. One important caveat must be noted, however. Where Weyland, for instance, locates affinities between the neo-liberal and populist agendas exclusively in the domestic political arena, the populist neo-liberalism invoked here clearly transcends national boundaries and must be seen as a reflection of transnationalized political structures. Hence, the populism that characterizes the donor–state partnership in Tanzania, for example, does not primarily refer to the means by which President Mkapa and his ruling CCM party seek to legitimize their electoral mandate. Rather, populist neo-liberalism describes above all the rhetoric and measures through which transnational actors evoke the interests of 'the poor' to legitimize their penetration of domestic political arenas.[7]

The pro-poor policy process as a political arena

Externally promoted demands for public consultation and civic empowerment translate, variously, into both mechanisms of increased control *and* expanded degrees of political freedom for different sets of actors. How the new conditionalities of consultation, ownership and partnership affect different groups is contingent on two parallel trends associated with (and catalysed by) the PRS policy process. These trends might be labelled the *depolitization of governance* and the *transnationalization of political space*. In concert, these trends work to consolidate the hegemony of creditor interests in the development policy arena. Unlike the aggressive modalities of SAPs, this hegemony is established under current conventions of 'post-conditionality' (Harrison 2001), less directly, via a rhetoric of mutual gain and through the decay of mechanisms of democratic accountability. The result is deepening control exercised by a delocalized class of transnational functionaries over the political space where public resource allocation decisions are made. In the longer term – to paraphrase Callaghy's (2001: 144) kindred analysis of debt relief in Uganda – the most significant consequences of the donor-imposed imperative for 'consultation' and 'civic participation' in public policy may not relate to poverty reduction at all, but to 'the new configurations of power and transboundary formations that it has helped to unleash'.

Policy coalitions The image of an iron triangle employed here captures the exclusive, interdependent character of the politics of pro-poor policy formulation, but it offers little to help understand the complex dynamics and tensions *within* the configuration. The geometrical trope of a triangle confines the configuration of actors to a two-dimensional plane of inclusion/exclusion that obscures, among other things, the dynamic relationship between public/private, on the one hand, and domestic/international on the other. One needs to ask to what extent does it make sense to think about a development partnership in the context of a nationally bounded, domestic policy process?

Graham Harrison's recent analysis of 'post-conditionality' policy processes in Tanzania challenges the view of a policy process as a discretely bounded domestic arena. According to Harrison (2001: 661, 669), 'the national–international boundary has been rendered so ... porous by a historically embedded "mutual assimilation" of donor and state power' that 'rather than conceptualizing donor power as a strong external force on the state, it would be more useful to conceive of donors as *part of the state itself*'.

Harrison's empirical observations concur with recent attempts to theorize the systematic incursion of external actors in domestic political processes. In the African context, again, Robert Latham's attempts to formulate generic concepts for characterizing the transnationalization of political space seem pertinent. Latham calls attention to the widespread 'transterritorial deployment' by external actors of more or less permanent 'installations' within domestic political space in Africa – embassies, multilateral missions, branches of transnational agencies and multinational enterprises, and so on (Latham 2001: 75 et seq.). The growing assertiveness of external actors in local political arenas through the agency of their transnational networks results in new hybrid forms of 'global/local linkages', and in a blurring of the boundaries between the internal and the external in political space, as Harrison suggests. Latham (2001) refers to such a political configuration as a 'transboundary formation'. He suggests that the ways in which such formations emerge – the dynamics of the interaction of domestic and transnational actors in national political arenas – is of increasing relevance for understanding the constitution of order and authority in the post-colonial world.[8]

A post-conditionality policy regime is reflected not only in aid discourse, but also in the aid business itself. The World Bank, along with the rest of the donor community, maintains that the failures of the past 'one-size-fits-all' policy prescription have been acknowledged, and that the old model has now been replaced with a country-tailored, locally-owned and participatory approach that customizes policies to fit local circumstances. The Bank even claims to have abandoned the rigid blueprints and stringent policy conditionalities of the structural adjustment framework: the number of macro-economic conditionalities on loans has been reduced by 40 per cent on average. This is because the Washington consensus policy package has been internalized to a very high degree in client countries' policy-making processes. Hence, there is little need for the kind of interventionist micro-management of economic policies that the BWIs routinely exercised into the 1990s. After some two decades of structural adjustment across the African continent, the Bank now affords a degree of flexibility in macro-economic policy while shifting its disciplinary attentions to new policy areas with a large potential for new lending: the social sector and state (governance) reforms.[9]

In practice, this change of approach relies on the Bank's intimate involvement in the management of state governance. While loan conditionalities have not changed in their essence, their adoption has become more subtle. The Bank is now enforcing them through advice and capacity-building rather than by external supervision. A system of audits, benchmarks, track records and Joint Staff Assessments (JSAs) have been put in place to inform loan decisions. The Bank is thus moving from ex-ante blueprints into a more nuanced ex-post assessment with adaptable 'triggers'. The idea is to create more competition for aid between developing countries by promising to reward 'good performers'. As a result of much traumatic experience, reinforced by training programmes financed by the BWIs, African civil servants in ministries of finance are well exercised in 'guessing what Washington wants'.

These arguments transect the recent work of Philip Cerny who argues on a general theoretical level for the need to see national policy arenas as subordinate to the interests of both private and public transnational actors. In Cerny's view, policy decisions are increasingly made within 'a complex, uneven and asymmetric set of multilayered cross-cutting processes and nodes of interaction'. The multilayeredness of policy arenas leads Cerny to embellish the concept of the iron triangle, supplanting it with the notion of a 'golden pentangle'. In addition to the conventional triangle of private, bureaucratic and political actors, Cerny identifies a coalition that encompasses two additional sets of transnational players: multilateral governance institutions (World Bank, IMF, WTO, etc.) and 'cross-border non-governmental structures and actors, from transnational markets to civil society' (Cerny 2001: 4). Cerny would have us see domestic policy processes as embedded in a

> transnational rearticulation of social and political coalitions, as actors attempt to cope with and control the implications of globalization. Sovereign national political structures have little intrinsic coherence in this model. On the contrary, the growing prevalence of transnational forces are seen to generate complex and fluid structures of governance that subsume domestic level policy processes ... and incorporate domestic actors into wider, cross-cutting arenas. (Cerny 2001: 4)

The structure of political opportunity In the history of the West, demands for public consultation and participation in policy processes have largely been championed by mass social movements representing the interests of domestic citizens. This is scarcely the case in much of the South. In all three countries discussed here, issue-based advocacy groups seldom transcend the social confines of a small, if visible, urban professional elite. Domestic political space is effectively colonized by a hegemonic political organization that controls the executive, legislative and, to a great extent, the judiciary branches of government. Organized forms of political opposition or citizen activism on the ground are negligible.

Thus the story of Poverty Reduction Strategies can be read as a tale about how the dynamics of an emergent transboundary formation affects social and political mobilization. The problem that arises is of a conceptual framework to deconstruct the complex articulations of the 'global' and the 'local' implicit in this formulation. The analysis of political opportunity structures offers a perspective on how various actors have been able to cash in on the political space opened up by the consultative imperative of the PRS (McAdam et al. 1996). In this connection, the notion of opportunity structure describes the range of factors that affect the relative success of various actors in promoting their respective agendas, as well as how they relate with one another (e.g. making alliances attractive or redundant) within the political space of public policy-making. Interventions or events such as the PRSP throw up new opportunities, reconfiguring relationships between actors within these spaces or bringing in new actors, and opening up the possibilities of a shift in direction (Grindle and Thomas, cited in Brock et al. 2002: 37).

These studies have employed a constructivist version of the opportunity structure concept. A constructivist perspective directs attention not only to the play of interests in the pursuit of agendas, but also to the iterative processes by which the interests (and self-awareness) of various actors are produced and negotiated as opportunity structures vary and alliances evolve and dissolve. A constructivist take on political opportunity theory has been developed to illuminate the political trajectories of issue-based social movements. Such an approach can suggest reasonable explanations concerning how specific policy coalitions impact on the formation of articulated demands for representation and accountability among the purported targets of public policy. It is especially germane to consider how changes in the political environment affect the strategic choices of the various players, as well as the way that individuals within corporate entities modify their aims and behaviour in response to rapidly transmuting opportunities.

Throughout the substantial sections of this book, the primary emphasis is on shifting alliances and coalitions within the policy arena. Continuities of creditor interests notwithstanding, the pro-poor partnership signals important shifts in the social relations of governance. Hence, the dynamics of the networks, alliances and competition among groups and individuals *within* these broad categories is of special interest. A central empirical concern is how the politics of 'partnership' affect relations among non-state actors (i.e. within 'civil society'), changing the relationships between groups that have been included in the partnership and those that have not.

In sum, the study seeks to address the following consequences of the consultative imperative: What social forces have advanced their capacity to exercise political initiatives? What political agendas have enjoyed an enhancement of their legitimacy? How have changes in political relations affected the accountability of those exercising power? What effects do pro-poor policy rhetoric and aid partnerships have on political selfhood? How do these events and processes affect the dialectic of domination and freedom implicit in the 'will to empower' driving demands for popular consultation and participation?

Case studies

Beyond the fact that the three countries analysed here are located in the main Southern regions (Asia, Africa, Latin America), they do not constitute a representative sample in any conventional sense. Indeed, the choice of cases was determined to some extent by the concerns of the agencies that funded our work. That said, the three country studies offer interesting contrasts and similarities that shed light on the range of contextual factors and experiences encountered when seeking to meet with donor demands for 'consultative' public policy formulation. The similarities and contrasts among the three case countries can be highlighted with respect to their size, external linkages and prevailing social relations of governance.

The three case countries differ, first of all, in respect to the size of their population, their territories and their economies. Tanzania, in East Africa, is a huge land mass of 35 million inhabitants; Honduras,

TABLE 1.1 Socio-economic indicators for the three case studies, 2003

	Honduras	Tanzania	Vietnam
Population (millions)[1]	7	35.2	80.5
Gross National Income (US $ billions)[1]	6.8	9.9	34.8
GNI/capita (US $)	970	280	430
Foreign aid/capita (US $)[2]	64.0	35.8	18.00
Human Development Index[3]	115	162	112

Sources: 1 World Bank on-line database at <www.worldbank.org/> 2 World Development Indicators (2003) 3 Human Development Report (UNDP 2004)

in Central America, is a postage stamp of a state, home to 7 million people. The long, narrow Southeast Asian dominion of Vietnam has only a fraction of Tanzania's land mass, but more than twice as many citizens. More importantly, for these purposes, Vietnam's Gross National Income (GNI) is more than three times that of Tanzania and nearly six times that of Honduras.

In per capita terms, Honduras's national income is more than twice the size of Vietnam's and the 'average' Honduran's monetary worth is nearly four times greater than that of an average Tanzanian. While there is a great deal of statistical poverty in all three countries, only in Tanzania do the majority live on less than a dollar a day. With per capita income nearing $1,000, Honduras can barely qualify as a poor nation. Although by some accounts (e.g. Piron and Evans 2004), a third of Vietnamese live in poverty, the country is rapidly joining the ranks of the Southeast Asian tiger economies.

The external linkages of the three countries also have a very varied history. Tanzania first entered the international community of sovereign nations in 1960 upon gaining independence from Great Britain. Vietnamese state institutions trace an unbroken lineage back a good thousand years, although Vietnam attained modern nationhood in its present form in 1954. Unlike Tanzania, which was 'created' as a state through colonial domination (first by Germany, then by Britain), Vietnam fell under colonial domination (first by China, and much later by France) as a full-fledged nation-state. In Honduras the colonial era ended in 1821, but the country transcended the economic status of 'banana republic' only in the latter part of the twentieth century. In other words, in so far as 'stateness' is a function of a government's external political relations (cf. Jackson and Rosberg 1982), each of these three countries represents a unique process of state formation.

The history and nature of their relationships to the international aid community also differ, albeit not so radically. Of the three, Honduras has most recently come under the tutelage of the aid cartel; most donors began operations in Honduras after the country was devasted by Hurricane Mitch in 1998. Vietnam has a longer relationship with donors; the support of some Nordic donor agencies (not to mention that of Russia and China) for Vietnam dates from the years of the 'American' war. But it was only after Vietnam demonstrated a more serious commitment to liberalizing its economy in the 1990s that the

BWIs and other major donors have begun issuing credits and grants. Tanzania, on the other hand, has been a major aid recipient almost since achieving nationhood, and its aid relationships have lived through a number of cycles of intimacy and rejection.

As one would suspect, the social relations of governance within each country also differ significantly. For all their many differences, Tanzania and Vietnam share the legacy of what Issa Shivji (1976) once termed a 'bureaucratic bourgeoisie' at the apex of political power. The economic bases of their entrenched technocracies are very different, but the main tasks of government in both countries have been exercised largely by professionalized civil servants with middle-class backgrounds and weak links to production. In both instances, the technocratic elite governs under the close supervision of a single ruling party, incorporating representatives from other social classes. In Honduras, the political class is organized within two competing political parties and has been more closely associated with the productive economy, albeit as a 'comprador' class subservient to external economic interests.

Forms of clientelism link the rulers and the ruled in all three countries. In Tanzania and Vietnam, client–patron relations have been more or less coterminous with the structures of the entrenched ruling parties. In Honduras, clientelism has worked through more 'feudal' arrangements by which the propertied classes have brokered support for political aspirants on behalf of rural voters residing on or around their holdings. The introduction of aid-backed non-governmental organizations as a new stratum of service providers among the rural poor, taking over some of the newly privatized functions of the state, has reshuffled brokerage relations in all three countries.

Finally, political culture is also a relevant variable for assessing the way the consultative imperative of PRS processes has affected the social relations of governance. The rhetoric of poverty reduction can resonate strongly in polities with a strong (rhetorical) commitment to values of social equity. This is true of both Vietnam and Tanzania, but not particularly so for Honduras. A passionate attachment to nationalist ideals and to the value of sovereign government (independent of external manipulation), on the other hand, can counsel reserve and suspicion in the face of too eager offers of 'partnership' with powerful external actors. Of the three countries under scrutiny here, Vietnam and Honduras seem to have been most resistant to the embrace of donors' policy partnership, while Tanzania has offered little opposition. Vietnam, while a zealous defender of national sovereignty, has demonstrated a very selective openness to the allures of partnership (and the lucrative investments it implies).

This cursory analysis does not exhaust the range of similarities and contrasts between the three cases. It does, however, underscore the fruitfulness of cross-country comparative analysis for fleshing out tensions associated with the imposition of a new bundle of populist neo-liberal aid conditionalities upon a diverse range of post-colonial states. The detailed analyses of the politics of poverty reduction in three such countries will, it is hoped, stimulate thoughts about the role that aid and aid modalities play in the perpetuation of global inequality.

2 | Tanzania: merging in the circle

JEREMY GOULD AND JULIA OJANEN

The state–donor partnership in Tanzania

In 1994, there was a virtual breakdown of relations between the Tanzanian government and aid donors, leading to the discontinuation of aid disbursements. The immediate reason cited for the aid freeze was financial mismanagement (corruption and under-taxation). The diplomatic rupture and concomitant freeze in donor funding were the culmination of a long roller-coaster ride in Tanzania's aid relationship since the late 1970s. Aid flows ebbed in the early 1980s when Tanzania's economy hit rock bottom, and President Nyerere resisted the neo-liberal reform package advocated by the World Bank and the International Monetary Fund. The hesitant liberalization measures introduced by President Mwinyi from 1986 were welcomed warmly by the donors, and aid levels were raised in support of structural adjustment reforms. As the social costs of the reforms became evident, the government voiced reservations over the scope and tempo of macro-economic reforms, the break-up of state ownership of national assets and market liberalization (Gibbon 1998). Reform measures agreed upon in government–donor negotiations stalled in the implementation phase, and despite a good performance in the macro-economic indicators (relative to other African adjusters), Tanzania came under a Bretton Woods-led attack for reneging on its commitments (Helleiner et al. 1995).

The Nordic donors – whose collective economic and political stake in Tanzania was substantial – sponsored a fence-mending operation in 1995. The result was a report on 'Development Cooperation Issues Between Tanzania and Its Aid Donors' prepared by a 'group of independent advisors' chaired by the Canadian academic Gerald Helleiner.[1] The 1995 Helleiner Report questioned the validity (or reasonableness) of donor criticisms, placing a large share of blame for the government's half-heartedness in complying with conditionalities on 'donor procedures'. The report specifically assigned the bulk of the responsibility for undermining government commitment on the World

Bank, which was characterized as 'an institution encouraged by its superior manpower and other resources to be self-confident to the point of arrogance, with little consideration of others' views' (Helleiner et al. 1995: 13). The operational prescription was to pay serious attention to government ownership of reform programmes.

Between 1995 and 1998, the World Bank responded to these and other criticisms with a new aid management strategy. The Tanzania country office became a forerunner in the campaign spearheaded by newly instated Bank president James Wolfensohn to reinvent the Bank, or at least its public image. Tanzania's Country Director, hitherto based in Washington, was 'decentralized' to Dar es Salaam, allowing for the Bank to respond quickly to feedback and initiatives from the Tanzanian government, civic groups and other donors. The World Bank/Dar es Salaam office recruited economics professor Benno Ndulu (one of the 'five wise men' behind the 1995 Helleiner Report), as a deputy to the Country Director, thus providing the Bank with a Tanzanian face palatable to both government and donors. During this period, the multilateral donors made a concerted effort to encourage Tanzanian government efforts to formulate 'home-grown' policy documents such as Vision 2025, the National Poverty Eradication Strategy and the Tanzania Assistance Strategy.[2] An important symbol of the change in donor attitudes was the shift, in 1997, of the site of the strategic consultative group meeting between donors and the government from Paris to Dar es Salaam.

By 1998/9, the electrical charge of the government–donor relationship had reversed, and the rhetoric of partnership had replaced the confrontational language of the mid-1990s. According to President Mkapa (1999), there was a 'need for a broader development agenda that goes beyond macro-economic fundamentals to include issues of social justice, equity, participation, political and economic sustainability and inclusion'. Things were in place for Tanzania to enter the HIPC pipeline, and thus qualify for a new generation of aid conditionalities, marketed under the 'broader development agenda' of poverty reduction.

The politics of harmonization Not only were the donors introducing a new rhetoric of social development, as Mkapa indicates, they were also changing the way the aid business was organized – its basic modalities. Simplifying what is in reality a many-stranded process, it would appear that a key to understanding the new development partnership (and its associated modalities of aid delivery) is the 'multilateralization' of relations *within* the so-called donor community. At the core of this process are the 'new mechanisms and modes of operation ... being set up so as to strengthen linkages between the World Bank and IMF in the day to day planning and administration of their respective and joint programmes' (Mbilinyi 2001: 1). Through this convergence, claims Mbilinyi, the Bretton Woods institutions 'are asserting ever more power over micro-policy as well as macro-policy at national level' (ibid.). This influence is exercised directly on the Tanzanian government, but also indirectly, via other donor agencies, through the 'harmonization' of aid.

In retrospect it is evident that Helleiner's 1995 report signalled many of the things to come, underscoring Tanzania's role as a forerunner in and major laboratory for experimentation with new aid modalities. Helleiner found that a major reason why the aid relationship in Tanzania had deteriorated so dramatically was because of the immense 'transactions costs' to the Tanzanian government of accessing aid. Transactions costs were seen to be 'an excessively heavy burden on the scarce financial and managerial resources of countries such as Tanzania' (Helleiner et al. 1995: 19). Every donor had its own Country Assistance Strategy (CAS), its own accounting techniques and reporting format. The fiscal years adhered to by donors differed from that of Tanzania and also among themselves. Each donor needed to send a separate mission to plan, appraise, negotiate, monitor and evaluate each of the interventions in its aid portfolio. And each mission demanded audiences with key officials in the Treasury and in sector ministries. Government had little time for anything other than catering to donor procedures.[3]

Helleiner's linking of transaction costs to poor ownership (read: non-performance on macro-economic reforms) crystallized a line of thought that had been gestating among aid managers since the early 1990s. In 1998, the OECD's Development Assistance Committee (DAC)[4] issued a 'Working Checklist for Strengthening Development Partnership'. A central element of the OECD/DAC recommendations concerned finding means of moving 'toward the simplification and harmonization of [aid management] procedures'.

Issues of aid coordination and harmonization have become critical

TABLE 2.1 Principles of aid harmonization in Tanzania

Main areas of activity	Instruments	Principles/goals
Reflecting development assistance in the budget	Harmonization of reporting	The DAC target is to include all development assistance in the budget book for FY03 (submission deadline in April 2002). Exceptions would be IMF PRGF assistance (disbursed to central bank) and some assistance to NGOs and private sector.
Working more effectively at sector/thematic level	Sectoral programmes and basket funds; joint sector reviews	Joint missions should move to replace bilateral consultations (and not present an additional burden on government). The timing and format of reviews must complement key processes such as the PRS review, the PER and the budget exercise.
Linking sector/thematic and macro-work	Calendar of key annual processes	Ensure appropriate linkages of sectoral investments to PER/MTEF, PRSP and poverty monitoring system. The calendar can also be used by the PRBS group to structure deliberations on levels of budget support.
Monthly DAC meetings	Use DAC meetings actively to seek ways to promote harmonization, identify best practice and to ensure that work of respective members contributes to the key processes in Tanzania, in line with TAS.	The DAC should: (i) assimilate examples of best practice, identifying a methodology by which sector/thematic work can link to key processes; (ii) ensure that best practice is disseminated; (iii) address cross-sectoral issues more coherently; (iv) gauge consistency of DAC assistance with TAS and assess quality of inputs to key processes; and (v) ensure timely, comprehensive and coordinated inputs to the budget exercise, PRS review and other major processes.

Source: Adapted from 'Principles for Promoting Harmonisation and Aid Effectiveness (Draft Two)', prepared by Tanzania DAC Secretariat (20 March 2002). The principles are 'based on two local DAC meetings held on 7th and 20th February 2002 ... [and] represent a general framework to be implemented on a voluntary basis by development partners'.

reference points in negotiations among donors, and constitute a cornerstone of the new development partnership. These procedural issues are at the core of the new modalities of aid and represent the main means by which multilateralization is being accomplished. Witness two central 'Principles for Promoting Harmonization and Aid Effectiveness' (20 March 2002) agreed upon by the Tanzania/DAC:

> 1. The Poverty Reduction Strategy (PRS) is the dominant instrument and overarching objective for Government and development partners. Efficiently/effectively linking our work with PRS is the main rationale for harmonisation.
> 2. However framed (harmonisation, effectiveness, transaction costs) we must evaluate our performance in terms of facilitating Government delivery of the PRS outcomes.

On one level, harmonization is a positive response to recipient demands for lowering transaction costs. Experienced aid managers are sympathetic to the plight of the harried Tanzanian civil servant. Many realize that the tax on administrative capacity resulting from uncoordinated aid has become a bottleneck hampering their own performance. Growing credence given to once heretical claims that the policies of structural adjustment are a source of instability may have also inspired some managers to reflect more generally on ways in which aid and its procedures were a part of the problem, and not a solution. Harmonization could thus be seen as an expression of self-critical, post-structural adjustment good will.

Yet, invoking matters of conscience can hardly explain the multilateralization process adequately. It is important to keep in mind that the degrees of manoeuvre open to donor agencies in their mutual negotiations are constrained by certain relatively inflexible imperatives. Despite the relative autonomy with which many agencies appear to work, their directorates are held accountable to taxpayers via national parliaments or boards of directors.

The imperative of accountability encompasses both weaker and stronger elements. The weaker elements relate to political consistency and financial management. In political terms, agencies must be able to defend their disbursements on the basis of the official policies of their governments. The weakness of this mechanism is that the policy pronouncements are generally vague (restating the abstract goals of poverty reduction, market integration and good governance), and measurable indicators of policy success are seldom specified. In practice, few expenditures cannot be linked in some way to such equivocal policy goals.

Given the current obsession with good governance, issues of financial accountability should be viewed somewhat more stringently. Yet the daily gossip of donor communities is rife with accounts of how such and such an agency 'lost' so and so many millions due to recipient malfeasance. Such mishaps seldom lead to a suspension of disbursements but, when they do, normal relations are generally restored before long.

Such behaviour expresses a double standard in the way donor governments view issues of financial hygiene. Events that would spark a major scandal in the domestic arena are quickly papered over in the domain of foreign aid. A reasonable explanation for this is that a second, stronger imperative affecting donor strategy concerns volumes of disbursements. Parliaments will react forcefully if approved allocations are not disbursed, and aid managers live constantly under the threat of cuts in their operational budgets (and possibly in staff) if they fail to move the money entrusted to them. For the financial agencies proper, such as the World Bank and the IMF, disbursement is the ultimate imperative; for the individual functionary, career advancement is largely contingent on the speed at which disbursements are effected. At the core of 'disbursement anxiety' are basic concerns of institutional survival, translated into tangible incentives for staff, mission and agency performance.

Paradoxes of multilateralization One might surmise that multilateralization is contingent upon the extent to which it is compatible with the imperative to disburse. Harmonization is, indeed, the site of a power struggle among donors in which nationalist and moralist tendencies compete. The flag-wavers (USA, Japan, Germany) resist the initiatives of the harmonizers who claim to speak for a good greater than that of the strategic or commercial interests of national entities. Harmonizers (the EU, the Nordics, Holland, Canada) have yet to advance their positions relative to flag-wavers in the primary game of disbursements. They compete heatedly among themselves to occupy the moral high ground. The harmonizers can none the less expect that their self-discipline will be rewarded as the norms of multilateralism come to dominate the partnership. They have committed a part of their bilateral aid to direct budget support through the Poverty Reduction Budget Support (PRBS) facility, and strongly emphasize that the PRS priority sectors are now the basis of their bilateral support.

The long-term scenario of harmonization aims to tackle the problems of 'capacity' and/or 'governance' which threaten volumes of aid disbursement. Harmonization is seen as a solution in that uniform procedures – the consolidation of individual national decision-making and monitoring processes into a single multilateral transaction – would free up large amounts of recipient administrative capacity to use, as against merely negotiate, aid. Or, to cite the Tanzania/DAC:

> Harmonisation should be seen not as an end in itself, but as a means to accelerating implementation of the Government's poverty reduction programme. In a simple 'input–output' equation:
>
> $$\frac{\text{Impact of aid (promoting poverty reduction)}}{\text{Transaction costs of delivering aid}} = \text{Development effectiveness}$$
>
> We can, therefore, promote harmonisation (and thereby increase development effectiveness) by becoming more *effective* – greater impact – and by becoming more *efficient* - lowering transaction costs.[5]

Aid managers also understand that future disbursements are threatened by unrecoverable debt. Multilateral coordination (the identification of mutual interests through the negotiation of procedural issues of harmonization) has been efficacious in putting HIPC in place quickly and in a way that did not imply dramatic concessions for the IFIs. The concrete achievement of mutual procedures around HIPC initiatives convinced many managers that it is in their long-term interests[6] to align themselves with the multilateralization agenda. These arrangements are now being further polished and institutionalized through the PRS.

The partnership between Tanzania and the donor community is increasingly justified – and consolidated – in line with the principles of multilateralism. There is little doubt that the harmonization of aid disbursement practices reduces the transaction costs of aid. Yet there is a double irony here: first, that the Tanzanian government is drawn into the auspices of an iron triangle of multilateral interests with promises of greater national ownership; and second, that the rhetoric of multilateralism ensures that those players with the greatest capacity on the ground to participate in preparatory drafting committees, and so on, are able to define the 'collective' agenda. Today, as in 1995 when Helleiner first recorded his cryptic observations, these players are the World Bank and the IMF.

Building the pro-poor policy partnership on a foundation of multilateralism delimits the range of issues which potential new parties to the partnership can influence. As the political basis of the multilateral policy partnership is expanded to encompass representatives of 'civil society', these new entrants are finding that certain basic principles are non-negotiable. One such principle is the hegemony of creditor interests and the sanctity of the disbursement imperative; a second is the concentration of policy-formulation power in the hands of a transnational technocratic elite, schooled in the populist neo-liberal mindset.

This trend can arguably enhance the 'efficiency' of aid management and allow for donors to keep better track of their collective monies. But it may well be costly for Tanzania's political system, and may have damaging effects for the deepening of a genuinely participatory, democratic and pluralist culture of politics.

Changing political opportunities of non-state actors

A new aid partnership has gradually been consolidated among aid agencies and the Tanzanian government since 1997. This is reflected in the reconfiguration of players participating in public policy processes. A novel feature of the PRS is the extent to which a certain category of private, non-state actors have succeeded in legitimizing demands for inclusion in the direct exercise of decision-making power.[7] The extent of domestic private or civic influence on the PRS and subsequent policy decisions has been slight, and in terms of practical outcomes the donor–government axis (in overall conformity with Bretton Woods priorities) continues to dominate public policy-making (Evans and Ngalwea 2001; McGee et al. 2002; World Bank 2002b). Yet, the new conditionality of consultation, championed by the World Bank and others, has established a moral leverage point via which non-state actors – self-proclaimed representatives of 'civil society' – can justify their access to the epistemic community that frames public policy.[8]

Forms of public participation that began with an informal consultative group civil society shadow meeting in Dar es Salaam in 1997, and led to ad hoc non-state participation in the PRSP zonal and national workshops in 2000, are gradually becoming more firmly established. The main context for further routinization of direct non-state involvement in public policy processes is the Poverty Monitoring System (PMS). The shift in the opportunities of actors outside the narrow political elite to participate in policy formulation is hailed on several fronts as a major breakthrough in opening up policy processes to civic oversight. Political space has indeed opened up for private, non-state actors to promote their interests, or those of their constituencies. But having recognized this basic fact, it is necessary to ask which actors have capitalized on this opportunity and to consider the tangible consequences of their 'empowerment'.

Participation of non-state actors The formulation process of the PRS document reflects an ambivalence about the status of non-expert views. While the World Bank imposes the 'process conditionality' of consultations in the formulation of a PRSP, it does not actually require that contributions made in this process would be taken into account in policy-making. After the Bretton Woods institutions indicated, in September 1999, that Tanzania would be eligible for debt relief under the HIPC initiative, two governmental bodies were established to manage the process of fulfilling the creditors' conditions. These were an Inter-Ministerial Committee and a Technical Committee of key civil servants. The immediate task of the Technical Committee was to draft an Interim Poverty Reduction Strategy Paper. In order for Tanzania to reach the PRSP 'Decision Point' for inclusion in the enhanced HIPC initiative, the I-PRSP needed to be endorsed by the boards of the Bank and the Fund. In addition to preparing an I-PRSP, reaching decision point required the government to sign a new three-year agreement with the IMF – a Poverty Reduction and Growth Facility – encompassing nearly three dozen non-negotiable conditions pertaining to the government's economic and fiscal policies.

No representatives of non-state actors or their organizations were invited to participate in either of the government's PRSP committees. In December 1999, however, 'a number of NGOs received letters individually from the chairperson of the Government Technical Committee on the PRSP' indicating 'the intention of the Government to involve NGOs in the process' (TASOET 2000: 2). The means of civic involvement were not stipulated in the letters. Recognizing both the opportunity for policy influence, and the risks of an uncoordinated response to the government's overture, some leading Tanzanian advocacy organizations formed a network to coordinate civic input into the PRS policy process.

At a workshop convened by Oxfam and the Tanzanian Coalition on Debt and Development (TCDD)[9] in January 2000, twenty-eight CSOs met to deliberate on how to respond to the government's offer of consultation. Some expressed the view that since the PRS was a conditionality imposed upon Tanzania by the World Bank and the IMF for HIPC debt relief, CSOs should remain 'outside' the process. The whole PRSP idea was considered 'foreign', since Tanzania had already formulated a National Poverty Eradication Strategy in 1997 and was at the time working together with the donor community to produce a Tanzania Assistance Strategy (interviews: TCDD; TASOET). This position remained in the minority. The majority felt that despite the dangers of being used to legitimize a Bretton Woods conditionality, the PRS process represented an 'open door' for engaging in policy dialogue with the government.

The workshop designated the TCDD/PRSP network as their 'focal point' for dialogue with government on the PRSP and established five sectoral committees which quickly produced a 'civil society input paper' that offered a commentary on the government's sketchy (five pages plus annexes) Interim PRSP document. Where the intellectual basis of the I-PRSP is extremely lean, the TCDD/PRSP contribution expounds at length on the 'conceptual framework of poverty and development' (TCDD 2000: 3–7). The TCDD/PRSP argues that the government's poverty reduction strategy should be founded on a

> holistic vision of people-centred, poverty-free development, based on full and equal access to food and nutrition for all; to education, health, water and other basic services; to sustainable livelihoods and incomes, and to the resources necessary to achieve the same; control over key resources; good governance and full participation in policy-making, implementation and monitoring; and strengthening of sustainability and self-reliance from the grassroots to the national to the global level. (ICDD 2000: 7)

The TCDD/PRSP document takes the structural roots of poverty as its point of departure and proceeds to assign a substantial share of the blame for Tanzania's dismal economic performance and its massive debt burden on the 'structure of the global economy' as well as on the 'creditor community'. A central thrust of the critique revolves round the undemocratic nature of development financing and the unsustainability of debt relief. The TCDD/PRSP position advocates making 'decision-making for loans and grants ... as participatory and transparent as possible' (ibid., p. 11) and rejects the established neo-liberal macro-policy measures. The document calls, among other things, for 'support systems ... to protect the livelihoods of smallholder farmers, livestock-keepers and small business people, including subsidies for farm inputs and progressive tax systems'. Domestic industry also 'needs to be protected, and economic development oriented to regional and domestic markets as much as the global market' (ibid.).

The message from the organizations participating in the TCDD/PRSP network to the government was clear: the 'home-grown' TAS constituted the valid policy framework to which the creditor community's PRS exercise is to be subordinated. The government should resist the pressures of external financers – whose previous poor advice and bad credits are a major cause of prevailing levels of poverty – and revive what might be termed a Nyerereist (Feza Lwaitama 2002) ethos of 'grassroots self-reliance'. In so doing, the advocacy groups presume to speak for the mass of primary producers – the workers, cultivators and livestock keepers – whose livelihoods have been undermined by neo-liberal structural adjustment programmes.

At root, the TCDD/PRSP document represents a nationalist response to the perceived threats of the mode of globalization championed by the transnational creditor community. The authors position themselves firmly in support of private local business and a domestically controlled industrial sector. This view is informed by the authors' 'prioritisation of increased employment as a cornerstone of economic restructuring and poverty reduction strategies' (TCDD 2000: 13).[10] The I-PRSP, in contrast, speaks euphemistically of 'higher growth', and of an improved environment for 'robust private sector development' in order to 'enhance private investment and lower the cost of doing business' (§4, 8), yet offers no concrete measures for stimulating domestic industry. The only direct reference to employment in the I-PRSP celebrates the *reduction* of state employment by 87,000 workers as part of the on-going civil service reform (Annex II, §4a).

The drafters of the official PRSP document patently ignored the TCDD/PRSP input. It is not mentioned as an element in the consultations feeding into the formulation of the PRSP. Critical views of national(ist) advocacy groups were buried under a blanket of silence.[11] Instead, the official draft of the PRSP festively cites the input of 'the poor' via seven zonal workshops as a major source of inspiration for the government's Poverty Reduction Strategy. For this round, the advocacy groups' aim of gaining access to the iron triangle of development policy formulation was singularly unsuccessful.

Zonal workshops Initially, unspecified government officials proposed that the Tanzanian Coalition on Debt and Development coordinate the zonal workshops. This arrangement with TCDD was later overturned, and invitations to the workshops went out via regional authorities (interviews: TCDD, Oxfam, UNDP). A total of 804 Tanzanians participated in seven zonal workshops. According to the official report, workshop participants comprised, in the aggregate, villagers (53 per cent), councillors and other elected representatives (27 per cent), district executive directors (14 per cent) and NGOs (7 per cent). The national policy advocacy groups withdrew from the consultations following the sidelining of TCDD, and there is no record of their participation in zonal workshop deliberations.

All in all, it is difficult to accede to the claim of the Bretton Woods' Joint Staff Assessment that the PRSP formulation would have been 'characterised by ... the broad-based participation of civil society' (JSA 2000, cited in Evans and Ngalwea 2001: 10). The consultations involved a minuscule number of participants who expressed a desire for improved economic infrastructure and better social services.[12] According to one external assessment, the consultations were 'hastily prepared' and 'rushed', and were heavily criticized by civic organizations as 'opportunistic and tokenistic' (Evans and Ngalwea 2001: ch. 9, v, vi, 10).

It is evident that the culture of state–society interaction evoked by the 'workshopping' mode of consultation employed by the government (interview, I. Shivji, 2002: University of Dar es Salaam) encouraged the articulation of what Judith Tendler (2000) has termed 'micro-ized and projectized' demands. There is no indication that workshop participants would have expressed opinions about the government's fiscal policies and macro-economic framework, about aid relationships or public indebtedness, about international trade policy, or about any other aspect of the nation's long-term development strategy. Nor were they asked to. One suggestion is cited (out of a total of 230 recorded recommendations), according to which the government should 'provide [a] conducive environment for agro-processing industries to be revived or established' (Tendler 2000: 70). Crucial economic issues, such as the need to promote employment by enhancing industrial development and inter-sectoral linkages, were passed over in silence.

A supplementary National Consultative Workshop was organized in Dar es Salaam in August 2000 to discuss the first draft of the final PRS document. This workshop initiated a wide-ranging policy discussion and was attended by 209 participants representing the civil service and the donor community as well as 'NGOs and the private sector'. The key analytical submission highlighted the necessity of stimulating 'export-led growth in the rural areas' (URT 2001a: 34). A representative of TCDD cautioned participants about the need to 'critically examine new loans', and a number of participants called for a clearer link between poverty reduction and employment creation, industrial development and international trade. The main focus of the deliberations was, however, poverty reduction as a function of social service provision and infrastructure development.

The 'full' PRSP In technical terms, the government's production of the PRSP was an impressive performance. The consultation and drafting processes kept strictly to the designated timetable (see Box 2.1). Of utmost political importance was the Bretton Woods endorsement of Tanzania's qualification for debt relief – reaching the HIPC Decision Point in March 2000. This entitled the government to a new tranche of IMF loans and allowed the government to take credit for hundreds of millions of dollars of new foreign assistance – a claim which the CCM government exploited immodestly in its campaign for the elections in October that year.[13] The final prize, Completion Point, was achieved in December 2000.

Reviewing the events and reading the document one is struck with how economically the Tanzanian government fulfilled the formal requirements for debt relief eligibility. The entire process from the establishment of the authoritative bodies responsible for managing the process (in November 1999), through the drafting of the Interim PRSP, the discussion of a draft PRSP at zonal workshops, a parliamentary briefing and a National Consultative Workshop and on to Cabinet approval took only nine months. Tanzania traversed the path from Decision Point to Completion Point in about the same length of time.

It is hard to avoid the impression that, from the point of view of the national leadership, the production of a PRSP was above all about accessing debt relief, 'another hoop to jump through', in the words of one senior civil servant. In any event, within the elected timeframe there was little opportunity for negotiation concerning substantive policy issues. Rather than being a 'participatory public policy-making process', the PRSP consultations in Tanzania were primarily about legitimizing

Box 2.1 PRSP Process in Tanzania

Nov. 1999	Formation of Inter-Ministerial Committee and Technical Committee
Feb. 2000	I-PRSP approved by Cabinet
March 2000	I-PRSP endorsed by IFIs; HIPC Decision Point; three-year PRGF loan granted by IMF; prospectus of final PRSP produced by Technical Committee
May 2000	Seven Zonal Workshops (simultaneously over two days)
June 2000	Cursory briefing in Parliament; draft final PRSP produced by Technical Committee; consultations with donors[14]
Aug. 2000	Consultations with Regional Administrative Secretaries; National Consultative Workshop
Sept. 2000	Final PRSP approved by Cabinet
Nov. 2000	Final PRSP endorsed by the IFIs; HIPC Completion Point; PRSP implementation began
March 2001	Seminar chaired by President and attended by regional and district leaders
June 2001	Seminar organized on environmental concerns in the PRSP; Poverty Monitoring Master Plan (PMMP)
Sept. 2001	1st PRSP Progress Report

the technocratic partnership and prioritizing public expenditure to be funded by new grants and loans. There was certainly no possibility of engaging with critical advocacy groups on the real causes of poverty and on the responsibility of the creditor community for the plight of the Tanzanian poor.

The Poverty Monitoring System: extending the partnership

The most institutionalized form of incorporating select non-state actors in the policy community can be found in the government's Poverty Monitoring System (PMS). It is significant that as the donors and the government move into the implementation of the PRS, the partnership is being expanded and a highly selective mode of non-state participation is now integral to the process (Evans and van Diesen 2002). This section focuses on the Poverty Monitoring System as an example of the transnationalization of public policy processes, examining the relations between 'local' and 'global' configurations of civil society.[15]

An examination of the PMS provides an opportunity to explore a subtle dynamic in the relationship between the state, donors and non-state actors that emerged via the PRS process. Two main points arise:

1. The depoliticization of policy feedback as 'independent professionals' (Helleiner 2002: 232) take over responsibility for brokering communication between policy-makers and target populations, crowding out elected representatives and the statutory structures of policy oversight.
2. The PMS acts as a catalyst for a realignment of relationships within the non-state sector. It appears that the transnational private aid agencies have been particularly successful in capitalizing on the political opportunities incumbent on the consultative imperative at the expense of Tanzanian actors and organizations.

The PMS is an official governmental institution intended to provide the 'data and information required for the monitoring and evaluation of the PRS'. The operations and findings of the PMS are to be incorporated in an annual report on poverty and human development as well as to provide factual input into the annual PRS Progress Report (URT 2001b: 2).[16] Non-state representatives, including four national lobby networks and one transnational private agency, have been included in the membership of the National Poverty Monitoring Steering Committee.

Openings for the involvement of non-state actors in the policy process have been established within two of the four PMS Technical Working Groups: 'Dissemination, Sensitization and Advocacy' (DSA) and 'Research and Analysis' (R&A).[17] In terms of direct non-state influence on substantive policy issues, the purview of the Research and Analysis TWG warrants close scrutiny. Chaired by a senior government official, it brings together a pivotal cross-section of the cosmopolitan community of development professionals. By overseeing the incorporation of a Participatory Poverty Assessment (PPA) within the Poverty Monitoring System, the Research and Analysis group has been responsible for spearheading the most direct and extensive opening for the influence of non-state actors on the PRS policy process.

PPA and fast-track democracy The Tanzanian PPA is an innovative and ambitious attempt to introduce a mechanism for policy feedback between policy-makers and beneficiaries. It has attracted intense interest among both donors and non-state lobby groups (interview: ESRF). According to the Poverty Monitoring Master Plan, the PPA is 'key in ensuring [that] the views and perspectives of the poor are fed through to policy makers' (URT 2001b: 4). In promising to provide a direct link between the poor and the policy elite, and by offering an evidentiary basis for assessing the impact of the PRS, the PPA possesses substantial symbolic value.

The PPA's specific goals are defined as:

1. Enhancing, through in-depth description and analysis, research participants' and policy-makers' understanding of key poverty issues.
2. Exploring the (a) different and sometimes competing priority needs of poor people, (b) likely impact of policies and (c) trade-offs and potential compromises between diverse interests in order to develop 'best bet' recommendations for poverty alleviation.
3. Facilitating the constructive engagement of civil society in pro-poor policy-making processes.[18]

The PPA data collection exercise involves a series of three-week cycles of participatory data collection and analysis at thirty sites around Tanzania. It is expected that the initial PPA will be the first in a repeating process of two-year cycles 'calculated to feed into the PRSP and other policy review processes' (interview: ESRF). The

PPA Implementing Consortium consists of fifteen Government and academic institutions, national and international NGOs, chaired by a Tanzanian policy think-tank as the Consortium's 'lead implementing agency'. A considerable investment of human resources was required of the agencies participating in the Consortium. Still, their involvement was presumably motivated by largely *strategic* considerations, geared towards accessing a seat at the 'policy table', rather than the expectation of an immediate reward.

Indeed, key players in and around the PPA see it as a project with a quite explicit political agenda (in the broad sense of the term).[19] Many see the Consortium as an opportunity to promote a coalition of reformists who reject the 'old-style' mode of political participation (through statutory channels) that, it is felt, has tended to exclude civil society. The PPA participants see themselves as involved in mobilizing, sensitizing and building up an avant-garde of progressive actors linked 'downwards' to grassroots communities, and 'upwards' to an emerging guild of pro-poor policy advocates.

A major outcome of the PPA was expected to be an enhanced sense of self-awareness among non-state advocacy groups as a political force and a clear strategy for political impact. In practice, however, the autonomous political agency of the PPA teams was compromised by the institutional set-up. In dealing with the local government and rural communities, the teams were perceived as working for the government, while in Dar es Salaam they emphasized their role of representing 'civil society'. This led to confusion among the participating CSOs and generated a lot of discussion in the PPA teams (interview: ESRF).

In both design and execution the PPA manifests a vision of fast-track democracy endorsed by a transnational corps of development professionals. Other elements of this vision embrace partnership with the multilateral financial institutions, scepticism towards local political elites and a relentless search for 'positive lessons' and 'best practices' that are portable from context to context and which are contingent on the technical input of transnational development professionals. The cornerstone of this perspective is confidence in the technical skills of transnational policy professionals, and in the capacity of 'independent professionals [to act] constructively as mediators and assessors' in the development arena (Helleiner 2002: 232).

The eventual division of privileges and duties within the PMS testifies to the strong strategic advantage of transnational actors in the competition for seats at the policy table. As noted, transnational private aid agencies (TPAAs) gained significant representation in the Consortium management, securing positions on four of the five research teams. Those areas of the poverty monitoring system which rate highest in resources, visibility, momentum and impact are characterized by an intimate alliance of the domestic technocratic policy elite, multilateralist donors and transnational private actors.

In its conception, the PPA has a clear potential for bringing the practical experience of poor Tanzanians to bear on policy-making. That said, there are two inherent risks in this configuration of powers around channels of policy feedback. One that has aroused critical comment is the likely marginalization of constitutionally empowered structures of representative democracy (Booth 2001; Eberlie 2001) discussed below. The second is that Tanzanian non-state actors and interests will be 'crowded out' of the policy process. This risk is especially large for those adhering to a vision of development means and ends that challenges the transnational policy partnership.

Crowding out After the TCDD/PRSP coalition had been sidelined from the zonal workshops, domestic and transnational non-state groups made a new attempt at a coordinated response to consultative space incumbent in the PRS process. The Policy Forum for NGOs, a network of advocacy organizations, was established as the successor to the TCDD/PRSP coalition. This newer network contains an expanded presence of transnational private agencies. In comparison with the TCDD/PRSP coalition, the Policy Forum could be seen as evidence of 'crowding out' as transnational private agencies penetrate the management functions of the roughly-hewn Tanzanian policy advocacy movement. This risk is recognized by the participants: the Strategic Plan of the Policy Forum states unambiguously as its first working principle that 'the Policy Group [sic] must draw its strength and credibility from being Tanzanian led and inspired'.[20] Far from actively conspiring to capture political space for its own sake, TPAAs insist that they would prefer to see domestic actors taking the lead.

This is reflected in the effort transnationals are making to 'Tanzanianize' certain functions in their organizations. Staff recruited into policy advocacy positions, for instance, are invariably Tanzanian, as are the participants in the PPA research teams. (Indeed, these are usually the same individuals.) Is the indigenization of the strategic policy advocacy function having an impact on the political orientation of the TPAAs? How do these young Tanzanian development professionals view their role and mission? Do they buy into to a policy partnership that caters to creditor interests, or are they inclined to push their organizations to challenge the 'micro-izing and projectizing' focus of the established poverty reduction policy framework? Some insights into these issues can be gleaned from the following excerpt from a discussion with two members of a PPA research team in March 2002.[21]

> GODFREY TWEVE [GT]: The move of the government to include CSOs in the PRSP process is positive. Government now recognizes that CSOs are part and parcel of development. The relationship has not fully matured, but it is off to a good start toward more concrete relations between civil society and government.
>
> Earlier on, PRSP was seen as just a government initiative. Some CSOs initially argued for staying out of the PRSP because of government domination of the agenda. These people argued on behalf of an approach based on activism and protest, not constructive engagement.
>
> They see PRSP as 'political' and their reaction is to shy away from the advocacy dimension. When we attempt to bring them up by focusing on PRSP, this political wariness is an obstacle. The political nature of PRSP is problematic for local CSOs because of the history of confrontation between civil society and government in Tanzania. Local CSOs are afraid that entering into policy debates will cause a negative reaction from government.
>
> There is now a partnership between government and the donor community. People are being prepared for self-reliance. CSOs are maturing now to insert themselves in the partnership. CSOs are being asked what they can contribute to the policy process; if they just want to criticize, they cannot 'merge in the circle'. Otherwise, if they have nothing to contribute they have to get out.
>
> We believe that engagement with government is a way to learn, to be involved. Government also gets experience of working with civil society. In our perception, this is not the time for a more radical, i.e. confrontational approach to government. At the moment, advocacy is being done at a very high level, but through the PPA we have begun to

see issues at the village level for advocacy through village government, wards and districts. We are identifying a number of things that we can take forward as advocacy issues at higher levels. It is better to work within the circle to influence policy directly.

JOACHIM NJOKI [JN]: Through the new forms of participation, CSOs are experiencing ownership of government programmes, even at the district level. We are the owners of development, of the country. The government has even demonstrated more openness regarding the ownership of the land, as in the case of resolving disputes between pastoralists and cultivators in some areas.

At the national level there is mutual understanding, but at district level, officials are not so responsive. Districts are jealous of government funds going to NGOs. Involving CSOs in decision-making is difficult.

GT: The problem is that the focus of most local CSOs is limited to service delivery. They are not involved in policy issues. At district level, organizations like Concern are building CSO capacity to engage with local authorities and promote local development more generally. Such organizations are reaching out from Dar es Salaam to local NGOs that have varied agendas.

The PPA is all about policy and feedback. The history of policy-making has been top-down ... Now the CSOs are learning what issues to carry forward. The problem is of the mechanism – whom can we see, whom should we talk to in order to get our lessons across and incorporated into policy.

JN: Our responsibility is to question our leaders. There also needs to be civic education of government officials by NGOs. 'Participation' has become something everyone is saying. But does it mean teaching or listening?

JEREMY GOULD [JG]: The issues you are raising have important implications for politics and political theory. The Tanzanian constitution provides for a political structure by which citizens can influence policy through representative organs and the ballot-box. Some non-state actors argue that these structures are not functioning effectively enough and demand more direct means of bringing the experiences of citizens to bear on policy. Are your organizations offering themselves as brokers or mediators in this more direct form of democracy?

GT: We think that many voices should be heard concerning the same issues. A loose coalition can be effective. MPs are also important and need to be taken into account. But CSO voices also need to be taken seriously. We are somewhat discouraged by MPs. Now people are saying: Parliament was much more lively under the one-party system. Now the MPs are only there to safeguard the interests of the ruling party. They call it 'working together' and 'collective responsibility'.

JN: We have a constitution, but no democratic content. Democracy should not only be limited to the arena of politics. There must also be democracy in education, in agriculture and other productive activities.

These statements express a clear, if implicit, political vision. It is rather dismissive of the statutory institutions and political mechanisms of the CCM party-state, perhaps justifiably so. It is also one of firm (self)confidence in the capacities of politically independent, professional development experts to act constructively as 'mediators and assessors'. It is, in other words, a vision highly sympathetic to a model of 'fast-track' democracy in determining the course of development policy. The interviewees appear as advocates for a system of democracy which would promote just and equitable outcomes; their predilection is also somewhat populist in that the ultimate vindication of their agency is contingent on their rapport with 'the poor'.

It is also evident that this vision reflects a convergence of interests between the strategic interests of the TPAAs (which seek to maximize their claims of policy leverage) and the professional habitus of the policy advocates (who benefit from a growing market for their specific skills). In seeking access to policy-making circles, it is the presumed status of the TPAAs as 'civil society', representing the interests of 'the poor', which constitutes their strategic edge. Similarly, the fast-track model of democratic feedback empowers a mode of development professionalism which can translate the outcomes of grassroots consultations into the established rhetoric of the policy community. It is not surprising that Tanzanian activists sympathize with political practices that privilege their particular mode of agency.

Fast-track democracy also has a selective affinity with populist neo-liberalism, a position that is not particularly popular in the Tanzanian NGO sector. Practices that permit the designers of neo-liberal measures to invoke the 'voices of the poor' in tacit support of their policies without subjecting these measures to representative popular assessment serve to legitimize a depoliticized, technocratically driven policy machine. From this vantage point it appears that facility with a 'consultative' instrument like the PPA makes TPAAs natural allies of the donors and civil servants upstream that are dependent on some mode of democratic endorsement in order to legitimize their iron lock on the policy process.

The Poverty Monitoring System does not wield direct political clout in any measurable degree, and the whole PPA exercise is separated from the policy-making core by a number of bureaucratic firewalls. The link between the 'voice of the poor' as conveyed by the PPA findings, and the budgetary framework through which Tanzania's Poverty Reduction Strategy works is also undefined. The Consortium management claims to be prepared for this struggle, however. According to the website, 'the entirety of 2003 will be dedicated to encouraging and facilitating the practical use of research results by policymakers and to preparing for the next cycle of research in 2004'.

In any event, the PPA has already proved to be an important site for forging deep alliances between national and transnational non-state actors, and has provided an opportunity for national and transnational non-state actors to seek out new kinds of alliances at district/subdistrict level. Finally, and perhaps most importantly in the long run, the PPA has been a testing ground for the crystallization of a new mode of professional habitus in the Tanzanian context – the policy advocacy officer. Perhaps (like the PRS more generally) the PPA will prove to be more important as a site of forging (transnational) alliances, political strategies and professional habitus than as an instrument of poverty reduction.

Discipline and empower: transnational actors and civil society

Transnational private aid agencies in Tanzania A large number of transnational private aid agencies have set up operations in Tanzania. Up until around 1998, most of these concentrated on programmes of direct development assistance to the delivery of basic services to impoverished citizens. More recently, there has been a general trend in the TPAAs of expanding their capacity to exert leverage on the government and multilateral institutions on behalf of so-called global policy agendas. An intrinsic part of this trend has been the establishment of dedicated policy advocacy positions within these agencies, which have strikingly homogeneous job descriptions. The new corps of policy advocates are not necessarily 'movement veterans' – grassroots activists with deep ties to a social cause – but development professionals whose vocational skills and social habitus have been moulded first and foremost by the bureaucratic demands of the development industry.

The multiagency global campaign on behalf of debt annulment, Jubilee 2000, was a catalyst to professionalizing policy advocacy functions and to expanding the budget share private aid organizations allot to these activities. The debt relief campaign provided the TPAAs with the strategic edge to penetrate the PRS policy process in Tanzania. Partnerships with Tanzanian organizations were deepened, and the rhetoric of local ownership familiar from public donor discourse took root in private agencies as well. Increasingly, TPAAs now seek to work with or through local organizations. From the perspective of the TPAAs, it is precisely the 'capacity' for policy advocacy – facility with the language of the global campaigns, and a familiarity with the routines of programme/campaign management – which forms the basis for partnership. Tellingly, building local NGO capacity in the realm of policy advocacy is a growing priority among TPAAs in Tanzania. Bilateral donors are very supportive of this trend.[22]

TPAAs as political actors The previous section outlined how TPAAs have come to exercise a more accentuated political agency under the auspices of the PRS process. Presumably, the efficacy of this agency would be evident in the TPAAs' increased leverage on national policies. While TPAA access to the policy elite has improved and their visibility has grown, actual impact on policy substance is negligible. Quite the contrary, in their role of surrogate civil society, the TPAAs might rather be seen as contributing to the legitimation of the populist neo-liberal hegemony.

A second dimension of the new political agency of the transnational agencies is visible via their impact on the constitution of domestic social movements, that is, on the organization and articulation of anti-hegemonic perspectives on post-developmental neo-liberalism. Despite (or perhaps due to) virtuous efforts to 'empower' local CSOs and build up their 'capacity', the role of the TPAAs in domestic social movement formation within the context of the PRS process has been problematic. We found TPAAs to be complicit in two distinct mechanisms: (a) that of 'crowding out' (discussed above); and (b) the exercise of 'disciplinary power' via instruments of 'capacity-building' and 'empowerment'. In the following, these mechanisms are explored through an empirical example.

CONCERN AND MANGONET In a training module on 'Policy Analysis' for Tanzanian NGOs prepared in early 2002, UNDP's civil society task manager outlines 'current plans' for 'CSO involvement in influencing national policy planning'. (*Whose* plans was not specified.) This model (see Figure 2.1) envisages a well-organized, hierarchical structure of 'civil society organizations'. At the apex is a National Umbrella CSO/CSO Network interacting in a subsidiary relationship with the government's Poverty Monitoring System. Below this is a matrix of district CSO networks (presumably one in each district) with bi-directional 'synergy/backward and forward linkages' with district administration, and 'direct input' into the upstream national CSO network. The district CSO network would also have weaker links with the political organ of the district council. The district-level network embodies the dual role of gatekeeper/facilitator vis-à-vis 'sectoral' NGOs that deliver privatized services to poor communities. The district network is also expected to gather 'policy input' from the grassroots-level CBOs for national-level advocacy work and coordinate contacts with donors at both local and national levels.

The UNDP model expresses elegantly the multilateral partnership perspective on Tanzanian social activism. 'Civil society' is to organize itself into a self-disciplined 'civic bureaucracy' that both mirrors and engages constructively with the depoliticized structures of the pro-poor policy partnership. Unfortunately, the main 'civil society' elements in this model are merely convenient fictions. National-level 'umbrella' organizations exist,[23] but none has the resources or the capacity to 'coordinate' the CSOs with an interest in policy advocacy. TCDD was intended to fulfil this function, but things didn't quite work out that way. With one or two ambiguous exceptions, district-level 'umbrella' organizations rarely exist independent of national- or international-level sponsors.

The main parties to the multilateral partnership (the state and the major public donor agencies) lack the means to conjure these organizations into existence. Instead, this task has been subcontracted to TPAAs, which have undertaken the requisite 'facilitation' and 'capac-

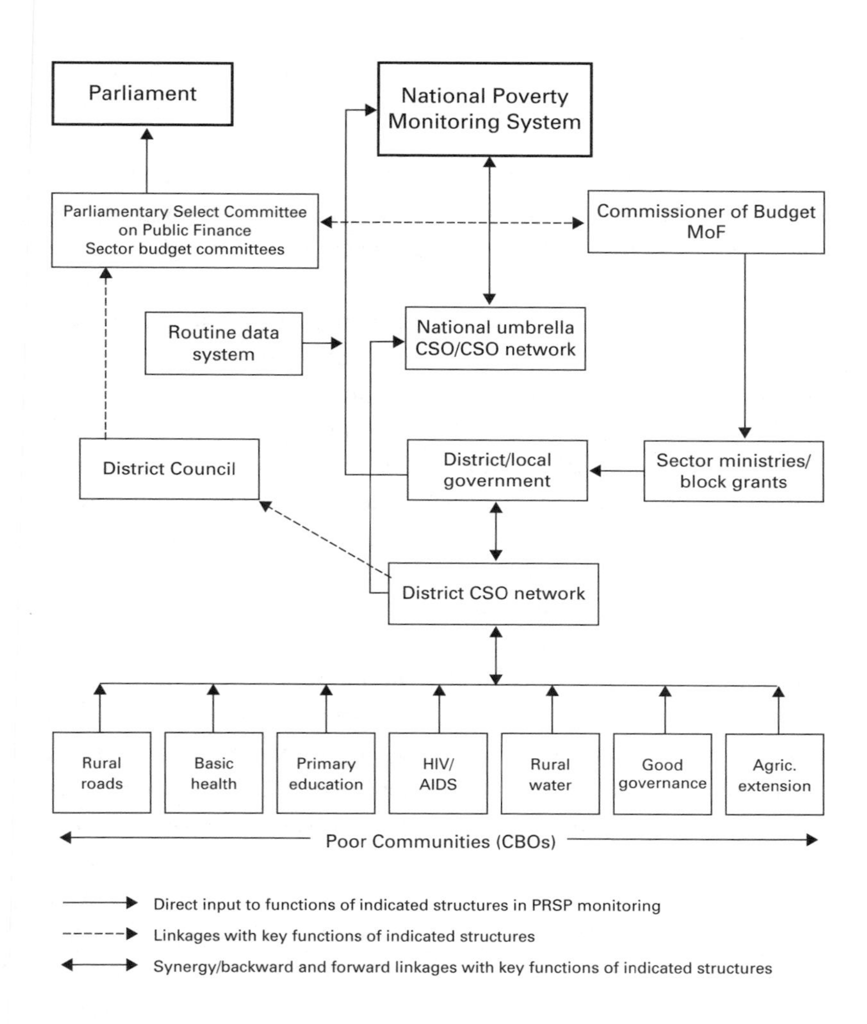

FIGURE 2.1 Model of CSO involvement in influencing national policy planning in Tanzania *Source*: UNDP, 'Training in Policy Analysis, Module 5: NGOs, CBOs, Trade Unions and Cooperatives' (mimeo, n.d.)

ity-building' activities in a number of districts across the country. The Masasi Non-Governmental Organization Network (Mangonet), operating in the southern Tanzanian district of Masasi (Mtwara Region), near the Mozambique border, is one such organization. Mangonet was established in 2000 under the facilitation of Concern Worldwide. The establishment of Mangonet was an outcome of Concern's Civil Society Development Programme through which Concern had established

'partnerships' with seventeen CSOs in Masasi District with the aim of 'enhancing their organizational development' (Concern Worldwide 2001a: 46).

Concern is a transnational private aid agency of Irish extraction with its HQ in Dublin, subsidiaries in Belfast, London, Glasgow and New York, a country office in Dar es Salaam (as well as in twenty-six other countries), and up-country offices in the regional centres of Mtwara and Kigoma. Concern mobilizes a little more than half of its resources (a total of €62 million in 2001) through public fundraising drives in Ireland, the UK and the USA. Roughly 40 per cent of its revenue comes from public donors; EU, Irish Aid, Dfid and UNHCR are the largest public contributors – Irish Aid provides a hefty block grant (Concern Worldwide 2001b). The Masasi Civil Society Development Programme runs on funds from Irish Aid, Dfid and private contributions to Concern.

As a transnational organization, Concern has different modes and layers of activity, the scope of which varies in relationship to the level of the office managing the campaign. At the Dublin/HQ level, Concern launches global campaigns, often related to its fundraising efforts. In addition to overseeing and coordinating up-country branches, the Dar es Salaam country office has actively sought to engage in direct policy dialogue with the government, for example via participation in the multiagency Poverty Monitoring System. Consequently, around 25 per cent of Concern's spending has been shifted internally from service delivery to policy advocacy (interview: Concern). Facilitation and support to Mangonet is managed by Concern's Mtwara office. Support has comprised a range of services from organizational capacity building, convening Mangonet's founding meeting to the provision of an office building in Masasi.

The capacity-building partnership with Mangonet deviates from the traditional role of Concern as a service provider. These days, Concern prefers to work with and through local non-state organizations. There are powerful interests at work influencing this shift of emphasis. As public enthusiasm for development aid wanes in the North, private transnational agencies are in intense competition for donations and support from both public agencies and private donors. *Credibility* is the pivotal asset (alongside financial responsibility) in this struggle for survival. Direct links to the grassroots via viable partnerships and networking with 'local civil society' and 'community-based organizations' contribute decisively towards consolidating an organization's image as a credible player. This legitimizes high-profile policy engagement in the capital which in turn enhances the organization's own visibility in the competition for resources. Local non-state organizations often have strong clientelist ties to the political elite, and establishing these links may require creating the organizations one needs to 'partner' with from scratch.

Another important source of credibility is a demonstrated ability to influence national policy (promoting the pro-poor agenda). In Masasi, Concern is working to establish credentials as a champion of grassroots policy advocacy. One of its first actions after facilitating the foundation of Mangonet was to assign this new 'Learning Network' (Concern Worldwide 2001a: 46) with the task of gathering feedback on the popularized (Swahili-language) version of the PRSP through small, rural member organizations. Concern's aim was to provoke critical debate among 'the poor', but the practical outcome was something else. In practice, Concern subcontracted with Mangonet to disseminate the neo-liberal views of the Dar es Salaam-based policy elite through its newly established grassroots networks.

Forging grassroots partnerships is a tricky endeavour. Local organizations have little or no experience in managing larger sums of money, and can find it difficult to adhere to strict reporting formats, sequences of procedures or timetables. An understanding of policy advocacy and 'rights-based, bottom-up policy engagement' continues to be thin on the ground. Concern has had to change its conception of voluntarism in local-level policy work in order to win over local organizations for the new activities. CBOs now receive financial compensation from Concern for doing policy advocacy. Needless to say, much organizational development is needed. It is certainly *not* true that Concern's activities *only* reflect self-interested considerations and pragmatic corporate strategy. All is not just about the political ecology of self-survival and resources mobilization. Yet in any development intervention, unintended consequences often surpass the desired objectives.

Concern's partnership with Mangonet and its member bodies is portrayed in reports and verbal accounts in technical terms. The focus of capacity building is to promote 'self-sufficiency' and make civic associations more 'effective'. Yet behind this sterile rhetorical gloss political tensions are brewing. A number of Mangonet board members are district councillors who have close ties to one or more local private organizations – mainly CBOs, district foundations and trust funds – as well as to local businesses, especially in the construction and transport sectors, the main arenas of public tendering. These local organizations, including many of Mangonet's members, mobilize their resources through development levies, from fees from their members, through private patronage from prominent individuals, from the CCM (especially in areas where the party's dominance is threatened by the opposition), as well as from bilateral donors and rents on public expenditure.

Subcontracting to the district council is one way through which these local associations gain access to local government spending. This is a procedure whereby councillors award themselves and one another contracts through the District Tender Board, or by direct council decision. In essence, then, the 'CSO sector' is not about advocacy, nor even service delivery. Civic organizations represent one of many mechanisms through which a core circle of the local elite, working under the all-pervasive patronage of the local CCM party machinery, orchestrate intricate stratagems involving MPs, councillors, district executive directors, district treasurers, etc., to extract maximum benefit from the thin stream of public resources that reach a remote rural district like Masasi.[24]

Understandably, not all local brokers were enthusiastic about Concern's intervention in the NGO sector. Relations between the district executive director and Mangonet have been tense, and the district council tried to bury Mangonet's application for a plot to build the office block Concern promised to sponsor (interview: Mangonet). Concern, like all donor agencies engaged in local political arenas, is also under constant pressure from politically influential partner-clients to provide support to these applicants' personal projects. An external actor such as Concern is poorly equipped to address these political tensions directly. Instead it must resort to the technical tools at its disposal in its competition with local power brokers for the allegiance of its partners. These include meticulous audits and a complex array of formalized reporting procedures: stakeholder analysis, project documents based on logical framework analysis, monitoring and evaluation reports, and financial summaries based on strictly prescribed formats. Indeed, the internalization of a rigorously formalized aesthetic for the production of such documents is considered a prime indicator of improved capacity. This capacity may, on the other hand, help a local NGO establish its position in relation to the local political structures. Masasi District Council had asked Mangonet's help in accessing donor funding by reviewing the council's funding proposals.

Capacity building and the disciplines of partnership It is characteristic of post-developmentalist policy discourse that economic objectives are eclipsed by those related to state reform. 'Governance' and 'performance' have replaced 'development' in the populist neo-liberal vocabulary, while 'capacity building' has been substituted for 'growth' as the operational goal of external interventions. The lack of 'capacity' is, among other things, a generalized (and depoliticized) means of legitimizing external intervention at various sites in post-colonial polities. Weak capacity (to perform administrative routines according to established standards, to deliver mandated services to clients, to manage and account for assets, to anticipate risks and opportunities in one's field of activity) is portrayed as a characteristic of, variously, government ministries and public agencies like the judiciary and the police; parliaments and political parties; local government institutions; as well as of 'civil society'. Capacity building is thus exercised by external actors on state and non-state institutions, and by domestic (state and non-state) actors within both the public and the private spheres.

Capacity building is portrayed as an act of empowerment, of providing a given institution or set of actors with the skills and resources to participate in a beneficial process. From another perspective, influenced by the work of Michel Foucault, capacity-enhancing interventions also constitute the exercise of disciplinary power (see Abrahamsen 2000) – of introducing (self-enforcing) standards of 'proper' behaviour. The cogent point here is that the disciplinary and empowering dimensions of capacity building are virtually inseparable. Yet the indivisibility of effects does not imply that discipline and empowerment accrue in equal amounts.

These efforts at capacity building might seem to reflect a technocratic 'will to empower' (Cruikshank 1999), a means of 'constituting and regulating citizens'. That is to say, capacity building represents a 'technology of citizenship' through which governments and other authoritative agencies seek to empower subjects defined as poor, apathetic or marginalized. Capacity building is thus one of many 'strategies for governing the very subjects whose problems they seek to redress' (ibid., p. 2).

In the practices of (post-)development aid relations, the recipient state itself becomes the target of a neo-liberal will to empower – state reforms represent an attempt to build the capacity of 'weak' Southern states to attain more responsible 'citizenship' in the international community of liberal democracies. Fiscal discipline, macro-economic stability, the rule of law and other basic features of a 'conducive investment environment' were already part and parcel of early SAPs. The populist trend in neo-liberal governance extends the reach of external regulation to the quality of state–society relations as transnational agencies fund and implement schemes for building the capacities of civil society to participate in consultation, policy advocacy and other political processes.

Technologies of citizenship, argues Cruikshank, are exercised 'both upon and through the citizen-subject at the level of small things, in the material, learned, and habitual ways we embody citizenship' (ibid., p. 124). The effects of these technologies, the constitution and regulation of citizenship, are not necessarily traceable to the explicit intentions of 'the state', or of any other authority. The political power that (re-)produces citizenship cannot always be confronted face to face. State actors are not simple 'targets' of the will to empower – some are absorbed into the coalition of forces responsible for designing the means and ends of enhanced capacity. The ideal of capacity building for good governance implies the internalization of 'democratic disciplines' – the goal is not simply good compliant behaviour, but a self-governing subject, a democratic citizen.

Donor funding is increasingly being made available to build and regulate the relationship between the state and civil society. Whereas previously CSOs were mainly funded directly by donors, reflecting the idea of 'democratization from below', now policy-oriented 'civil society participation' is also mandated at the top end of the political power spectrum, by the national government. The drafting of the government's NGO policy has been supported by aid; the vice-president's office under which the NGO unit operates has grown significantly and part of its staff costs are financed directly by aid; the World Bank funds studies on civil society for the use of the government. Donors also finance secondments to individuals from CSOs into the Ministry of Finance and other state institutions. This new approach reflects strong pressures to adapt the state–society relationship to a model commensurate with the consensual views of the emerging policy community.

The modes and relations of 'governance' promoted by state reform are seldom the direct outcomes of explicit 'programme objectives' (as entabled in a project logframe). Since donors tend to deny their own political agency, such outcomes are complex, contradictory and largely unintentional. We suggest that one can better understand these political implications and the sort of capacity that is transferred by interrogating the discursive and stylistic conventions adhered to by the actors driving the reforms.

Aesthetic discipline In her study of NGO networks, legal anthropologist Annalise Riles (2000) takes the critical analysis of empowerment and capacity building into previously uncharted areas. Riles undertook ethnographic research among women's organizations from the Pacific region as they prepared for the Beijing Conference in 1995. The establishment of many of these organizations was heavily 'facilitated' by donor agencies, and they were also the target of much transnational 'capacity building'. Riles became interested in how routines and formalities dominated the agency of network members and in the way that these networks appeared to be a self-referential mode of political action. Her observation was that participating in the network was an end in itself. Members had little in common: nationality, values, background, even education. Despite the pervasive rhetoric of 'equality', 'participation', etc., most of the activity of the 'focal points' in the network organizations was about inclusion and exclusion, about who could claim membership in the network.

Networks were purportedly about 'sharing information', yet key players in the network worked hard at restricting the spread of certain kinds of information. Instead of sharing (or even networking), key participants were obsessed with what Riles refers to as the 'aesthetic' dimension of action. Much of this had a textual referent: countless hours were spent debating and refining formal procedure as well as the style, semantics and graphics of documentation. These aesthetic standards provide the network with its transcendental logic – a concern with stylistic elements rather than policy substance – that ordered and patterned the behaviour of those in the network.

Riles discovered no secret or hidden logic behind evidentiary patterns of action – the routines, procedures, and aesthetic concerns. Network women did not come to govern themselves and one another in order to achieve some higher, more valid goal (justice, equity, empowerment). Rather, the aesthetic of the network was its substance. If there was an ulterior motive underlying the obsession with style, it was to enhance access to funding, to aid-rents. Yet the two were inseparable: experience demonstrated that a 'proper' aesthetic was most successful in attracting funding.

Reflecting on Riles's observations, it is evident that a mastery of stylistic elements is a vocation. It implies a certain professional habitus, a certain mode of utilitarian calculus, one for which rhetoric is substance; presentation is product, quantity (of funding) is quality. Thus, through the mechanisms of capacity building and empowerment, self-organized, largely unregulated forms of socio-political action adhere to mechanisms of self-governance that are relatively uniform across multiple sites (and at multiple levels or layers). These mechanisms of self-regulation emerge without the direct coercion of a central authority; it is through them that indigenous social movements become (self-)disciplined clients of donor agencies. The incentive to perform according to pattern is largely linked to national and multinational public and private aid agencies, and to their recognition and funding. The mode of reward-delivery is in the form of a 'project'. Our anecdotal evidence from Tanzania corroborates this view and suggests that (a) TPAAs are becoming an instrumental link in these disciplinary/clientelistic structures; and (b) the PRS process was a significant catalyst for expanding and consolidating such structures.

As aid-rent extraction surpasses local resource mobilization as the main source of value, clientelism multiplies. Increasingly, these rents are extracted through local NGOs and CBOs created to access aid flows, many of which are patched into transnational networks. Resources flowing 'down' from transnational donors to CSOs are by far a more important asset than block grants from a central government to a local authority; often higher than, for example, the state's sectoral expenditures within a given constituency. At this level, it is often aesthetic considerations (mastery of logical framework analysis, for example) which determine success in securing a project and thus ensuring the availability of assets for elite accumulation. Because 'aesthetic' discipline is about form as against content, there is little overt conflict between the rhetoric of 'empowerment' and demands to conform to externally imposed criteria of 'style'. This form of disciplinary power can comfortably co-exist in a patron organization with an empowering self-image and the rhetoric of partnership.

Depoliticizing civil society Concern is certainly not unique in its strategic analysis and pursuits. The move to establish 'networks' and 'partnerships' with local non-state associations is the predominant trend among transnational private aid agencies in Tanzania. Similar narratives could no doubt be recounted for the far richer and more powerful ActionAid, Care, Oxfam, Save the Children and others. To a large degree, these transnational private aid agencies act in a subcontracting capacity for the major bilateral donors (DfID, USAID) and multilateral agencies (such as UNDP). This subcontracting is no longer aimed only at traditional service delivery activities; it is increasingly shifting towards policy advocacy in the capital, and towards poverty monitoring, networking and capacity building at the district level.

The transnationals sit together (in 'partnership') with their patron organizations and other international donors, including the World Bank and representatives of the Tanzanian government, on a plethora of multiagency task forces, technical committees and working groups to which the formulation of public policy issues has been devolved. Some Tanzanian non-state organizations also participate in this 'policy triangle', most notably the semi-private policy consultancy companies who do much of the intellectual subcontracting (one could say, policy indigenization) for the World Bank and other donors.

One can see, then, two consequences for the constitution of local political arenas. On the one hand, there is a chain of relations via which a technocratic consensus around the World Bank/IMF poverty reduction agenda – institutionalized in a partnership of state actors, donor agencies and transnational private aid organizations – is being disseminated via grassroots 'partnerships' among an important segment of the local political elite (development brokers, local politicians and decentralized civil servants). At the same time, through the agency of their facilitation and capacity building, transnational private aid agencies are promoting the proliferation of a uniform organizational form, predicated on a depoliticized, bureaucratic aesthetic of 'good documentary hygiene'.

On the other hand, the engagement of the TPAAs (as 'surrogate civil society') with the inner circles of the policy elite (e.g. by providing grass-roots policy feedback via the PPA), legitimizes the populist neo-liberal partnership. Taken together, this is Ferguson's (1990) 'anti-politics machine' run amok. On a general level, policy discourse and policy feedback mechanisms are debugged of any reference to the stuff of 'real economic development': terms of trade, employment, industrialization, labour productivity, sectoral linkages, pricing mechanisms, even land reform – all such issues are swept under the sanitized euphemism of 'pro-poor growth'.

These public resource allocation policies (both the substance *and* the modes of delivery agreed upon by the 'transnational policy partnership') naturally have economic and political effects in local political arenas (via sectoral programmes; decentralization, civil service reform, pro-poor social funds, etc.). Local social processes are deregulated from the managerial oversight of the state; this creates new opportunities for local political entrepreneurs, just as it does for transnational actors. One might term this localization, but it can also be called 'micro-ization' – a 'focus on the project and the micro world [that] is distracting or diverting attention from social-policy problems that require more aggregative solutions' (Tendler 2000). With no aggregate economic momentum promoting the transformation of the economic infrastructure, accumulation cycles revolve in place and the formation of productive classes is stunted. The political options of local elites are limited to devising innovative strategies of rent extraction, or the self-serving flamboyancy of micro-nationalist provocations.

Parallel to this, the potentially volatile political energies of the educated, professional stratum of elite actors – the potential 'agents for change' – are herded into standardized associations of self-regulating functionaries who are forced to balance their allegiances between a parasitic political elite and a transnational corps of delocalized, 'voluntary sector' technocrats. Another way of putting this is to speak of 'ngo-ization' (of social movements, of the not-for-profit associational sector, of municipalities – see Bagić 2004). From the point of view of the converging transnational policy elite, the self-disciplined, self-managed non-state technocrat is a very convenient partner for carrying out an agenda of post-developmental poverty containment.

Transnational actors and local politics The model of 'fast-track democracy' clearly coincides with the interests of transnational private aid organizations; its penetration into the instruments of public policy via the consultative imperatives of the PRS represents a tremendous empowerment of these agencies. This does not imply that the transnational aid agencies would be malevolent conspirators. Their inroads into the policy community are more a reflection of the evolutionary success of their organizational model than of an intentional will to usurp public authority. Neither, however, are they passive recipients of this 'empowerment'. The current internal discourse of these organizations stresses their proactiveness in achieving leverage in domestic policy arenas.

Success in penetrating domestic policy arenas might be, and is, portrayed as a victory for 'global civil society'. Yet the mainstream concerns of global social movements (justice, greater equity in benefit from public goods, diversity, pluralism in global governance, fair trade, etc.) do not seem to be affecting the core economic policy positions of the partnership. Participation of civil society legitimizes (and perhaps improves the quality of) expanded social spending, but at the cost of marginalizing structural concerns: continued accumulation of unsustainable new debt (and persistent aid dependency); the deterioration of domestic productive capacity (industrialization) and of economic integration (agro-manufacturing links).

The TPAAs' success is problematic both directly and indirectly. Directly, via a lack of accountability and indirectly, by virtue of the fact that it strengthens the depoliticization of development policy ends and means, and legitimizes unsustainable lending to the bottomless budget lines of social spending, thus entrenching aid dependency. TPAA strategies also indirectly contribute to the consolidation of a 'parasitic' class alliance at the core of state power that has a strong symbiosis with quasi-feudal political configuration at the base.

Given their independent resource base, the transnationals have a relative autonomy vis-à-vis the domestic and international public agencies. The transnationals have a strong interest in joining the state/donor policy coalition (influence, visibility) but not in subsuming their identities under that of the public partnership. Elements of competition thus persist – among agencies (for credit and, ultimately, for contributions), at the level of national policy arenas (a need to maintain a distinction between the 'non-governmental' and the governmental) and, significantly, at the site of policy implementation, where advocacy networks compete with the quasi-feudal local party–state apparatus for the allegiance of their natural class allies, the professionalized development experts. The emerging system of social relations of governance thus encompasses a dialectic of brewing political tensions.

One may find the beginnings of a tug-of-war between donor-sponsored TPAAs (perhaps working through domestic CBOs or 'umbrella organizations') and local political elites. Competition is accentuated when local elites have an independent revenue base of their own (as when there is an export crop to tax). This struggle is not about 'transparency' or 'accountability', although this political imagery may well play a role in the rhetoric by which the tug-of-war is carried out. Nor is it about 'deepening the public sphere'. Inasmuch as there is any genuine concern for 'empowerment' and 'capacity building', these are first and foremost practices of 'private government' by which the 'disciplines' of self-subjectification are being promoted in the interests of rerouting the networks of clientelism towards private (politically unaccountable) actors.

All in all, the increasingly assertive role that transnational private aid agencies are playing in policy processes and (possibly) in local political arenas is leading to a very specific kind of privatization of civil society – or, should we say, to the emergence of new, unpredictable structures of 'private government' of very ambiguous accountability (cf. Mbembe 2001). These observations pave the way for an analysis of the political context of the implementation of the Poverty Reduction Strategy, the focus of the next chapter.

Representative democracy and the politics of policy implementation

The disjuncture between policy and politics The process of formulating a Poverty Reduction Strategy has been dominated by a multilateral coalition of donors, driven by creditor interests and closely coordinated by senior technocrats in the Ministry of Finance. One feature of such depoliticized policy design is that conventional political actors like the Parliament have been largely bypassed in the PRSP process. It is evident that populist neo-liberalism privileges 'civil society consultation' instead of statutory political structures as the main source of policy legitimacy. This calls into question the model of representative democracy enshrined in the Tanzanian constitution.

It is often argued that strengthening national parliaments would resolve dilemmas of political unaccountability typical of elitist oligarchies like post-developmental Tanzania. Strong parliamentary oversight of national policies, it is claimed, would be the best way to strengthen the national ownership of development programmes and to enforce democratic policy sovereignty. Observers advocate a closer involvement of parliaments in the PRSPs because these institutions 'constitute a society's democratic forum for the reconciliation of interests' (Eberlei 2001: 30). They are inclined to view parliamentary debates and a formal approval of the PRSP as an important symbol of the national ownership and transparency of the PRSP process (cf. McGee et al. 2000; Evans and Ngalwea 2001).

There is, however, much scepticism about the practical feasibility of a strengthened policy role for the Parliament. While in theory the Parliament is an important arena of representative democracy, in practice 'Parliaments lead a shadowy existence, are often powerless, and in not a few cases represent interests of patrons and clienteles' (Eberlei 2001: 30). The competence of the Parliament and individual MPs to make informed judgements on crucial policy matters is being strongly questioned.

The World Bank is not alone in confessing to 'considerable uncertainty in terms of how to deal with the institution' (World Bank Institute and Parliamentary Centre 2002: 15). In general, donor attitudes towards Parliament are rather paradoxical: on one hand Parliament is an institution without which a modern political system cannot function credibly, and on the other, the politics of representation in which it is embedded is seen as undemocratic, lacking both transparency and accountability. Moreover, open engagement with Parliament might be seen to endanger the 'apolitical' public image sought by donors.

The marginalization of Parliament from participatory processes raises a number of questions related to the Tanzanian 'social relations of governance' at large. For one, has the Tanzanian ruling party, Chama Cha Mapinduzi (CCM) lost political control of the state apparatus to an aid-financed technocracy? If so, why don't the politicians protest? Why, on the contrary, has CCM chairman and national President Benjamin Mkapa thrown his weight so vigorously behind the PRSP?

We argue that in contrast to the consensual policy-making practices of the technocratic iron triangle, implementation structures are highly contingent on increasingly competitive social relations of governance at the local level. This reflects a profound disjuncture between what is conceived as 'policy' and what takes place within the party-based sphere of 'politics'. The former is the substance of a consensual and technical problem-solving exercise, the purview of a cosmopolitan professional elite, while the latter relates to informal, personalized competition between local interest groups, revolving around the patrimonial deployment of public resources.

Aid-sponsored commissions, committees, working groups and task forces in the interstices of the Ministry of Finance, the vice-president's office and the World Bank represent the sphere of policy, while Parliament and the CCM dominate the shady realm of politics. While formal representative democracy in Tanzania is weak – due both to the 'non-political' aid relationship and to de facto one-party rule – the informal aspects of political representation provide a basis of power for parliamentarians.

For the purposes of this analysis, two conceptually separate spheres of politics can thus be distinguished in contemporary Tanzania: the politics of aid (governing policy-*making* within the iron triangle of state, donor and non-state actors), and the politics of representation (governing policy *implementation* as struggle over material and political resources among and between clients and patrons in national and local arenas). These two spheres are interdependent. The politics of aid presumes the ability of political institutions to deliver development resources, while the politics of representation presumes the availability of external assets for establishing and maintaining patrimonial bonds.

One reason for the lack of attention to Parliament in the current configuration of governance relations in Tanzania lies in the idea of an 'apolitical' role for donors, their allies in the government and the non-state sector vis-à-vis policy processes. If poverty is to be reduced, these actors maintain, there is a need to insulate sober technocratic decision-making from populist political pressures and the possibly destructive logic of political games (cf. Callaghy 1990). Shielding central decision-makers and the state administration from distributive claims, and from the burden of electoral cycles, is seen to enhance the state's capacity to launch new reform initiatives and maintain political momentum for reform. This thinking reflects a strong belief in the rationality and commitment of the country's leadership to distribute available resources in the interest of the poor majority. Donors claim not to be involved in supporting one or another political group or individual; in practice the politics of aid consolidates the hegemony of a specific urban-based, professional class of transnational policy community.

Parliament and policy formulation The participation of parliamentarians in defining Tanzania's Poverty Reduction Strategy was limited to a two-hour PRSP seminar held on a Saturday in June 2000. As a result, few elected representatives are familiar with the PRSP, and even fewer can unpack the acronym (cf. KK Consulting Associates 2001). The HIPC debt relief initiative is slightly better known, presumably because of the CCM election campaign in the autumn of 2000 where the HIPC card was played ostentatiously to the ruling party's advantage.

Formally, the political weakness of the *Bunge* (Parliament) can be attributed to the country's legal framework (a Westminster parliamentary system with strong presidential powers). Within this framework, Parliament is supposed to be at the *receiving end* of policy.[25] An informal division of labour exists in Tanzania's political system: Parliament has responsibility for the enactment of government policies into legislation, while all its other functions, namely oversight, budgeting, policy debate and even representation, are performed more effectively in aid-conditioned arenas.

The budget process itself has become primarily an aid coordination exercise, as the development budget is mostly composed of aid resources. The World Bank is closely involved in the coordination of aid in the budget via various administrative mechanisms.[26] It is striking that the cornerstone of government expenditure – loans and agreements with the international financial institutions – is not scrutinized by the Tanzanian Parliament.

Unlike in neighbouring Uganda, Parliament cannot become involved in the prioritization of public expenditure during the preparatory stages of the budget. 'Technical' information such as expenditure and revenue estimates are not open to parliamentary scrutiny and amendment.

Second, the Finance and Economic Affairs Committee is not allowed to increase expenditure beyond sectoral ceilings outlined in the MTEF. The third handicap is that Parliament is not constitutionally empowered to initiate bills with financial implications (Msekwa 2000).

A serious shortcoming in parliamentary oversight is the fact that public funds are simply not always spent the way they have been spelled out in the budget.[27] The newly introduced cash budget system may in effect undermine financial transparency, as the Ministry of Finance is now able to decide more or less unilaterally which of the allocations approved by Parliament will actually be disbursed. Hence the resulting budget outturns can diverge greatly from the allocations approved in the budget and spelled out in the PRSP.

These observations raise fundamental and alarming concerns about accountability and political oversight over the executive in Tanzania. One might ask, what is the value of a potentially open and participatory policy process at the national level, even if Parliament was part of it, if the actual politics of public spending takes place behind the scenes through administrative cash rationing?

The politics of policy implementation Ironically, the transition to a multiparty system since 1992 has not strengthened parliamentarianism based on political pluralism. Instead, one finds an increasingly 'privatized' and localized mode of politics within a de facto one-party system. The transition to a multiparty system has mainly been 'a way to restore the legitimacy and popular support to the CCM – and to re-establish the party's effective dominance of politics at both the national and the local level' (Evans and Ngalwea 2001: 6).[28]

The intensification of political competition at the constituency level accentuates the economic contingencies of political representation. MPs are not only brokers entrusted with overseeing party interests in local political arenas; the constantly rising cost of maintaining patrimonial bonds with their constituencies ensures that they are also entrepreneurs with one eye on the look-out for an opportunity for personal benefit.

With few exceptions, parliamentarians have not seemed particularly concerned about their marginal position in the PRS policy process. MPs stand behind party leaders, who in turn claim ownership of the PRS and other aid-financed reforms. Parliamentarians apparently have no difficulty accepting that a depoliticized policy community manages the allocation of public expenditure as long as their capacity to extract rents at the site of spending is not threatened. The main political prizes that MPs are pursuing in the parliamentary arena relate to securing projects for their constituencies, or to promoting themselves or their allies into senior political posts. As long as the aid funds continue to flow, and assuming that the social relations of local governance facilitate fungibility and rent extraction at the site of implementation, policy leverage is a very secondary consideration.

As aid coordination and policy dialogue have increased, the number of administrative reforms has also multiplied. Currently more than twenty major reform programmes are being implemented in the Tanzanian state sector and economy. Reforms entail shifts in power relations and are driven by political conflicts and opportunities. The donors' self-proclaimed non-involvement in the internal politics of the country positions them outside the power struggles and rent-seeking that permeates the implementation processes. Indeed, direct donor involvement in the phase of policy implementation is on the wane.[29] Meanwhile, the politics of public spending at the point of policy implementation is dominated by the CCM through its intimate control of district-level politico-administrative structures.

The transnational policy technocracy, with its aversion to political institutions and processes, oversees the production of policy guidelines. Politicians broker the instantiation of these intentions at the site of implementation. MPs are the main link between the party's strategic leadership and its power base in the rural periphery, and thus act as the linchpin of 'national' political aspirations in a political system wrought by deepening localization. The informal aspects of political power as they work through personal relationships and social networks are thus crucial for understanding the logic of policy implementation in Tanzania.

The localization of political and economic opportunity The outcomes of the current Poverty Reduction Strategy will depend on the social relations of governance prevailing at the site of implementation. We argue that the faltering and abridged implementation of the Local Government Reform Programme, coupled with a decade of steep socio-economic stratification, has created conditions for the appropriation of resources earmarked for poverty reduction by shifting alliances of local elites. This thesis will be advanced in general outline based on observations from Southern Tanzania (and Masasi District in particular) in March 2002.

Tanzania has demonstrated a passion for multilayered governance reforms. The Local Government Reform Programme (LGRP) launched in 1999 has increased the autonomy of district-level directorates from central government sectoral ministries, implying the virtual dismantling of the once-powerful regional level of public administration. Moreover, as a result of semi-spontaneous processes catalysed by neo-liberal policies, medium- and larger-scale capital has undergone a geographical localization process, which also creates resources and incentives for social and political districtization (Gibbon 1998: 49).

Officially, the expansion of local autonomy is to be accompanied by strict mechanisms of financial accountability in order to enhance the capacity of elected representatives to exercise democratic control over the civil service. For various reasons, however, the LGRP faltered in its first cycle of implementation. In brief, the administrative powers increasing local autonomy and discretion were devolved, but without the concomitant tightening of controls and oversight. The half-baked implementation of the LGRP has facilitated the rent-seeking ploys of the local political class, who have been left cut off from the central government apparatus that enforces bureaucratic accountability. Local government officials exploit their bureaucratic powers to ensure that decisions of the district council and its tender board award projects and contracts to their allies.

Socio-economic stratification and political competition Socio-economic stratification has had a fundamental impact on the social relations of governance in the 1990s, driven by privatization and market liberalization. In Southern Tanzania, which provides the empirical backdrop for this discussion, the primary force fuelling stratification has been the deregulation of cashewnut marketing. From the early 1990s, the Southern Tanzanian market has been aggressively coopted into the Southern Indian cashew industry as a source of cheap raw materials. Throughout the 1990s, local farmers benefited incrementally from a steady rise in producer prices. A few large growers and rural brokers benefited significantly from this development. District councils also benefited from the levies on the cashew trade, absorbing the increased revenues in 'allowances and conspicuous consumption such as the purchase of luxury vehicles' (Chachage and Nyoni 2001: iv).

Informal mechanisms also prevailed. A multifarious and complicated array of taxes affecting sales, transportation and export provide lucrative opportunities for district officials and their political allies to extract rents from the nut trade. The entrepreneurial agency of the political elite in the cashew sector echoes a general trend in an economy marked by stratification and the transformation of opportunity structures. These opportunity structures also affect national-level politicians: there is now a growing tendency for competition over political office to degenerate into a competition over the spoils of the liberalized economy (Kelsall 2000). MPs are also more dependent than before on party nomination due to increased political competition within the CCM. Altogether, the impacts of decentralization, political liberalization, donor involvement in service delivery, the outsourcing of public works and services as well as privatization have created an added incentive for politicians to build strong local support bases. As Evans and Ngalwea (2001: v) note: 'The liberalisation of the economy has provided a crucial boost but it has also opened the way for a more overtly patrimonial style of politics.'

Small-scale business projects and micro-finance institutions established or supported by the MPs are becoming increasingly common in Tanzania. A locally based NGO or trust fund can also be a convenient vehicle for the purpose of 'mobilizing' and 'sensitizing' the voters.[30] In his study of the politics of local development in Tanzania, Kiondo (1994: 58) argues that the role of home district organizations in social development activities has grown strongly since the mid-1980s, when political and economic reforms were begun and donors increased their funding to civil society. Kiondo points out that the rise of a variety of community development associations has by and large been initiated by the state and by CCM – the tactic of the party has been to shower resources and money on areas where popular support for the opposition is strong (ibid., p. 61).

This brief sketch confirms a rapid process of elite accumulation in district centres as well as in villages. In order to exploit the new opportunity structures offered by the price boom, the urban-based elite was obliged to cooperate with an emerging stratum of rural brokers.

This suggests a significant shift in the relation of district elites to village communities. Where, under the centrally regulated economy, urban elites extracted rents via the parastatal structures they controlled, market liberalization has promoted alliances among urban and emerging village elites based on complicity in rent-seeking. If nothing else, this development casts grave doubts on the likelihood that ad hoc village-level political structures will be motivated to carry out policies to the benefit of the poorer and marginalized sectors of the population.

Village institutions nevertheless appear to play a central role in the emerging strategy for implementing the PRS. The World Bank, especially, promoted the direct transfer of development resources to village institutions – largely bypassing the district bureaucracy – and the direct deployment of these resources by local committees. In the first instance, village-based school committees have been selected to test this implementation model.

The politics of policy implementation is mediated by political agents who operate through party structures and patrimonial relationships in an environment rife with opportunities for rent-seeking and personal enrichment. These trends are accentuated by growing political competition within the main party and in relation to the political opposition, as well as by an emerging socio-economic stratification at the district level. The marginalization of the party and the Parliament from the PRSP policy process is best understood against the background of political and economic localization and the deregulation of local government. On the other hand, the vagaries of Tanzania's aid relationship would appear to pre-empt opportunities for reinforcing popular structures of political accountability through the politics of representation.

Poverty reduction and democratic politics

Our interpretation of the politics of the PRS process may strike some readers as somewhat severe. We suggest that the prevailing ethos of the pro-poor policy partnership – thoroughly consensual, triumphalist and self-congratulatory – should be viewed with scepticism. The terms of the partnership – above all, the way that key elements of prevailing neo-liberal economic policies are left unchallenged – undermines political accountability and the democratization of public oversight. From this core premise it follows that the complicity of previously independently-minded actors – we have in mind certain bilateral donors and the transnational private aid agencies – erodes the democratic potential of policy consultation and occludes significant room for manoeuvre for critical domestic actors and grassroots social movements. At worst, anti-hegemonic views are crowded out of the public dialogue, or their interlocutors are domesticated into depoliticized icons of populist legitimization via the disciplines of 'capacity building' and 'empowerment'.

Another reading of these materials is also possible. The consensual view, propagated most avidly by the World Bank, DfID and their think-tanks, highlights positive elements in the ongoing process. Unfolding events in world politics render multilateralism an attractive alternative to non-negotiable unilateralism. Tanzania's peaceable partnership is certainly preferable to the unmanageable conflicts in which several of its neighbours are engulfed. Many would argue that a system of financial management controlled by a transnational technocracy is far better than a kleptocratic regime. Even rhetorical attention to the 'voice of the poor' is better than the arrogant disregard of non-expert views, and consultation, however curt, is an advance over a self-referential oligarchy. And many would agree that the accumulation of performative capacity and the empowerment of civic associations are vital preconditions for both democracy and efficiency.

This upbeat reading presents the PRS process, and the partnership that has managed it with a particular 'spin'. Our assessment spins the data a different way. Are both spins equally true (and thus equally false)? What might the unspinned truth about Tanzania's public policy arena look like?

This simple question cuts to the core of the dilemma facing all social and political analysis. How to portray configurations of interests and power in a neutral, disinterested way? In truth, the Tanzanian public policy arena will never stop spinning, at least not as long as it attracts approximately one billion dollars of foreign aid per annum. It will never even slow down enough to allow for a clearly focused snapshot that might be scrutinized at leisure. There are, alas, no technical or methodological tools to eliminate the spin – to neutralize the interests, strategies and asymmetries of power in which all actors, including researchers, are enmeshed. All observations must be made on the run, chasing a rapidly moving object which appears differently depending on where you are standing (or running, as the case may be). Most confounding, all sources of information, down to the most innocuous of statistics, express the point of view of one player or another. There is, in fact, no genuinely authoritative knowledge about such political arenas. Underlying all the rhetoric, fancy titles and impressive aesthetics there are only 'battlefields of knowledge' (Long and Long 1992), struggles over whose truth will be most widely accepted.

Does this not mean there are no 'facts', that empirical study and careful argumentation are a waste of time? We certainly wouldn't have spent many months researching and writing this study were that the case. But one must also acknowledge that the systematic search for information, its careful analysis and informed interpretation do not necessarily produce 'authoritative knowledge', especially when the findings run against the grain of established narratives and, most decisively, prevailing interests.

The claims put forth in the name of the pro-poor policy partnership appear reasonable, and a great many actors in Tanzania – domestic, foreign, transnational – take them at face value and allow them to guide their actions. We have argued that the consensual narrative is a self-referential construct through which a cosmopolitan elite of middle-class professionals, firmly under the sway of neo-liberal ideology, justifies its hegemonic grip on budgetary process. Perhaps this is not such a bad thing. As a Danish team of consultants pronounced in their assessment of the Tanzanian PRSP: 'Questions might be raised about placing too much influence in the hands of a small group of technocrats, but it is a virtually universal aspect of all successful policymaking that at a critical stage responsibility for drafting coherent policy document [sic] has to be clearly located with a small team capable of effective drafting.'[31]

Our concern is neither with the coherence of the document (coherence is merely a formal property), nor with the capabilities of the people who wrote it. Our misgivings revolve round the procedures of policy formulation, and the political character of the process. Was the PRSP formulated in a manner that promoted the routinization of democratic procedures in the Tanzanian political system? Did the actors in control of the process exercise a democratic mandate? Are the actual procedures, and the coalitions of actors that established them, likely to encourage inclusiveness and transparency in future cycles of policy-making? Did the policy process encompass a wide range of views, and carefully consider the implications of different positions before the document was finalized?

It is hard to respond positively to any of these queries. One must inevitably wait and see whether the current path does indeed lead to poverty reduction and improved governance. Meanwhile, it is worth reflecting on the following cautionary elements in our findings:

1. The prevailing domination of creditor interests (streamlined disbursement, guarantees of repayment) without increased controls on lending policies.
2. The empowerment of cosmopolitan middle-class positions in the policy elite (and their populist legitimization) at the expense of deepening popular democratic influence and oversight.
3. The abuse of 'consultation' to legitimize predetermined policies (and duplicity in the portrayal of the process as participatory).
4. The one-dimensional focus of public policy on social investments without parallel attention to productivity.
5. The affinity between the productive social forces excluded from the policy process (the domestic middle class, small-holder producers) and the absence of corresponding economic elements in the policy framework (agriculture, manufacturing).
6. The reinforcement of quasi-feudal political relations at the grassroots as a result, in part, of the depoliticization of public policy-making.

Of greatest long-term concern are perhaps the negative implications of the consensual hegemony for the resurgence of a genuinely pluralist debate on Tanzania's development options, one rooted in the broad range of social and environmental conditions that characterize this vast country. The increasingly systematic exercise of disciplinary power over actors and associations with social movement potential is especially worrisome. But the most immediate problem undoubtedly is that of 'crowding out' and its impact on the structure of political opportunity for effecting democratic policy formulation and implementation.

'Crowding out' depends on operative standards of inclusion. The criteria by which an actor is deemed competent, responsible or representative enough to be included in a political process are not arrived at by divine decree, they are politically constructed, defined and negotiated by self-interested parties to the same process. The above narrative recounts a number of incidents by which domestic organizations were excluded from various aspects of the PRS process. In all cases, their exclusion was the result of 'insufficient capacity'. But how has the measure of sufficient capacity been defined?

Our evidence suggests that these standards – professional, ethical, and aesthetic – emanate from practices established within the aid industry. As coordination and harmonization within the industry deepens, the most powerful members of the aid 'cartel', the large multilateral agencies, set these standards. In this sense, the multilateralization promoted in the name of harmonization and coordination looks increasingly like a process of unilateralization, as collective donor aspirations converge on the interests of the main creditor institutions. For semi-commercialized institutions like the World Bank and the IMF, standards of performance echo both the formal requirements of a massive bureaucracy and, however circuitously, the demands of hysterically competitive global markets. As Tanzanian organizations struggle to conform with these standards – a goal which only the thinnest elite precariously achieves – alternative ways of thinking about time and process, respect and reciprocity, power and efficiency, are peeled away, leaving a uniform and unchallenged sense of normality and acceptability. Only those who can adhere to these stringent standards of civility are considered legitimate members of 'civil' society.

What might be done? Given the complexity of these issues we are more comfortable posing questions for further reflection rather than assigning guidelines for action. Different actors may need to reflect on different aspects of their strategies.

In the *non-state* sector, more attention is needed to ensure that emerging social movements can speak with an independent voice. Mechanisms of accountability need to be deepened and radically reformed, not merely coopted under a hierarchical model of civic bureaucracy. The private aid agencies have much cause to rethink their role in this respect.

In the *state* sector, the national leadership may need to consider how it could recapture policy autonomy by forging alliances with the productive middle class. The local technocracy may also need to reflect on its political strategies. Some lessons could be learned from Uganda where the senior civil servants allied themselves with critical advocacy groups to leverage greater leeway from the creditors.

For the *donors*, it may be worthwhile to reconsider the importance of pluralism in the policy arena. Harmonization is positive when it lessens the transaction costs of aid management, but less so when it sharply reduces the policy options open for debate and experimentation. One should perhaps be less obsessed with form and procedure, and pay more attention to policy substance. Genuine autonomy is also an important criterion of ownership. Politics and interest representation are messy, but there is no democracy without them.

3 | Vietnam: dealing with donors

IRENE NØRLUND, TRAN NGOC CA AND NGUYEN DINH TUYEN

In May 2002, the Comprehensive Poverty Reduction and Growth Strategy (CPRGS) was endorsed by Vietnam's Prime Minister Phan Van Khai. The strategy's main Vietnamese architect, Dr Cao Viet Sinh, from the Ministry of Planning and Investment (MPI), stated with confidence that Vietnam was the first Asian country to write a full PRSP by itself (Wolff et al. 2002: 33).

The CPRGS is the Vietnamese version of a Poverty Reduction Strategy Paper (PRSP). The reference to 'growth' in the title underscores Vietnam's independent approach to the PRSP model. Contrary to suspicions that the Vietnamese government may have capitulated to the demands of the World Bank, the leading donor, to highlight growth, it was in fact the Vietnamese who insisted on the wording of the title.

The formulation of a PRSP was a prerequisite for the Vietnamese government to access new credits from the Bretton Woods institutions. In accordance with the policy of the new post-Washington consensus, the World Bank took the initiative to create a new type of donor–government–NGO relationship to back up the process.

The process of formulating the CPRGS and its predecessor strategies started in 1998. In the autumn of 2002, the strategy started a process of being 'rolled-out' at the provincial level, and it continues, in early 2004, to be in a fairly early phase of implementation. The formulation process was spectacular in that it opened avenues for new types of cooperation between donors (including the so-called international non-governmental organizations, INGOs) and the Vietnamese government. The CPRGS has an aura of success around it, and the process of inclusion by which many had a say in the formulation of the strategy resulted in widespread satisfaction among stakeholders. Criticism was raised during the process and after, but that does not distort the overall picture. Donors adhere to the new strategy as a central approach to future development cooperation.

Seen from a distance, the process surrounding the CPRGS added some new dimensions to development cooperation in Vietnam. The implications of the incumbent power-plays for politics in Vietnam, beyond the formulation of a new development strategy, are similarly significant.

It will be argued that in spite of new references to poverty reduction, more openness around the CPRGS and the inclusion of new actors from the non-state sector, state–society relations have not fundamentally changed. Rather, innovations in the policy process should be seen as part of an opening up in Vietnamese society which began more than a decade ago. Secondly, the relationship between the government and donors is not uniform beyond fairly superficial interactions at the central level. Policy formulation continues to take place on two parallel tracks, with government and donor policies having two distinct logics and two different ways of operating. However, interests common to groups that were empowered by the process have generated better cooperation and mutual understanding between government and donors.

New alliances were shaped in the process of formulating the CPRGS, and this opened the door for groups that had not earlier contributed to policy discussions. The political dynamic of the process can be understood only by looking closely at the government's relations with the emerging non-state sector (local NGOs and business communities), and with the donor community (the World Bank, bi- and multilaterals and INGOs).[1]

Central questions informing this analysis concern whether or not the process surrounding the CPRGS opened doors that would lead to further convergence between the two systems. How far has it created political space for the non-state sector, particularly for a more vibrant 'civil society'? Which groups were empowered and disempowered in the process?

Other questions will be dealt with from a broader perspective: Do the new active policies by the transnational donors in cooperation with the government in the name of growth and poverty reduction lead to policies and interventions which undermine the relatively high level of independence characteristic of Vietnam? Do the policies of transnational donors improve shortcomings in the present system? Will cooperation between transnational donors and government through the PRSP process lead to more democratic rule?

The answers to these questions cannot be uniform and clear-cut, as the outcomes vary between major groups in the new alliances, and are changing over time. However, new types of cooperation have implications going beyond the outcomes of the strategies. Who has the power to determine the language in which artificial formulations and analyses are couched? Whose language is being spoken: that of donors or of the government? Will the diverging vocabularies and definitions be merged in new strategies outlined by the government and party for the next party congress scheduled for 2006?

A number of features of Vietnamese society differ from many other countries entering the PRSP process:

- Vietnam can no longer be considered a HIPC country and at the outset the government volunteered to write a PRSP document primarily to ensure access to concessional funding.
- In spite of still being a poor country, the Vietnamese economy has experienced dynamic growth for more than a decade.
- Vietnam was successful in reducing poverty in the 1990s, even before the donors instigated the new, comprehensive strategies.
- Donors perceive Vietnam as a successful example of a PRSP process and the country is presently viewed in a positive light by the donor community. Accepting Vietnam as a 'donor darling' may result in an overly optimistic perception of the difficulties the country is facing.
- Vietnam proclaims itself a socialist country where equity plays a key role in government policy and in the perceptions of the people. National independence is a fundamental value – historically, as well as today.

The Communist Party plays a core role in society at all levels, overseeing development ideas and policies that penetrate society down to the grassroots. This hampers the development of civil society in the Western sense of the concept, but in other ways it facilitates more inclusive and participatory processes via what might be termed multipolar consensus governance.

Historical context

From war to reform and globalization Vietnam is a middle-sized country of 80 million inhabitants, one of the fifteen most populous countries in the world. The Cold War and, related to that, the American War (1964–75), remain important for the country's history and identity today. After the exit of the French colonial government in 1954, the country was divided between the capitalist South, supported by the United States, and the North with a socialist government under President Ho Chi Minh, with alternating support from the USSR and China. After the collapse and takeover of the South by revolutionary forces in 1975, marking the end of the American War, a socialist government was installed in the whole country.

Continued conflicts with neighbouring Cambodia under Pol Pot, culminating in Vietnam's military intervention, along with increasingly tense relations with China in the late 1970s pushed Vietnam towards closer cooperation with the Soviet Union and Eastern Europe. Around the same time, the centrally planned socialist system sank into deep economic crisis. This crisis spawned grassroots initiatives on behalf of economic and political change, and pushed central government to adopt a reform agenda. By the early 1980s, the country entered a slow reform process which speeded up after the decision to renovate the country's policies from late 1986 (*doi moi*). More far-reaching transformations toward a market-oriented economy were introduced from the late 1980s.

When Eastern bloc countries began to reform and the communist governments finally collapsed in the late 1980s and early 1990s, the barriers between 'East' and 'West' started to disintegrate. Vietnam had no other option than to find new alliances and to integrate in the globalizing world of the 1990s. Whereas internal reforms were the key to change in the 1980s, closer interaction with the international community was limited by a continued blockade by the USA until the final issues in Cambodia were settled in the 1990s. The American blockade made it difficult for many of its allies to approach Vietnam, but contacts were nevertheless slowly established in the late 1980s and early 1990s. By 1994, the USA and Vietnam had decided to establish official relations; cooperation with transnational donors also speeded up from this time onwards. Foreign direct investments expanded in the belief that Vietnam would be the next Southeast Asian 'tiger' economy following in the path of South Korea, Singapore and Hong Kong. Some foreign investors had, however, been overly optimistic and were increasingly critical; investing in Vietnam proved more difficult than expected. The economy was still at a stage of transformation and the government was hesitant to open up too liberally for a market economy; moreover, local institutions were not functioning according to the needs of foreign donors and investors, and would not do so for a considerable time to come.

When, in 1997, financial crises suddenly struck several of the strong economies in the Asian region, particularly Thailand and South Korea, Vietnam was not hit hard because its financial policy was still regulated by the government and it could protect the Vietnamese currency (*dong*) from collapse and depreciation. However, FDI from important investors like South Korea and Taiwan fell sharply, and major trading partners crumbled in Asia. New diversified trading links to Europe and other parts of the world nevertheless provided a buffer and Vietnam experienced only a mild impact of the crisis.

Lessons of the crisis were multiple. Bad debts of industrial companies were a weakness of the Asian economies, and that was the case in Vietnam as well, even if the state-owned enterprises (SOEs) were still protected to some extent by the state. The fate of apparently strong and vigorous economies in the region falling into crisis and the humiliating conditions imposed by the IMF and the World Bank also changed the direction of official development thinking in Vietnam. The government's *doi moi* reforms appeared to be paying off in the mid-1990s: open doors and gradual reforms coincided with a high growth rate of around 8 per cent per annum. Party and government strategy aimed at high growth models based on the South Korean path of export-oriented industrialization. The Asian crisis, however, strengthened the position of the less optimistic circles within government, who emphasized the importance of slower changes and more equal development in the country, focusing more on rural areas. As Vietnam's development and integration into the world market was considerably weaker than that of Korea, supplying mainly agricultural produce, oil and light industrial products (garments and shoes) on subcontracting arrangements with countries like Japan, Taiwan and South Korea, this adjustment in thinking was probably fairly healthy.

Reform processes in Vietnam The core of the *doi moi* reforms consisted of a transformation of the centrally planned system in Vietnam to a more market-based system. The centrally planned economy was based on the ideology of Marxism-Leninism as it had been spelled out in a number of countries that had undergone socialist revolutions. Capitalism, characterized by the exploitation of man through the private ownership of enterprises and land and the economic enslavement of people and countries by the international imperialist powers, was perceived as the main enemy. Before the reforms in countries like Vietnam and China, even small-scale private production and trade were considered negative, likely to lead to the revival of capitalist relations of production. The party, administration, mass organizations of women, workers, youth and peasants and the National Assembly were closely linked to each other, with the party as the deciding partner. The party-state was the owner of the means of production, e.g. all industrial and trading enterprises. Peasants were organized in agricultural cooperatives which had to deliver a considerable amount of their produce to the state. In return, basic needs were secured through rationed systems of consumer goods, as well as access to basic education and healthcare.

The reform process started to open up in the economic field with larger returns to the peasants in the early 1980s, followed by the decision to de-cooperativize agriculture from 1988. Finally, a land reform law which gave the land to the peasants on long-term leases was passed by the National Assembly in 1993. This land reform was one of the cornerstones of the policy which catered to the establishment of free commodity markets and to individual planning by peasant households. Production increased steadily after each step of the reforms.

Reforms in the industrial sphere also took place, followed by measures to establish a macro-economic framework with a financial and monetary system and adjusted currency rate linked to international markets. Means of finance were urgently needed, and the liberalization of foreign trade and foreign investment, along with increased development cooperation, were chosen as a means to achieve resources. But it was difficult for Vietnam to admit that it had to use the same instruments in planning and development as the capitalist countries of the region. Moreover, reforms were to be carried out in almost every field of economy and organization.

While *doi moi* is largely seen as a package of economic reforms, it also brought about a number of changes in other fields. The roles of different organizations were redefined and separated. The party today increasingly plays the role of the organization which defines society's general orientation, whereas government takes care of daily tasks in public administration (confirmed by the 1992 constitution). The National Assembly has gained a much more central role in the huge project of establishing the 'rule of law'. From the late 1980s, legislation has been reformed in all the major fields of social organization, and from the end of the 1990s a second or third round of legal reform is still ongoing, resulting in new laws on foreign investments (1987, 1990, 1992, 1997, 2000), the Company Laws (1990, 1994, 2000), Land Laws (1987, 1993, 2001), financial institutions (1997) and the Enterprise Law (1999, 2000) (Arkadie and Mallon 2003).

From hunger to growth In spite of institutional obstacles, the economy started to grow quickly in the 1990s, with sharp increases in the industrial and service sectors. Even if the productivity of agriculture did not expand relatively as much as the other sectors, production and diversification increased enormously. From experiencing food shortages in 1980, food was produced in huge amounts and hunger reduced to specific areas and times in the annual cycle. Rice and food production increased from 15 million tons in 1981 to 21.5 million tons in 1990, a fairly moderate but important increase. From 1990 to 1995 output increased to 26 million tons, and Vietnam became a net exporter of rice. Since 1996 Vietnam has exported around 3 million tons annually, as the second or third largest rice exporter in the world. Even though rice is one of the less value-added commodities, this was psychologically important in Vietnam where hunger is still a recent memory.

The 1990s saw a transformation of production to include higher-value agricultural products such as coffee, tea, groundnuts, cashewnuts, rubber and pepper. For all these commodities Vietnam became one of the largest suppliers to the world market. Manufactured goods in the medium range of value-added, such as garments and footwear, besides exports of oil and aqua-cultural products, constituted the main export earners. Exports increased from US $2.4 billion in 1990 to US $18 billion in 2003, and in 2002 the combined export and import trade reached the level of the total GDP of the country.[2] All things being equal, agricultural and aqua-cultural transformations are probably the key to understanding the striking reduction of poverty that took place in the 1990s, since the majority of the population still lives and works in rural areas. De-collectivization and land reforms were crucial to increased production and consumption by the rural population which accounted for 80 per cent in 1990 and still accounted for a large share (75 per cent) in 2002 (*Statistical Yearbook 2002* 2003: 21). Most foreign investment went to the industrial sector which had fairly limited impact on employment. It enhanced, however, the dynamism of the urban sector, but also resulted in a widening of the gap between urban and rural incomes. Another important factor is the quick expansion of the service sector, ranging from informal to large-scale activities, and huge investments in infrastructure.

Economic reforms led to the growth of a private or non-state sector, partly through the legalization of private activities, Foreign Direct Investment projects and through the growth of the number of international NGOs (INGOs) and of local NGOs (LNGOs). As with the central–local dichotomy, however, the public–private dichotomy has been a contested area, largely due to overlaps between the two sectors by many types of hybrid ownership which obscure the distinction.

Three-sector approach In the 1990s, Vietnam began to develop from one sector into three sectors. This came to play an important role in the new approaches to poverty reduction embedded in the PRSP process. Whereas previously the government (party-state) had monopolized policy-making, towards the end of the 1990s, three sets of actors became involved: the government, the donors and the non-state sector. The private sector plays an increasingly important role in society, but fairly indirectly when it comes to decision-making, as it submits its opinions through the Vietnam Chamber of Commerce and Industries or smaller associations. The foreign investment sector often uses government-to-government channels to lobby for its interests. In donor–government discussions related to the PRSP, the non-state sector was mainly represented by INGOs and to a minor extent by local NGOs. Although donors – some more than others – often advocate on behalf of the business community, the private sector was barely represented in the process, albeit consulted from time to time.

The context of the CPRGS

Foreign resources pulling in Reforms in all fields in the 1990s were necessary to accommodate the changing structure of society, particularly

TABLE 3.1 FDI inflows and ODA, Vietnam

	No. of projects[a]	FDI, total implemented capital, (US $ million), govt source	FDI, total inflows, (US $ million), IMF sources[b]	ODA, new commitments	ODA disbursement (US $ million), UNDP, Dec. 2002[c]	ODA disbursement (US $ million), govt source 2001[d]
1988	37	288				
1989	68	311				
1990	108	408			448	
1991	151	664	620 (1988–91)		338	
1992	197	1,418	295		356	
1993	269	1,469	869	1,810	274	413
1994	343	1,730	1,048	1,940	635	725
1995	370	2,987	1,780	2,276	612	737
1996	325	2,914	1,813	2,430	985	900
1997	345	3,215	2,074	2,400	950	1,000
1998	275	2,368	800	2,200	1,200	1,242
1999	211	2,535	700	2,210	1,300	1,350
2000	371	2,413	800	2,400	1,600	1,650
2001	502	2,450	900	2,400	1,360	1,650
2002	754	2,591	1,100	2,500	1,500 est.	1,794
2003		2,650	1,200 est.	2,600 plan[g]	1,800 plan[h]	
2004		2,600 plan[i]		2,700 plan		
2005				2,800 plan		

Source: a. *Statistical Yearbook 2001* and *2002*. The figure excludes supplementary capital licences in previous years and Vietsopetro projects. b. Arkadie and Mallon (2003: 212), based on IMF information. The two columns are not in accordance because of two different IMF sources. Information on years 2001 and 2002 derives from *Vietnam Development Report 2004*, based on WB and IMF information. These figures are more conservative than government figures, and are included to show the wide discrepancy between the information, which probably reflects implemented capital as aggregate disbursement schedules of the projects, including equity and loans. Official figures might include a part of the domestic borrowing from joint ventures. Inflows are estimated based on average shares of foreign and domestic equity investors and lenders, plus information about major project disbursement (*Vietnam Development Report 2003*: 12). c. UNDP and MPI (1997: iv); UNDP (2002a and b: 1), taken from graph. d. Socialist Republic of Vietnam (2001a and b; 2003a and b. e. From 1996 to 2003, statistical annex 'FDI status'; MPI, quoted in *Vietnam Economic Times*, no. 119, January 2004. f. *Taking Stock* (2003b: 9); IMF estimate. g. Government of Vietnam 2002: 29. h. ibid., p. 39. i. Information from Minister of MPI, vnnews-l, 10 December 2003.

after inflows of foreign direct investment (FDI) and official development assistance (ODA) speeded up and the private sector began to expand. The government came to play a much stronger role as coordinator and facilitator of the new initiatives. Vietnam was considered to be an HIPC country due to its high debt to Russia and the new inflows of ODA. Trade was still limited in the early 1990s, resulting in high debt-service-to-exports ratios, one of the common criteria for measuring the level of indebtedness. Donor–government discussions took place at annual consultative group meetings (CG). Vietnam was a very poor country with a GNP per capita estimated around US $200 in 1990 (World Bank 1995). By 1999, the figure had increased to US $375 per capita and to about US $435 by 2002.

Figures for FDI and ODA are contested by various sources, but suffice it here to establish the overall trend whereby FDI reached considerable levels in the mid-1990s. FDI fell sharply in the years after the Asian crisis, but was again on the increase from 2002 (see Table 3.1). ODA has, on the contrary, demonstrated steady growth to the present level, where it has probably become more important than FDI.[3] The government is optimistic about achieving higher levels of both FDI and ODA in the coming years, but ODA has taken a more important role than before for the government. At the CG meeting in December 2003, the donors committed US $2,839 million for 2004, even higher than predicted. FDI contributed to 25 per cent of total development investments in 1998, falling to 18 per cent during 1998–2002;[4] the two sources together account for about half of total investments.

Most ODA funding is transmitted to programmes and projects through government institutions. It has to be added that, since the end of the 1990s, two-thirds of ODA consists of soft loans, while the rest consists of grants which are free but also more controlled than loans. As for FDI, the major share was channelled through government as joint ventures in the early and mid-1990s. As investors achieved more experience in operating in Vietnamese society, however, the number of fully foreign-owned enterprises and businesses started to increase.

The number of donors has expanded considerably. Currently, there are twenty-five bilateral donors, nineteen multilateral donors and roughly 500 INGOs operating in Vietnam. Japan, the World Bank and the Asian Development Bank (ADB) are the three largest donors; their disbursements account for 80 per cent of total ODA capital. The largest bilateral donors are Japan, France, Germany, Denmark and Sweden. The largest multilateral stakeholders are the World Bank, ADB, UNDP, the IMF and the full EU grouping. There have been nine CG meetings since 1994 with a total commitment of over US $20 billion between 1993 and 2003, of which about half (US $12 million) has been disbursed (UNDP 2002b and 2004).[5] INGOs have steadily increased in number from seventy in 1989 to 514 in 2002 and have committed US $807 million in total. The combined annual INGO development support is the largest after Japan, WB, ADB and EU, and it consists of grants not loans, unlike much of the 'official' aid (Delany 2003).

Vietnamese way of governing The government is obviously interested in attracting as much capital as possible in order to achieve a high growth rate, and to reach the growth target of the five-year plans laid out at the party congresses every fifth year (i.e. 1991, 1996 and 2001). In accordance with the principles of Marxism-Leninism guiding the leaders, the party has since its formation adhered to the idea that the forces of production must be transformed to build up a modern industrial society. Similarly, the means of production should be in the hands of the state and the people. The core goal today is that society should strive for industrialization and modernization. 'Poverty alleviation' is not one of the ideas inherent to official ideology and policy, but it is a clear policy objective that people obtain a decent living standard. In the management field, the motto is that society is 'led by the party, managed by the state and owned by the people' (*Dang lanh dao, Nha nuoc quan ly, Nhan dan lam chu*). During the reforms of *doi moi*, these ideas had to be transformed in some respects to be compatible with the development of markets based on a multisector commodity economy. Still, the socialist principle of the state as manager endured (Communist Party of Vietnam 1996: 15).

Since 1987, the party has gradually retreated from direct control over state affairs and promoted the rule of law, increased autonomy of the government and National Assembly, including greater separation of legislative and executive functions to replace customary party rules (Painter 2003: 18–20). The party nevertheless retains its central and decisive role in most of the important aspects of economy and society (Phong and Beresford 1998). From the mid-1990s, the strategy was to 'closely combine economic renewal with political renewal, with the focus on economic renewal while conducting political renewal step by step'. Political renewal implies exercising socialist democracy and promoting the people's right to be their own master, while countering 'fanatic democratism', i.e. the use of democracy and human rights to stir political trouble, and not accepting pluralism and multipartyism (Communist Party of Vietnam, 1996: 27–8).

The members of the National Assembly are chosen in regular elections. The candidates were earlier recommended by the Fatherland Front, but today it is possible to run as independent candidate, although the percentage of independents actually elected remains low. Legislation is discussed, often lengthily, and revised several times in the Assembly before being passed. The government is the executive body running day-to-day policy, based on suggestions from line ministries. The administration is organized in a concentric system from the centre to the province, district and commune level; the party and other organizations are also organized in concentric circles at all levels.

One large and difficult task is the Public Administration Reform (PAR), a continuing process which started in the 1980s and which has received donor support and technical assistance since the early 1990s. It relates closely to ongoing discussions concerning centralization and decentralization. Whereas donors often consider Vietnam as a centralized political and administrative system that has to be decentralized, the dichotomy between the centre and lower levels is an ancient and complicated theme in Vietnamese history. In the 1980s and early 1990s, central government was influenced by a decentralized system in which the provinces were fairly self-sufficient and independent. The peasants were able to increase their incomes because of new economic initiatives and market possibilities, and because of less appropriation by the state. When the economy started to expand and foreign trade, an important source of tax income, increased, donor funding also began to arrive. These developments allowed the central government once again to increase its control over the provinces.[6]

Donor support through ODA has strengthened the central administration which allocates the bulk of the funding to the provinces. A de facto division between the central ministerial and government organizations on the one hand, and the local, particularly the provincal, level, on the other, is one obstacle to donor–government strategies, including the CPRGS. The PAR aims at changing 'the centralised and subsidised bureaucratic management mechanism', based on 'give and take relations' into a modern 'management mechanism responding to the needs of people and ensuring efficient and effective management of all aspects of economic and social life' (Government of Vietnam 2001: 3). A core goal of the PAR is separation of party and administration, and to ensure appropriate administrative skills, resembling new public management ideas in other countries. However, the reforms are running into traditional ways of managing and a lack of competence, if not direct resistance. PAR challenges power relations at all levels and is faced with many difficulties hindering the rapidity of change.

In spite of the reforms, governance can still be characterized by a 'two-track' policy, according to which national planning and operations are distinct from foreign donor activities. State governance still exhibits a distinct form of organization and logic, combining planning and distribution from the top with consultations at many levels. It is inspired both by Confucian ideas and socialist planning, with many organizations involved in a finely meshed network. The provinces are still not very dependent on central allocations, and cannot be controlled from the centre that way (*Vietnam Development Report 2004* 2003: 102). At each level consensus has to be reached before a decision can be implemented, and agreement can require long discussions and cumbersome procedures. It has an inclusive function as well. This type of management has been characterized as 'consensus governance' (McCarthy 2002), or as a system of 'polycentric power sharing' (Painter 2003). Tolerance of irregularities is fairly wide, and the provinces enjoy a fairly large degree of independence, reflected in a diversity of governance from province to province.

In discussions with donors and other foreign organizations, the contrast with governance ideas is obvious, leading to difficulties in dealing with core issues related to the reform process. Reforms like the equitization of state-owned enterprises (SOEs), banking reform, the public administration reform and the improvement of conditions for private sector activities are some of the main areas of contestation. Donors, particularly the World Bank and the IMF, have at times been dissatisfied with the slow speed of transformation, and have used a stick-and-carrot approach to push the reforms. Discussions have been hard-wearing and complicated due to differing views on the timing and pace of change. Towards the end of the century, the government did in principle agree with the necessity of the above-mentioned reforms, but consensus governance has obviously been an obstacle to faster change because it takes time to overcome inertia at lower levels. At the same time, donors applied pressure to liberalize the private sector which is smaller but more dynamic than the state sector. So far, the government has succeeded in opening more room for private business without limiting the state sector.

Many of the reforms have assumed a Vietnamese form of the models originally proposed by donors. For instance, the 'privatization' of SOEs became 'equitization', implying that the companies should be transformed into shareholding companies. Only a certain percentage of shares can be sold to foreign interests, and as the state and employees are encouraged to buy shares, it is not straightforward privatization. Privileges for SOEs were maintained through the 1990s in the form, for instance, of continued access to low-interest loans. The number of SOEs has been reduced and employee-owned shares 'made redundant', but the SOEs have also been restructured in order to improve efficiency and productivity so that they can compete with the upcoming private sector. A backbone of socialist ideology and social organization, industrial enterprises and their employees are core units and interest groups for the government, both in economic and political respects. However, the early years of the new millennium witnessed new efforts at reforming the SOE sector and at facilitating private sector expansion. The private sector absorbs a considerable amount of new labour entering the market, an important function given the need to create between 1 and 1.5 million new jobs each year.

Poverty reduction While the government is clearly committed to increasing the growth of the economy, increasing incomes in a fairly equitable way is also on the agenda. Growth is considered a precondition for improving living standards with a philosophy fairly close to the neo-classical vision of 'trickling-down' resources from the better-off to the poorer members of society. Concern for the poor is deeply embedded in Vietnamese social thought, at least in parts of it, and there are many forms of humanitarian support for poor and calamity-stricken people through government programmes and mass organizations. One of the achievements in the first half of the 1990s was spelled out as follows: 'The material conditions of life for the majority of the population have improved. The number of medium-income and wealthy households has risen while the percentage of poor households has decreased ... The campaign for hunger eradication and poverty alleviation and philanthropic activities continues to expand, becoming a new and fine feature of our society' (Communist Party of Vietnam 1996: 15–16).

The hunger of the 1980s has been firmly left behind and the country is in a process of rapid development and transformation. The nationally-targeted programme for Hunger Eradication and Poverty Reduction (HEPR) approved at the 8th Congress in 1996 was one of the specific programmes introduced by the government. The campaign was started in the early 1990s by local initiatives, and later sector programmes started to operate through the central government, but only in 1998 did it expand nationwide. The HEPR programme, also called Programme 133, sought to eliminate hunger and reduce poverty among the poorest and most vulnerable through combined relief and development efforts (Evaluation 2004). From the beginning about 1,000 communes were selected to be part of the programme; this was later expanded to about 2,000. A special programme, no. 135, aimed especially at the most disadvantaged ethnic areas, was established for socio-economic development in communes faced with extreme difficulties. These programmes operate through regular budget mechanisms by making special grants available. The structure and operation of the programmes has been improved in the 2000s. The Ministry of Labour, Invalids and Social Affairs (MoLISA) was the government agency responsible for the poverty-oriented policies. MoLISA was also responsible for assessing the national poverty situation, mainly based on income analyses.

In recent years, Programmes 135 and 133 have been much contested. Some found that the central level still wielded too much power, and the communes were not able to make their own decisions concerning the allocation of funds. There are also stories and open cases related to the abuse of funding. An evaluation of the programme is underway, but the World Bank has recently assessed the impact by using information from the 2002 Vietnam Household Living Standard Survey (VHLSS no. 3). The conclusion is that a fairly high number of the poor are living in the targeted communes, which indicates that the programme's design is more appropriate than was supposed (*Vietnam Development Report 2004* 2003: 84–6). Efforts to strengthen commune planning, moreover, have been included in many ongoing donor/government programmes in recent years.

Before donors started supporting the large-scale living standard surveys and poverty analyses of the State Planning Committee and the General Statistical Office (GSO) with funding and expertise (Sida and UNDP funded the survey which was executed by the World Bank), little was known of the overall poverty situation in Vietnam. The first Living Standard Survey (VLSS no. 1) was carried out 1992–93 and presented in a comprehensive report by the World Bank in January 1995 (World Bank 1995). Based on methods from international surveys (expenditure analyses), the poverty frequency in Vietnam was pegged at 51 per cent of the population, whereas the measurement of food poverty indicated that 25 per cent were food-poor.[7] The first report revealed a bleak picture of the poverty situation in the country, and methodological issues of poverty assessment became a discussion point between national agencies and donors as the national approach focused more on food-poverty. In 1994, GSO released an analysis carried out at the end of 1993 which estimated a poverty rate of 20 per cent in the whole country.[8]

The debt agenda Debt has never been a hot issue in Vietnamese debates despite that fact that it reached dangerously high levels during the 1990s. The government took advantage of the easy access to new credits to ensure quicker growth, adding to the debt burden. The share of grants in the ODA transmitted to Vietnam grew in the early 1990s, but from 1995 it remained stable at around US $400 million per annum, whereas the total amount of ODA increased considerably from year to year (see Table 3.1) (UNDP 2004). From 2001 to mid-2003 alone, US $4.7 billions of loan and US $1 billion of grant agreements were signed. Because much of the debt from the 1980s was owed to Russia, debt was estimated differently depending on the conversion rate of the rouble. The IMF estimated the debt at US $8 billion in 1989, whereas the World Bank estimated it at US $19 billion and considered Vietnam a heavily indebted country all through the 1990s. Moreover, Vietnam had to settle old debt from the former South Vietnamese regime with the IMF before contacts could be established in 1993, and by 1998 the World Bank estimated the debt at US $20 billion, about 72 per cent of the GDP (CIEM 2003; World Bank 2003; *Taking Stock* 2003b).

Two factors contributed to making the debt manageable by the end of the 1990s. First of all, the debt with Russia was finally settled in 2000 at a rate of US $1.7 billion, much lower than was earlier assessed even by the IMF; the second factor was the quickly expanding export trade and a growing economy, which diminished the debt in relative terms (Table 3.2).

TABLE 3.2 Vietnam's external debt and debt service, 1998–2002 (US $ billion)

	1998	1999	2000	2001	2002
Total external debt	19.9	20.5	11.6	12.2	13.3
Debt/GDP (%)	71.6	72.4	38.5	36.9	37.2
Debt service/total export	13.8	13.8	10.5	9.8	7.8
Debt service/GDP (%)	6.4	6.8	6.0	5.1	4.3

Sources: CIEM 2003; World Bank 2003; *Taking Stock* 2003b

The debt decreased considerably after the settlement with Russia in 2000, and Vietnam fell far below the threshold of HIPC eligibility (150 per cent ratio of external debt to exports). In 2003, the debt-to-exports ratio was 50 per cent. Total debt is on the increase again, however, and even if prospects for future debt are still considered within reasonable limits by the multilateral agencies, Vietnam may easily run into new troubles. Projections point to an increase of debt-to-GDP to 50 per cent in 2005, remaining at this level for a couple of years when, according to the IMF, it should be falling again (*Taking Stock* 2003b: 14). The projections are nevertheless based on continued high levels of economic growth, and assume high inflows of FDI and ODA. This raises questions concerning further changes in society in the coming years. The ongoing transformation is closely linked to means projected and suggested by the multilateral agencies, and this path of development will to some extent force Vietnam to more rapid and perhaps less sustainable adjustments in order to be able to repay the debt. Exports, for instance, are not as promising as in recent years and are growing considerably more slowly.

The external environment is crucial for exports and the United States, for one, has limited the quickly expanding garment trade by quotas. The USA has also lodged complaints against Vietnam for dumping catfish on the American market and, with an upcoming case on shrimps to follow, two major exports are challenged. Vietnam is, moreover, constantly in competition with China, which is able to sell many commodities of better quality and at lower prices. One consequence is Vietnam's application for quick entry into the World Trade Organization, in 2005, in the belief that it can avoid trade restrictions more easily in this forum, and better manage Chinese competition and trade disputes. However, entrance into ASEAN, APEC and, in the future, WTO demands a fundamental restructuring of production. Present protection is already on the decline and further decreases will come. The main danger for Vietnam in the future is to be too dependent on exports in order to repay the debt. If this strategy is not successful the debt trap might build up quickly and reverse the positive outlook.

Compared to many other countries, Vietnam's transformation started well before aid and FDI increased massively in the mid-1990s. The economy thus got off to a start on growth and poverty reduction at a time when transnational resource flows were playing a minor role. The point of departure was very low, however, and growth seems more spectacular when measured from this low level. Because the economy had already started to grow before the increase in transnational flows, it is argued (Arkadie and Mallon 2003: 215; interview: World Bank staff, Hanoi) that foreign capital is still complementary to the national financial situation, and that Vietnam has avoided excessive aid dependence. The next phase from the mid-1990s onwards is nevertheless based on much higher levels of transnational inflow, as shown before, and cooperation with donors has been built up in new ways.

The process leading to the CPRGS

Post-Washington consensus The World Bank played a key role in the new aid relationship that was built up in the late 1990s. Since the structural adjustment policies of the 1980s had been a failure in many low-income countries, particularly in Africa, the 'post-Washington consensus' introduced new ideas and policies into multilateral development cooperation. While some have argued that the new policies were old wine in new bottles, specific themes of importance for both governments and donors were part and parcel of the new thinking. These ideas – spelled out in the Comprehensive Development Framework (CDF) – include emphasis on

- a comprehensive, e.g. multidimensional (holistic) development framework including all relevant policies including the donor side
- result-orientation for outcomes benefiting the poor
- long-term perspectives for poverty orientation
- a country-led and country-owned process
- widespread participation in policy formulation
- improving the aid relationship[9]

Some of these principles were difficult to translate into the Vietnamese context and even contradicted one another, as when the principle of 'local ownership' clashed with a donor notion of 'participatory process' that was new and unfamiliar in Vietnam. Moreover, to 'coordinate all relevant policies' was contrary to institutional and political traditions in Vietnam where the institutions' horizontal and vertical linkages are weak. The coordination of domestic and donor policies was a challenge to both parties, as government and donor coordination usually took place on two tracks. Moreover, the coordination of donors among themselves was an area with great difficulties. Other issues, such as 'long-term planning', and 'benefits for the poor', were easier to implement in Vietnam, with its long tradition of planning and an ideological commitment to equity.

The World Bank activates a new forum In 1997 Andrew Steer, the first Country Director of the World Bank, was stationed in Hanoi, and donor coordination was invigorated through a stream of new initiatives. The decentralization of World Bank operations from Washington to recipient countries was taking place simultaneously, and Vietnam was among the countries with a large portfolio. From about eight employees in 1997, the staff exceeded eighty by 2002–03. At the Consultative Group (CG) meeting in December 1997, the World Bank Country Director and CG chairman called for new rounds of reforms, and the donor community complained about a lack of aid efficiency. The Vietnamese side presented its own reform agenda, but remained mostly observers (Jerve et al. 2002: 5). In 1998, the World Bank started to develop a Country Assistance Strategy (CAS) for Vietnam, a format that the World Bank has increasingly used as an instrument to outline three-year plans. According to principles of CAS formulation, development issues should, in theory, be discussed with all societal partners, including NGOs.

According to the CDF, poverty reduction was to be the central objective. In 1998, the World Bank suggested a new poverty assessment based on data from the second Living Standard Survey (carried out in 1997–98), combined with participatory poverty assessments. Cooperation within the donor community was revitalized considerably with the World Bank as the leading agency, based on a new approach to 'participatory' cooperation. In early 1999, the Bank suggested that the Ministry for Planning and Investments (MPI), the leading ministry handling donor business, set up a joint government–donor–NGO Poverty Working Group (PWG), as well as a smaller, more flexible institution, the Poverty Task Force (PTF), which was introduced to handle urgent issues and the implementation of the poverty assessment. It was decided that an annual report to the CG meeting, the Vietnam Development Report, would address poverty and that the report would not only be the product of the World Bank, but of the whole Poverty Working Group. This began a process of poverty assessments, eventually published as *Vietnam: Attacking Poverty*. The report was to be presented to the CG meeting in December 1999 and the PTF worked intensively on quantitative and qualitative analyses.

On the Vietnamese side, planning for the 9th National Congress of the Communist Party began around 1997–98. The five-year plan was to be approved at the party congress scheduled for 2000–01. The decision was to approve two plans: a five-year plan for socio-economic development from 2001 to 2005, and a ten-year strategy for socio-economic development in the period 2001–10. The planning of these documents coincided with the emerging partnership processes with donors. During 2000, several drafts of the party plans were discussed at all levels in government, party and mass organizations around the country. A fairly refined draft version was published in newspapers before the congress, the most public of any five-year plans to date. The plans were finally passed at the 9th Party Congress in April 2001. Government cooperation with the donors in the Poverty Working Group, and the outline of a Comprehensive Poverty Reduction Strategy were not mentioned in the party documents, the political report, the five-year plan or the ten-year strategy.[10]

Attacking Poverty The process surrounding *Attacking Poverty* is regarded by some donors as a showpiece for innovative policy partnership involving the international community, central and local government and the INGOs. *Attacking Poverty* was based on data both from the government's qualitative measures in the first and second VLSS, and from qualitative assessments of poverty based on four Participatory Poverty Assessments (PPAs) implemented by three British INGOs (Oxfam UK, ActionAid UK and Save the Children UK), and a Swedish development programme in the Northern Mountains. The four PPAs brought 'hundreds of decision makers at various levels of society together, local officials from village level to ministry level together with local Vietnamese professionals and NGO structures in workshops to discuss the findings, and district and provincial authorities have agreed that these studies reflect the realities' (*Attacking Poverty* 1999). At the presentation of *Attacking Poverty* at the CG meeting in December 1999, twenty local NGOs were invited for the first time to participate with the other representatives.

The outcome of the second poverty assessment in Vietnam attracted intense interest from the donor community up to the release of the report. The results of the surveys depicted a country that had, despite persistent poverty, achieved a steep reduction in poverty levels. The core message was that from 58 per cent living under the poverty line in 1993, the number had fallen to 37 per cent in 1998, while the rate of food-poverty had fallen from 25 per cent to 15 per cent.[11] Moreover, the reduction of poverty was widespread and had taken place in a fairly equitable way. Poverty remained thus largely a rural phenomenon, even if pockets remained in urban areas. Poverty was concentrated in certain regions including the Northern Mountains, Central Highlands and the North Central Coast of Vietnam, all areas where ethnic minorities constitute a high proportion of population. The report pointed to an increase in farm income of 60 per cent, and to overall improvement in employment and delivery of services in education and health. At the same time, it warned that the dramatic gains in poverty reduction remained fragile, and that the incidence of poverty might be more safely put in the range between 30 and 45 per cent (*Attacking Poverty* 1999). The general results were nevertheless overwhelmingly positive. It encouraged all partners in the partnership of government, donors and INGOs. The combination of quantitative and qualitative research was convincing both for the donors and the INGOs which had carried out the poverty assessments. The government, usually sceptical of qualitative methods, seemed, to some extent, to accept the findings, even if the government's own investigations and criteria estimated poverty at a lower rate.

In early 2000, the government invited the Poverty Working Group (PWG)/Poverty Task Force (PTF) to give advice on a new ten-year poverty strategy, the Hunger Eradication and Poverty Reduction (HEPR), prepared by MoLISA (Ministry of Labour, Invalids and Social Affairs). The grand prospect for the donors was to better bridge the obvious gap between the donor and government paths of the two-track planning system.

The Interim PRSP To obtain further credits, the Bretton Woods institutions required that the government outline a Poverty Reduction Strategy Paper. As in other countries, the first step consisted of outlining an Interim PRSP (I-PRSP). In April 2000 the government asked the MPI to prepare the I-PRSP, and in June it requested the PTF to support this process.

The drafting of the I-PRSP was undertaken by a team led by the Ministry of Planning and Investment together with other ministries, but in cooperation with other organizations. At first it was supposed that MoLISA's HEPR plan could be taken as the point of departure, but the government obviously designated MPI to be the main drafter of the new document.

The Poverty Working Group, and particularly its 'executive committee', the Poverty Task Force, was revitalized under stronger leadership consisting of the World Bank together with the MPI. UNDP and MoLISA had pioneered the 'partnership process' from the early stage – MoLISA as the ministry most engaged in social issues, and UNDP as the long-term coordinator of the donor community in Vietnam – but now they came to play less prominent roles. The World Bank outlined concrete criteria for membership in the PTF: the donors contributing the most time and money to the process, regular seats for three INGOs, and three local NGO leaders were invited to take part in the PTF. A first draft of the I-PRSP document was circulated in September–October 2000 to be presented at the CG meetings in December 2000. Seven drafts in all were outlined before final approval of the document by the government in March 2001. The document was presented to the boards of the IMF and the World Bank in April and May of that year (UNDP 2003). It was approved, not so much because of its comprehensiveness, but because it was appreciated that the document was outlined by the government. It was moreover perceived as a document developed via the government's own planning process, that included a poverty reduction strategy, and was based on consultations with donors, INGOs and other organizations (Wolff et al. 2002: 21). At the same time, criticisms of the I-PRSP indicated that the document was still at a fairly rudimentary stage. The timing of the I-PRSP's approval coincided with the party congress taking place in April of the same year, and with the approval, by the IMF, of a US $386 million Poverty Reduction Growth Facility, also in April. The World Bank followed suit with a US $250 million Poverty Reduction Support Credit in June 2001.

Heading for the PRSP 'Partnership groups' in about twenty-five different areas (poverty, industry, forestry, environment, etc.) were established to facilitate cooperation between donors, ministries and some INGOs, to discuss strategies of common interest. After the approval of the I-PRSP, the full PRSP was the next step to achieve. Starting in March 2001, the document was again outlined by the MPI as the lead agency, with a larger team of seventeen persons from various ministries and agencies (Nørlund et al. 2004: 58, 66; Wolff et al. 2002; UNDP 2003). The Poverty Task Force gave input in a number of areas, particularly related to key development targets. New consultations took place based on the I-PRSP at national, subnational and community levels, including 1,800 interviews at household level in poor communes. The government insisted on the inclusion of the word 'growth' in the title, resulting in the name Comprehensive Poverty Reduction and Growth Strategy. Various interest groups worked and lobbied intensively at the end of the process to make sure that their specific areas of interest were included; a number of women's organizations were particularly successful (Vu et al. 2003), but also organizations working with children made sure that children were included in the strategy. One of the weakest points was the environmental agenda, where environmental groups were less successful in getting their points across. This might be explained by the fact that the environment is an area of less concern for growth-oriented economists, whereas the other interests were easier to include (Buch-Hansen 2003). After enormous efforts and fanfare, the final PRSP was presented in May 2002.

INGOs in partnership INGOs in Vietnam numbered more than 500 towards the end of the 1990s, and 100 of them have offices in the country. They have been welcomed by the government to work in Vietnam, but also limited to carrying out activities according to the rules and regulations of society. Government–INGO relations reflect a specific attitude towards foreigners, perhaps a legacy of wartime, but also affirm a need for foreign funding and expertise. INGO projects must be channelled through the People's Aid Coordinating Committee (PACCOM) which provides support to and control over the activities of foreign organizations, often quite restrictively. INGOs are considered private funding bodies, but also as humanitarian organizations.

In general, INGOs have been supportive of the government's development efforts, by and large cooperating with local government and mass organizations, particularly the Women's Union, all over the country. Local NGOs were almost non-existent until the mid-1990s and INGOs had difficulties finding local partners.

INGOs comply with the restrictions, both in order to work in Vietnam and because social and economic progress has been encouraging. Considering their knowledge of problems at the local level, however, they have been surprisingly quiet. By and large INGOs in Vietnam have kept a very low profile towards both the government and multilateral donors, particularly the World Bank and the IMF, which in most other places are hot targets of criticism.

The Poverty Working Group invited the INGOs to take part in the 'partnership process' because they represent the World Bank's new policy – expressed by the Comprehensive Development Framework – of cooperating with INGO and NGOs (i.e. 'civil society') alongside governments, in order to make policy formulation more inclusive and participatory. In the first phase of outlining *Attacking Poverty*, three INGOs – Oxfam GB, Save the Children UK and ActionAid UK – became involved because of their experience with participatory assessments and their grassroots contacts in some of the provinces. Moreover, the Northern Mountain Rural Development Programme, a Swedish (Sida) bilateral programme to support the development of communes in some of the Northern Mountain provinces, organized one of the four participatory assessments for the *Attacking Poverty* report. It was also co-financed by Sida – one of the key reasons why the Swedes were included in the PTF. The World Bank encouraged more poverty assessments but could not identify any other organizations versed in carrying out such large and complicated research undertakings (communication from the WB). During the compilation of *Attacking Poverty* and its successful presentation in December 1999, cooperation between government, donors and INGOs in the PWG took a positive turn. The World Bank saw the opportunity to perpetuate the partnership in a more formalized fashion, and INGOs were invited to take part in the subsequent PTF in 2000 if they were able and willing to deliver a substantial and coherent input.

At the initiative of the NGO Resource Centre, a forum for INGOs in Vietnam since the early 1990s, INGOs started an internal process to decide who should be members of the PTF. Substantial discussions took place within the organizations in 2000, but the handful of large INGOs already involved in the process were keen on continuing the 'partnership' for outlining a full PRSP, well knowing that they would represent the LNGOs. Their rationale was that they would be able to give substantial input, as with the first round of poverty assessments, and challenge discussions in the PTF. The process had also contributed to the internal learning of INGOs. A few INGOs found they could not set aside resources and opted not to spend their time with the demanding work of the Poverty Task Force. Some INGOs found that the process was basically unsatisfactory, including only INGOs from the central level (Nørlund et al. 2004).

Six INGOs were involved in the second round of participatory assessments leading up to the CPRGS, and they also contributed to the PTF with a number of papers. INGOs participated in a number of partnership groups and in groups discussing the development goals to be included in the CPRGS. To the satisfaction of most of the partners, it was decided to adopt the Millennium Development Goals and adjust them to Vietnamese conditions. Some discussions took place among INGOs about representation in the PTF, and INGO seats increased from three to four in order to let Oxfam GB, one of the most active INGOs, continue in the group. According to the organizations concerned, one of its tasks was to ensure that the discussions maintained a poverty focus.

The main achievement of INGOs was their new role in the policy process, which allowed them direct participation in discussions both with the government and with multi- and bilateral donors. The criticisms raised by them focused on issues such as poverty, gender, children and the impact of trade, but not much on the broader technical issues of budgeting, expenditure review, macro-finance, SOEs and infrastructure. They were much less critical of the process and the organizations involved, as they were now a part of it. Almost all of the participating INGOs were British or of Anglo-Saxon origin, with better training and a clearer focus on advocacy activities than most other INGOs. They also benefited from close relations with Anglo-Saxon donors.

Local NGOs with less partnership Representatives of local NGOs were invited more as personalities than as organizations, partly because most of the organizations have charismatic leaders who are outspoken and dare to question the authorities. The character of NGOs in Vietnam is still different from that in many other countries: they are not organized in strong networks and they cooperate closely with the government, even if they might be critical in specific areas of operation.

LNGOs in Vietnam can be categorized by type. Mass organizations, which are considered political forces of society by the government, were originally set up as the arm of the party that reached the grassroots. Particularly before the reforms, they functioned as conveyor belts between the grassroots and the higher levels of the party and administration in various enterprises and localities. The traditional mass organizations were the Women's Union, the Trade Union, the Youth Union, all of which were large organizations under the umbrella of the Fatherland Front, which conveyed instructions from higher to lower levels, carried out mobilization campaigns, as well as taking care of the ill, disadvantaged and the elderly. Today there are several new mass organizations which are assuming new and different roles in accordance with changes in society. The Farmers' Union was established after the agricultural reforms in the late 1980s and expanded considerably in the 1990s. The Veterans' Union was established after the end of the American war. In addition, senior citizens are organized in almost all communities and enjoy considerable respect in Vietnamese society. Today these organizations provide training and small-scale loans to their members and facilitate networking in the localities. The Women's Union, more than any other organization, cuts across social groups and issues and by virtue of its unique grassroots presence enjoys widespread cooperation with INGOs. This has bolstered its organizational capacity and increased its influence in the regions.[12]

The more recent NGOs can be divided into groups according to their various origins: organizations headed by former government officials; those operating primarily as research or consultancy agencies, often headed by well-educated younger staff; and smaller organizations in the regions, Community-based Organizations (CBOs), with specific issues such as credit, water user groups, farmers' groups and so on.

In the partnership process, the government embraced INGOs in the PWG/PTF, whereas local NGOs were accepted but not encouraged. They were not, for example, invited to take part in the government drafting committee. Had it not been for the invitation of the World Bank they would probably not have been invited to join the PTF. Those who were invited are among the prominent personalities of the Women's Union and the National Committee for Advancement of Women; a lawyers' organization, the Centre for Legal Research and Services (LERES); and three independent NGOs: the Rural Development Centre Service, the Centre for Reproductive and Family Health, and Eco-Eco, an environmental NGO. At the end of the day, however, LNGOs did not play a key role in the process (Dang Ngoc Quang and Nghiem Hong Son 2001b: 14, 21).

Some LNGOs receive economic support from INGOs as a part of their campaign to develop civil society. However, many INGOs are critical of LNGOs whose leadership is often culled from retired state bureaucrats, and do not find them sufficiently 'alternative' or 'vibrant'. From the INGO perspective, there are greater benefits in supporting the administration at lower levels and mass organizations than in funding ex-civil servants.

Did INGOs exclude LNGOs by acting as a surrogate civil society in the policy partnership? LNGOs still have little influence, although it is growing, and they are neither well organized nor experienced in advocacy. As they are not a part of the government or its thinking, they are not considered a natural partner. They work under ambiguous legal frames, as research organizations under the Vietnam Union of Science Technology Association or as private consultants, and are accepted as such. With Decree 88 of July 2003 (Decree 88/2003/ND-CP), the government took a long awaited step towards establishing a more formal legal frame for the organization, operation and management of LNGOs. Yet this decree mainly deals with 'associations' and not with many of the other types of organization that constitute the LNGO sector. A more complete legal frame is scheduled for tabling in the National

Assembly in 2007 (*Taking Stock* 2003b: 33). LNGOs have nevertheless developed along with the increasing openness of society, occupying niches that are expanding for operations and projects in the social field. Still, they are playing according to the rules of the government and the party. Some of them have been encouraged by the partnership process, and have more recently taken part in poverty assessments in the new phase of the rolling out of the CPRGS. In this sense, one can say that INGOs have complemented the limited role of the LNGOs rather than excluding them from the scene.

The government's increasing openness and inclusiveness at the grassroots level has been underscored by the Grassroots Democracy Decree of 1998. This important decree was a reaction to widespread rural dissatisfaction and unrest generated by corrupt cadres in some provinces. The decree opens up space for consultation with local people over important policy decisions, and promotes transparency in the local bureaucracy. In 2003, the decree was improved with respect to organizations and associations in the localities (Decree 29 of May 1998 and Decree 79 of June 2003).

Donors diversified in the process In the final round of the CPRGS preparation, multilateral donors were represented on the PTF by the World Bank, UNDP, ADB, IMF and FAO. Of the bilaterals, the Japan Bank for International Co-operation (JBIC), Japan International Co-operation Agency (JICA), the UK development organization DfID, and Deutsche Gesellschaft für Technische Zusammenarbeit (GTZ) were members. Sweden (Sida) lost its seat when it did not contribute financially to the activities in the second round, and the World Bank tried to keep donor and government participation balanced. Denmark entered the group at a fairly late stage.

Multilateral donors were clearly under the leadership of the World Bank; although UNDP was pressured to take a less prominent role, it loyally followed the process. UNDP contributed by ensuring the broader participation of 'civil society', the introduction of the Millennium Goals, monitoring and giving support to mainstreaming the CPRGS in provincial planning. UNDP also pointed fairly early to the dangers of increasing social inequality (UNDP 2003). IMF and the ADB, which had much smaller staff in Hanoi, took more passive roles, although ADB supported the process financially.

Bilateral donors were at first dissatisfied with the newly assertive leadership of the World Bank. The Bank entered into the scene as a big brother with extensive resources, a rapidly increasing and efficient staff, and with ideas about how to manage development cooperation in a new spirit of greater openness and inclusiveness. Each of the bilateral donors has a different history and relationship to the Vietnamese government. Moreover, they need to be accountable to management systems in their respective countries. The Vietnamese government has tried to treat each of them specially, like the Swedes who were among the only donors throughout the difficult period from the early 1970s; the French who came back in the 1990s; and the Japanese with their massive development programmes, infrastructural credits and frank ideas on how relations between bigger and smaller brothers should work. On the other hand, donor participation in the partnership process has been unavoidable, since they are all a part of it one way or the other. At the same time they are also competitors and concerned with not losing their strongholds. The CPRGS process also offered opportunities for new influence and alliances, exemplified by the Japanese effort to be better integrated in the international community.

A number of donors formed a 'likeminded donor group' (encompassing the Nordics, the UK, the Netherlands, Canada, Switzerland and Australia) which raised a number of critical questions about the CPRGS. They were, however, still active in the process, particularly DfID, which was among the leading organizations in the PTF and the one which ensured financially that the World Bank had qualified expertise on poverty analyses. DfID also secured funding for British INGOs that carried out poverty assessments and which, to a large extent, provided the intellectual framework for poverty analyses.

In the early phase of partnership, the Japanese development organizations promoted a more straightforward growth orientation and had difficulties coping with the excessive 'poverty language'. Yet Japan, as the largest bilateral donor in Vietnam by the end of the 1990s, felt it had a rightful place in the PTF. To safeguard their position, Japanese organizations began to accommodate the demands of cooperating with other donors, while also starting to act more proactively. After the completion of the CPRGS, Japan insisted, with support from the Vietnamese government, that a new chapter on large-scale infrastructure should be added to the strategy, one of the most important pillars in the Japanese strategy for development. This happened towards the end of 2003.

Partner agendas

When the CPRGS was presented in 2002 by Andrew Steer, the dynamic Country Director of the World Bank, he was about to finish his term in Vietnam. He had succeeded in starting and completing the PRSP process in Vietnam, and could move on to the next position in the Bank, together with other core staff members. The partnership process had started at a low level in 1998 and had built up through several phases to a dramatic climax with the donor/government community as both spectator and participant. With a considerable amount of the participants' time and money involved, and with enormous efforts put into research, meetings, consultations, discussions, publications and strategies, the first round of the process had reached completion. The new leadership of the World Bank in Vietnam had to start the difficult phase of 'rolling it out'.

The CPRGS is a new type of document in the history of development cooperation in Vietnam. In spite of taking its point of departure in the five-year plan and ten-year strategy, it differs from these in placing more emphasis on poverty and on integrating poverty into policy thinking, while also building on liberal models according to which people, and not the state, have to take the initiative in solving their own problems. The strategy documents from the party and government separate growth and poverty: growth is related to the development of the economy, while poverty is a concern of the social sectors, like education, health and employment. It was probably in the process of including broader issues of development, including those not strictly within the social sectors, that the Vietnamese leadership of the policy process shifted from MoLISA to MPI. The CPRGS was formulated under heavy time constraints and with many stakeholders trying to influence it. As a result, the document is not particularly clear. It is what it is: a document compiled by many partners in which a diversity of interests – including those of donors – had to be accommodated.

MPI strengthened its authority during the process vis-à-vis more socially-oriented parts of the central administration. MPI is dominated by reform-minded, growth-oriented economists who are preoccupied more with economic indicators and are less sensitive to social and environmental issues. MPI was, however, able to demonstrate that it could stand shoulder to shoulder with the big powers of the donor community, and could show the government that new credits and support were achieved for the development of the country. Although the strategy was outlined by an inter-ministerial task force under MPI leadership, many donors' ideas penetrated the document (Nørlund et al. 2004). The 'poverty language' of the CPRGS tends to portray almost everybody as poor, with the poorest situated in special regions rather than showing poverty as endemic across society. In that respect the 'poverty language', e.g. the frequent reference to 'poverty' and 'the poor', tends to substitute for the word development, but with a sense not so different from earlier meanings, that growth will lead to poverty reduction. Furthermore, liberal ideas are included fairly coherently – albeit not fully: the poor have to help themselves and not expect support from the state in all respects. In some sections, however, the state still plays the leading role.

The government claims that the CPRSG will be used in planning at central levels and will be integrated into provincial planning in the rolling-out phase (Government of Vietnam 2003; *Vietnam Development Report 2004* 2003). However, the CPRGS is not a strategy that can be adopted or implemented as a whole. The government regards the CPRGS as an action plan to translate the five-year plan and the ten-year socio-economic strategy into concrete measures (Socialist Republic of Vietnam 2002b). It might be used in parts, combined with existing national sectoral plans and general strategies. At the CG meeting in December 2003, the government reported that the CPRGS and national target programmes have been integrated at all levels in order to increase participation in poverty alleviation activities (e.g. the existing development and social programmes; Government of Vietnam 2003). If that is the case, it can be argued that the CPRGS is being implemented in some respects and not in others, without diverging much from the situation before the CPRGS. The government may, however, be more committed to achieving the goals of the strategy, the Adjusted Millennium Goals, if and when they are integrated into other plans.

In early discussions about the role of the CPRGS, there was much concern about whether or not it was owned by government, whether it was written simply to satisfy donors, and whether it reflected a genuine wish for change. In the beginning, most donors thought it was a donor-driven process; later on, post-festum, most writers conclude that the process was controlled by government. The problem is that the CPRGS differs from the usual government documents, complicating its reconciliation with established procedures. The outcome is obviously a result of give and take among donors and government representatives and recognizing this fact might be more important than trying to determine who the main owner is. It is obvious that the provinces and localities did not control the policy process; even the fairly broad rounds of consultation do not constitute ownership.

If the broader ideas of the CPRGS were to be applied as stated, it could signal the beginning of the end of the dominant 'two track' policy process. This is what the donors want, being frustrated about the poor impact of some projects and programmes. The government, in turn, would rather use the positive elements, learning from donor experience, without buying the whole package. Nevertheless, the government is not a monolith and there are diverging views within various institutions. The powerful language and humanitarian thrust of notions such as 'poverty reduction' and 'improved planning' are positive formulations from the Vietnamese point of view. The broader implications of cooperating with donors – leading, for example, to new procedures in budgetary planning and accounting from the top to the village – are not yet to be known, but the language may well filter through over time.

A clear alliance was established between donors, particularly the World Bank, and core ministries involved in formulating the CPRGS. Both of these groups were winners as a result of the CPRGS process. In a short time, the government secured credits from large multilateral agencies for developing the country. The World Bank, in particular, could claim credit for organizing the government–donor–INGO community to undertake common action, led by government, to increase poverty orientation and promote reforms in accordance with core Bank policies. Best of all, the World Bank, IMF and the ADB were able to continue lending to a country with a stable economy and political environment confident that the credits would produce a safe return. The two parties – the government under MPI leadership and the donors under World Bank leadership – have found agreement in managing a large-scale planning process along the lines of the Millennium Development Goals.

Bilateral donors were less involved in discussing the process. At first, some were hesitant and provoked by the World Bank's charm offensive, equipped with a new poverty rhetoric and networking across the three sectors (state, donor, non-state). Others were encouraged by the new leadership dynamics and followed the new leaders with more admiration. Almost all bilateral donors had the problem of not having extra staff for the new demands of policy networking, or of not being equipped for extensive dialogue. The speed of the discussions made it especially difficult to contribute substantively. UNDP found that the haste of the process made it less sustainable than it could have been (UNDP 2003; Nørlund et al. 2004). Today most donors claim to adhere to the CPRGS, but at the same time an amicable dialogue is taking place between the like-minded donor group and the World Bank about its usefulness. One of the goals – to harmonize donor strategies – is being discussed and strategies are being outlined, but the multilaterals, bilaterals and the government have obvious difficulties complying with one another's strategies, and the results are as yet fairly modest.

The CPRGS process also worked much to the advantage of INGOs. They improved their policy impact vis-à-vis both government and donors in a forum where they had not earlier been accepted. They could moreover harness local contacts established in the course of the participatory assessment exercises for further reform efforts and to ensure projects in the future. The CPRGS document can be used to push for greater openness to INGOs and even to some extent for the LNGOs. The INGOs were represented in the process by a few very active professionals trained in policy advocacy. Even among INGOs, the CPRGS process was relevant for only a few organizations.

LNGOs were more marginal and benefited less from the CPRGS process. Those that had the opportunity to become involved were nevertheless positive towards it. Poverty assessments involved some local NGOs, particularly in the rolling out phase. The mention of 'civil society' in the CPRGS document and the importance of the Grassroots Democracy Decree underscore the possibility of future openings in the localities.

In spite of the consultations, the partnership process mainly took place on the central stage with a fairly limited number of institutions and people involved. This stands in contrast to the way that large party and government plans and decrees engage the Vietnamese political and administrative system at all levels, institutions and communities.[13] Interviews with a number of government agencies at the central level and some at provincial level during the summer of 2003 reinforce the view that the partnership process is not known beyond the core ministries, or even among core units of the ministries. From the viewpoint of rank-and-file civil servants, the CPRGS is a minor incident amid daily routines characterized by a huge number of other plans (Nørlund et al. 2004). The rolling out of the CPRGS into the provinces started in summer 2003 with a number of seminars, and it is still too early to know if and how it will actually work. Perhaps it will be possible to introduce the CPRGS in provinces such as Tra Vinh, where UNDP and Oxfam have a pilot programme to transform the CPRGS into annual and five-year provincial plans (UNDP 2003). In most provinces, however, government plans will be carried out as usual, since the CPRGS is not an action plan for the local level and is far too complicated to be included in local government planning. What remains are some of the Millennium Development Goals, which may be integrated into new and existing strategies.[14]

The National Assembly (NA) did not discuss the CPRGS. The government explained that it was not necessary to have an action plan based on the five-year plan and ten-year strategy passed by the NA. A CPRGS that had been assessed by the National Assembly would, however, have been a much more inclusive and better-known document. If the wish to make the strategy public and inclusive was genuine, it would have been logical to involve the National Assembly. That would have prolonged the process, however, and thus would not have complied with the timing demands of the government or the World Bank and the IMF.

The national private sector did not participate in the partnership discussions. Business organizations were occasionally consulted, but in such cases it was not clear to the representatives what the partnership process was all about. They thought it concerned only donor relations (UNDP 2003). The Federation of Trade Unions, another group with no influence in the process, should have participated in one of the larger sessions. In the rolling-out phase contacts were established with the Vietnam Chamber of Commerce and Industries, where the ILO is the cooperating agency.

The provincial level took part in the process only to a limited degree. Provincial representatives and some local poor people were involved in some consultations and in the participatory poverty assessments, but it was hardly an inclusive process of participation. It was consultative and driven by instrumental concerns related to analysis and strategy formulation.

Broader perspectives on the process

Is the commitment to poverty alleviation stronger in Vietnam because of the PRSP process? It is possible that the proliferation of poverty talk at the central level will have an impact on forthcoming policy documents and that ideas are trickling down. The message of the CPRGS is that reforms in various areas are connected. Some of the targets identified in the course of the partnership process might not be new, others will be adopted irrespective of the CPRGS. The process might result in increased support to forces and institutions in favour of poverty alleviating initiatives at the central and provincial levels. It might also reinforce institutions that benefit from donor support to rapid growth without being particularly committed to poverty alleviation. It might even enrich individuals who just happen to get access to funds in the process. These are simply hypotheses.

The PRSP process in Vietnam came into being in the midst of change, characterized by rapid growth, success in attracting FDI and ODA, and far-reaching reforms with a tendency towards greater pluralization. However, the administration and the party still have limited relationships with the globalizing world. The transnational aid industry is welcomed because of its funding and development advice, but reform is primarily viewed as an internal affair. This supports the maintenance of the two-track policy road, where donors continue to have difficulties penetrating the Vietnamese system and culture.

Some central ministries might be more reform-minded and open to new ideas by virtue of having a highly educated staff which actively communicates with the larger world. They might believe that reforms advocated by donors are unavoidable and even progressive, but by following this line they also broaden the gap between central and local government. Another result is that the provinces are unevenly developed. Productive investment tends to go to the more dynamic provinces where the prospects for growth are better, while government allocations for social services target the poor provinces (*Vietnam Development Report 2004* 2003: 73–4).

The involvement of the transnational donor community can be seen as an attempt at reforming Vietnam's social and organizational culture in the image of Western ideals of greater democracy and transparency (Northern Europe). It can be seen as a way of expanding capital investment and loan portfolios (international financial agencies), or as a way of promoting trade (Japan). INGO interest in participating in donor discussions is partly humanitarian, but they are also increasingly part of the transnational donor community who want to expand their share of projects and influence. All these interests benefited from the alliances donors established around the CPRGS, each serving specific purposes.

Through the partnership process, the World Bank succeeded in establishing itself as the lead donor agency in Vietnam. It also secured a core position vis-à-vis the government while expanding its profitable credit portfolio. At the same time, the Bank can claim to have raised the level of concern about poverty while maintaining its commitment to growth and private sector development. Like most large institutions, the World Bank is divided into different sections and factions. Many core Bank staff are growth-oriented economists but in Vietnam a strong section has also worked on 'soft' issues: social welfare, governance and poverty. The 'soft' faction has been successful in raising the profile of poverty and social issues in reports and in partnership dialogue. Most recently, the report to the CG meeting in December 2003, *Poverty*, analyses findings from the third Living Standard Household Survey combined with a new round of poverty assessments. The report points to Vietnam's 'amazing' achievements in poverty reduction, with statistics showing a decrease in poverty to 29 per cent compared with 37 per cent less than five years ago. A more nuanced problematization of the achievements is also presented based on new research, and for the first time the Bank is openly worried about growing income gaps between poorer and richer households (*Vietnam Development Report 2004* 2003). Nevertheless, the image conveyed to national and international audiences remains one of Vietnam's overall successes in growth and poverty reduction.

During the course of the PSRP process, the 'soft' sections of the World Bank country office also voiced concern about poverty and governance in Vietnam. But are their ideas being applied to the hard-core economic programmes of the World Bank, or do they remain merely on paper? It should also be noted that subsequent World Bank and IMF programmes, such as the Poverty Reduction and Growth Facility and the Poverty Reduction Support Credit, have much stronger conditionalities attached than the CPRGS. Negotiations around these programmes have been more similar to the traditional donor–recipient relations, and discussions have not been open for public scrutiny.

The extensive accumulation of data has another implication: the World Bank has to a large extent monopolized the definition of what and where poverty is in Vietnam. The Bank has been able to carry out the broadest analyses of existing material – the Living Standard Surveys and the poverty assessments – and it has published its results quickly and competently. What could be disputed, however, is the definition of poverty based solely on economic criteria and quantitative material measures. Such an approach has advantages for comparative purposes, but it excludes a deeper understanding of the Vietnamese way of thinking and ignores the importance of culture, traditions and relations between people in daily life.

The three-sector approach employed in this study suggests that Vietnamese society opened to the non-state sector, including the private sector, during the 1990s. Through PRSP formulation process, donors and the government became closer to one another, but mainly at the top level. The non-state sector was not really included in these discussions, with the exception of the INGOs. This is problematic since, while INGOs consider themselves to represent the non-state sector, they can also be seen as donors. Private capital does not feel bound by the same terms of accountability because they were marginally involved in the process. LNGOs, the National Assembly and the provinces were not active partners in the dialogues. Had they been included, this could have strengthened tendencies toward diversification in Vietnamese society. In fact, of the three sectors examined, non-state actors were most weakly represented in the PRPS discussions. This reflects its marginal status in society, but also testifies to the fact that the framework of negotiations precluded a policy process that was genuinely inclusive.

4 | Honduras: transforming the concessional state?

MAARIA SEPPÄNEN

Country context

The policy regime of Honduras displays characteristics of three different social, economic and political configurations. After a decade of economic, institutional and administrative structural changes and adjustments, Honduras exhibits many characteristics of a neo-liberal post-developmental policy regime. But there are also active mechanisms and frames of mind that date from the developmentalist, reformist state in the 1970s as well as from the long-term specifically Honduran historic configuration, termed here the 'concessional state'.[1]

The concessional state was characterized by a mechanism whereby political decision-makers derived their legitimacy from capital accumulation by and for foreign companies, through providing concessions for the extraction of natural resources. The reformist state, on the other hand, was an interventionist regime, whereby capital accumulation was based on an alliance of the state and a 'nationalist' comprador[2] elite whose interest was to provide products and services for both expanding consumer masses and foreign companies. In this phase the Honduran policy elite became practically identical to the economic elite. The latest phase corresponds to post-1990 democratization and liberalization, a phase in which new actors have entered the scene of policy-making, and the structure of political opportunity has changed profoundly.

It was precisely in the mode of the formulation of public policies that the policy regime in Honduras changed profoundly in the 1990s. It was here also that the PRS process – and, even more importantly, its precursor, the multinational response to hurricane Mitch – clearly played a role. Whereas earlier (up to 1998), policy formulation in Honduras was the almost exclusive domain of the two main parties and their closed circles of political and economic power, often connected to US investments, after Mitch policy formulation was opened to the wider participation of both domestic and transnational actors. In short, non-governmental organizations (NGOs), international private development organizations and donors have occupied an important political space in the formulation of public policies, far beyond the external influence typical of the 'banana republic'. There is a seat for Honduran NGOs, INGOs and donors at practically every table where public policies are formulated (sectoral policies, appointment committees of Supreme Court judges and judges of the Court of Auditors and in several fora for government–civil society deliberations and social auditing initiatives). The news is not that external actors sit at the tables of power in Honduras – that has been the historical legacy of the concessional state – but that political space has been opened to a new kind of actor, both domestic and transnational: bilateral donors, NGOs and INGOs.

It is important to note that this has happened in spite of a political unwillingness further to democratize Honduras, regardless of what the official discourse claims about democracy and participation. According to an interviewee who had closely followed and participated in the PRS process on behalf of the government (interview: Ministry of Finance), the government 'only thinks it is fulfilling conditions of access to HIPC but instead, without realizing it, it is opening political space'. This observation explains why there has been, parallel to the opening up of political space, constant and fierce opposition by several state actors (Parliament, president, most civil servants) to the participation of private development organizations, and, in some cases, to the participation of certain persons representing 'civil society'. In this context, donors have played a major role in pushing towards greater civil society participation in public policy formulation, by stressing the issue in consultative group (CG) meetings and by funding civic participation.

It is questionable how far private organizations can influence policy; such organizations expressed doubts and frustrations about the usefulness of sitting on the *mesas sectoriales* (sectoral committees) (interviews: Oxfam; G-15). This is not the main point, however. The significance of this sea-change lies in the impact that the opening up of space in decision-making, however small the power to influence policies might be, has on the public/private distinction in Honduran politics. It has become increasingly difficult for politicians to continue dealing with politics as a *private* matter of personal power and, consequently, of personal wealth. And this may well be the reason why there is opposition by the political establishment towards popular participation in public policy formulation. In these circumstances it is no wonder that 'politics' and 'the political' sound like curses to the ears of the general public in Honduras, and, consequently, the term 'professional' (that is, technocrat) has more positive connotations. The specific Honduran policy regime makes the country especially prone to the generalization of a (transnational) technocratic habitus and the depoliticization of policy processes.

The political configuration in Honduras thus favours external influence when this implies increased foreign investment and 'free' external resources from development cooperation. The government will undertake administrative reforms if these are seen to attract foreign funds. At the same time, the elite can be inflexible in defending its accumulation regime based on joint concessions and comprador interests. The hard core of Honduran politics resists modernization,[3] even when it is imposed from the outside as a condition for financial benefits for the national budget in the form of foreign debt alleviation.

In the PRS process, the pattern inherited from the concessional state, in which external actors actively participate in domestic policy formulation, has been strengthened. The domestic/external boundary has been further blurred, if possible, and external actors are increasingly important, occupying a larger political space than ever, even when compared to the heyday of the banana republic. This expansion of political space occupied by external actors is mostly due to a diversification of the kind of external actors that participate in public policy formulation in Honduras and the mechanisms employed. Whereas traditionally it was first the plantation companies, then the US military and later international financial institutions (IFIs) that participated in policy formulation, now bilateral donors and private transnational development agencies are also present. Not that foreign business interests have disappeared, but now they occupy a less visible role in public policy formulation.

The difference lies not only in the extent to which external actors occupy political space, but also in the legitimacy with which this is done. All progressively thinking Honduran interviewees underlined that external donor pressure is 'the only way of bringing about changes'. Only one interviewee – and, interestingly, the only expatriate – said that donors occupy a political space that should be occupied by Hondurans.

One aspect of the policy regime of the concessional state is conspicuous in Honduras: that external influence in domestic policy formulation is considered normal and is even celebrated by most political actors, both state and non-state, though for different reasons. It is as if Honduran citizens considered that change in the political system has to come about through external not internal influence. This situation has turned donors into brokers between the government and civil society.

Another consequence of the same process has been the ongoing redefinition of the public/private distinction. The gradual development of a new kind of political subjectivity at the grassroots level, that of the active citizen, and the opening up of political space in public policy formulation are interrelated. For politicians and the domestic policy elite in general, the current trend challenges the privacy (and, therefore, the impunity and unaccountability) of decision-making – and the privileges emanating from this privacy.

The social relations that govern the state–society interface are also undergoing subtle transformations. The main narrative of legitimacy that underlies most policies is to make Honduras attractive to foreign investments. There is a slight change to be noted, however, in the way in which that attractiveness is constructed. The elaboration of the PRSP is one of the factors behind this change; the other being the changes in the logic of global capital accumulation as perceived by Honduran business sectors. In order to attract foreign investment under the traditional concessional state, it was sufficient to guarantee cheap, disciplined and uneducated labour. Now it is increasingly acknowledged that the low educational level of the population encourages low levels of productivity. Low productivity, in turn, prevents economic growth and is one of the factors that maintains high levels of poverty – thus hindering further foreign investment. (The translation into action of this understanding, however, is still very rudimentary.)

Internal security shines as the brightest (or rather, darkest) immediate problem the government has to face.[4] Security issues bubble up into the public eye through unresolved 'social cleansing' cases of murdered youth, and the war that youth gangs have declared against the Maduro administration. The government has consequently taken a hard line, with severe punishments for youth gang members. The registers of authority (and loyalty) in the Honduran social relations of governance include a strong presence of intimidation at the foundations of state–society relationships. A large part of delinquency is directly or indirectly related to poverty, but instead of starting a campaign of internal security from the roots of delinquency (creation of employment, support to families, rehabilitation of youth criminals, etc.), the government has chosen the strong-arm approach with the support of the police and the armed forces, supplemented by judicial inactivity in cases of social cleansing. Therefore, it could be argued that the reduction of poverty is not a real political priority for the Honduran political elite; it is easier to start a security campaign based on repression. There is a general consensus among those who participated in the formulation of the PRSP that the Honduran political elite does not really understand the necessity of reducing poverty, the official political discourse notwithstanding.

Poverty and the poor are largely absent from the Honduran imagination and self-perception of the country, as expressed in media portrayals of political events.[5] Whereas in other Latin American countries poor people are the favourite interviewees of journalists in denouncing price hikes and the doings of the government (and sometimes as grateful recipients of development projects), in Honduras the poor have no voice. They are portrayed, from far away, as the ever silent, submissive peons of the elite. The fact that the Honduran media are owned by the very same politicians who prefer not to talk about poverty certainly has something to do with the poor's lack of voice in the press and TV, but no matter what the explanation, it is evident that the political elite in Honduras does not see poverty as *the* problem of the country.

Coming back to registers of authority and loyalty: there is always a curious and very conspicuous mechanism at work in Honduras when different social classes meet. This is an unconscious frame of mind or way of thinking about social categories, a 'dispositif' in the Foucaultian sense, that is used for (re)producing social distinction. In other Latin American countries there is a similar mechanism at work,[6] but the specific Honduran variant concerns the educational level of persons, normally expressed by 'low cultural level'. This dispositif is used instinctively by those who consider themselves superior, and normally is not contested by the person finding him/herself in the inferior position. Whereas some mechanisms of social differentiation – such as Bourdieu's *distinction* (Bourdieu 1984) – regulate an upward movement in social hierarchies,[7] the Honduran dispositif of low cultural level 'points downwards' (Nugent 1992). It is used with surprising regularity to dismiss some segments of the population (the poor, people without university degrees, people from the provinces ...), and prevents them from being credited with full-fledged citizenship, and from being heard and listened to, as happened in the PRS process. But as I will later try to show, there is an increasing contestation of this dispositif at the grassroots; i.e. a change in the mode of political subjectivity that has traditionally been passive and submissive to different forms of paternalism.

The organization of aid relationships

Background Until very recently, Honduras was relatively virgin territory for development aid. The country lacked the kind of social situation that would attract sympathy from bilateral donors, such as existed in Nicaragua in the 1980s (the Sandinista government). The position of Honduras as the launching pad for the US military's 'low intensity' war in the region also deterred donors from becoming involved with the Honduran government. At the beginning of the 1990s, it was mainly the international financial institutions and INGOs that had operations in Honduras, in addition to a few bilateral donors. Nor was there any aggressive policy of 'selling' the country's misery to the international development community for the reasons analysed above but worth repeating here: the politico-economic elite's perception of the country largely excludes the poor and poverty, and the accumulation regime which they are a part of is based on an alliance with international capital as concession givers and compradors, not on their position as brokers in the channelling of development aid.

Hence, when the first HIPC initiative was launched in 1995, the Honduran government remained passive, and only some sectors of the Honduran intelligentsia, those who eventually became the NGO sector in the participatory PRS formulation, were interested in the initiative (see below). The reason behind this lack of initiative in attempting to get Honduras included under HIPC was also statistical. The GDP was too high (US $722 per capita in 1998 according to UNDP; PRSP 2001a: 22) and the external debt too low (112 per cent of GDP and 35 per cent of exports in 1995; d'Ans 2002) to fit into the regulations of the first HIPC initiative.

In October 1998 something happened that changed the opportunity structure and, consequently, the configuration of aid relationships in Honduras. Hurricane Mitch devastated the country, destroying or damaging 85,000 houses, leaving over 400,000 persons homeless and increasing the number of poor by 2.8 per cent (an increase of 165,000 poor people). According to the estimates of CEPAL, the direct damage caused by Mitch represented 70 per cent of the GDP ($3.8 billion), and economic growth fell to −1.9 per cent in 1999, instead of the 5.5 per cent growth earlier projected for that year (PRSP 2001a: 18–20).

It seems hurricane Mitch changed the aid relationship in Honduras for good. It also marked a transnationalization of Honduran political space to a different degree and form than had been the case under the concessional policy regime. The new president, Carlos Flores Facussé (1998–2001), descendant of a famous family of businessmen (and politicians) and a successful businessman himself, was able to convince the development community of his government's commitment to developing the country at the consultative group meeting in Stockholm in May 1999. Honduras thus entered the international scene of development aid as a recipient country. In the same year, the Honduran government, also under pressure from civil society organizations, made an effort to be included in the enlarged HIPC initiative (HIPC II). A double process made the inclusion of Honduras possible: the lowering of the criteria for HIPC eligibility, and the deterioration in national statistics caused by Mitch. Once in the HIPC pipeline, a participatory Poverty Reduction Strategy formulation became a condition to be fulfilled in order to reach the Decision Point.

From G-5 to G-15 Hurricane Mitch and the international media coverage given to it sensitized the international aid community to the cause of Honduran reconstruction. Shortly after the extent of the damage was known, a rush of emergency aid flooded the country; over one hundred private aid organizations started operations (interview: Trocaire), chaotic and disorganized, whereas before Mitch only thirteen INGOs, eight of which came from European Union countries, had worked in Honduras.[8]

For the bilateral donors the hurricane represented a window of opportunity to establish operations in Honduras. The first consultative group meeting in Stockholm in May 1999, coordinated by IDB, laid the foundation for donor cooperation. In August 1999 the G-5 (Grupo

5) was established, originally called the Stockholm Declaration Follow-up Group. The members were the first bilateral donors operating in Honduras – Sweden, Spain, USA, Germany and Canada; a month later Japan joined to make up the G-6. The donor coordination committee, the 'G-X', has since grown to include more bilateral donors, and financial institutions. In addition to the above-mentioned six bilateral donors the UK, Italy and the Netherlands have subsequently established themselves in Honduras, and now the multilaterals – the World Bank, IMF, IDB, UNDP, European Union (EU) and the Central American Bank of Economic Integration (CABEI/BCAIE) – are also invited to sit at the G-15.[9] The stated purpose of G-15 is to harmonize aid in order to 'prevent overlapping, duplication of effort, contradictions and/or saturation' of development aid in Honduras (*Lineamiento* 2002: 2).

On the other hand, in mid-2004 it was obvious that the tide had turned and there was a movement of separation from the group, largely because of most donors' policy decision to concentrate on poorer countries. Since the early years of the present century, Honduras is no longer classed as a low-income country, and is presently in the category of low-middle-income countries.[10] Of the above-mentioned bilateral donors, the Netherlands and the UK have stopped operating in Honduras.

According to the statistics of OECD/DAC, the largest bilateral donor to Honduras is the USA with almost US $100 million annually (average 1999–2000), and the second is Japan ($58 million), followed by Spain, Sweden and Germany (with 41, 35 and 31 million, respectively). The largest lender in the period 1990–2000 was IDA (WB) with an average of $156 million annually, followed by IDB, offering half of the former amount.

The 'rush' to Honduras after Mitch was also given a boost by the situation in Nicaragua, where most donors were losing faith in the commitment of Arnoldo Aleman's government to the principles of good governance (at the end of the 1990s), which led them to search for alternative aid recipients in the region.

The 'bible' of donor involvement in Honduras is the Stockholm Declaration, a basic guideline of objectives and principles signed by the donors and the government in May 1999. It establishes six areas of action: (1) reduction of ecological and social vulnerability; (2) transformation of Honduran society based on transparency and good governance; (3) consolidation of democracy through strengthening decentralization and civil society participation; (4) human, gender and minority rights; (5) reduction of foreign debt; and (6) coordination of donor activities in respect of priorities set by the recipient country. In the words of a *pro-tempore* presidency[11] of G-15, the objective of the donor coordination committee is to 'transform Honduras into a modern, equitable state of law' where 'even the wealthy have to learn to pay taxes' (interview: G-15).

The political space occupied by G-15 is large. It participates in the seven trilateral (government–civil society–donors) sectoral committees (*mesas sectoriales*) where sectoral policies are debated.[12] The organization of the group follows a scheme in which the principles of the Stockholm Declaration are harmonized with PRS, giving, in addition to the sectoral committees, two mechanisms of political influence. The first is the level of ambassadors and resident representatives, in charge of 'contributing at the political level to the harmonisation of national policies with the principles of the Stockholm Declaration and HIPC' (*El concepto de transformación* n.d.: 4). The counterpart of the highest level mechanism are the Honduran ministers of the presidency, finance and the vice-minister of development cooperation (Interview: G-15). The second is the Technical Follow-up Group (*Grupo técnico de seguimiento*, GTS), which brings together the representatives of aid agencies present in the country (e.g. AID, Sida, GTZ, JICA, the European Commission) with the counterparts of UNAT, the vice-minister of the presidency and others (Interview: G-15). Their task is to promote the incorporation of the transversal themes of PRS into the implementation of development programmes and projects (*El concepto de transformación* n.d.: 4).

In October 2000, UNDP established its own forum, the Foro de Fortalecimiento de la Democracia (FFD), the president of which is Cardinal Rodríguez, the highest Catholic authority in the country and one of the future 'popeable' (*papable*) cardinals at the Vatican. The Forum contains representatives from a large range of Honduran civil society organizations, including political parties, private enterprise and media, and all foreign embassies in Tegucigalpa, plus eleven UN agencies. In addition, according to the Law on the Poverty Reduction Fund of 30 April 2002, donors have two observer seats (one multilateral and one bilateral) at the meetings of the Consultative Committee of the PRS that is in charge of monitoring and setting the priorities for the use of funds channelled for poverty reduction. The political influence exercised within this political space occupied by the donors is, at least potentially, considerable. It has been admitted openly that poverty reduction as an objective was written into the present government's programme only because of donor pressure (interview: FOPRIDEH).

The internal dynamic of the donor community is a topic about which it is difficult to say much without lengthy participatory observation. On the basis of the interviews and later observation it is, however, possible to reconstruct a picture of differences in priorities of different donors and internal divisions within the G-15 group. According to the holder of the rotating presidency of G-15, some donors within the group are more 'procurement'-oriented, 'down-to-earth' donors with an emphasis on service delivery, infrastructure and other tangible things such as rural development (Canada, Japan). Two others are distinguished by their stress on human rights, good governance and minority rights (Sweden, USA).

Non-state actors point out a certain ambiguity, as they call it, in the behaviour of bilateral donors (interviews: FOSDEH; Oxfam). In the experience of these non-state organizations, the bilateral donors are open-minded and can even raise 'sensible' issues, such as skewed income distribution and land reform, with the Honduran government. But when it comes to 'real' decision-making at the tables of power, none of the donors challenges the policies imposed by IMF. In the eyes of Honduran NGO actors, European donors appear (especially) dishonest: reformist, socially-oriented and pro-poor on the outside, yet submissive to the ideological hegemony of the IMF on the inside.

Several interviewees reported rivalry between multilateral donors (IFIs) (interviews: Ministry of the Presidency; FOSDEH). First, there were differences in the way poverty statistics were designed. The Inter-American Development Bank (IDB) produced its own statistics as if trying to minimize the credibility of the Bretton Woods institutions. One should remember that the HIPC initiative came from the World Bank, and because of the moral pressure of Jubilee 2000 and allied civil society organizations, other multilateral lending institutions (and bilateral donors) had to follow suit (Callaghy 2001). This in spite of the fact that the decision to alleviate debt implied a loss of revenue for the creditors; bilateral grants, however, often compensate for this loss.

Both state and donor actors also pointed out a lack of clarity on what a PRSP and its participatory formulation were supposed to mean (interviews: UNDP; Ministry of the Presidency; Sida). According to them, the World Bank left these definitions to the Honduran government, which created uncertainties and unnecessary disputes among actors about what constitutes participation.

During the process of formulating the PRS, Bretton Woods institutions appeared as two different partners in the eyes of NGO actors. In Honduras, the World Bank was 'open', i.e. supportive of larger non-state actor participation by organizing workshops and contributing to networking, and engaging in dialogue with civil society organizations (interview: Trocaire). On the contrary, the IMF was, if not invisible, at least hermetic,[13] providing no information about the macro-economic framework. This was not made public before the submission of the I-PRSP to the WB/IMF, and was not made an issue for discussion during the consultation process (Bertelsen and Jensen 2002: passim). According to the interviews carried out by Bertelsen and Jensen (2002: 75–6), on the other hand, the IFI resident representations have been generally suspicious of, if not directly hostile towards, a participatory formulation of the macro-economic part of the PRSP. This impression is confirmed by the reluctance of the WB/IMF resident staff assessment report (PRSP 2001b) to mention that Interforos had stepped out of the PRS process and formulated a PRS of their own (interview: FOSDEH; see below).

Yet it would be too hasty to impute a zero-sum game to the donor coordination committee G-15. In spite of rivalries, different approaches and probable institutional jealousies, the donors have a stronger influence together than they do apart. Bilateral donors do not propose macro-economic policies of their own but rather leave these to the Bretton Woods institutions; at least they refrain from challenging the recipes imposed by IMF because all of them are 'shareholders' of the lending institutions. Open cleavages are to be found with more probability in inter-IFI relationships, one of these being the extent to which 'participation' and 'partnerships' are integrated into the practical workings of respective international financial institutions. In the Honduran PRS process the result was that the bilateral donors, the World Bank and UNDP supported and encouraged the participation of non-state actors but did not object when IMF imposed a part of the PRSP without public consultation.

The result was a certain depoliticization of policy processes. Honduras has a poverty reduction strategy, with a neo-liberal PRGF sealed in with the blessing of the international development community.[14] The strategy was approved as the result of a (supposedly) participatory policy formulation but a significant part of it was, in reality, the result of direct imposition, totally excluded from participatory scrutiny.

To summarize, the opening of political opportunity in the aftermath of hurricane Mitch prompted the donors to occupy political space in Honduras, and the Honduran government welcomed them to an increasing degree as the prospects of new external funds have materialized. The main mechanism for achieving political space has been the conditionalities of poverty reduction necessary for the access to HIPC. With the 'carrot' of HIPC, donors have been able to open space in public policy formulation and impose an agenda of poverty reduction on the government – at least on paper if not always in spirit.

The same conditionalities have worked in a different way for civil society actors. Here the prerequisite for HIPC has been civil society participation in the preparation of PRSP. The donors have been instrumental in opening up and consolidating political space for non-state actors and thus have intervened, and mediated, in the relationship between the state and civil society. The PRS process and its catalyst, hurricane Mitch, have been crucial in increasing donor support to non-state actors in Honduras. Donors have financed capacity building and international networking of non-state actors for the PRS process, prompted by the (then) new discourse on participation of the World Bank. The result is that whereas before Mitch the established political elite was in charge of policy formulation, in collaboration with economic and/or military (as in the 1980s) actors from abroad, after Mitch there is a wider diversity of actors involved in policy formulation.

The main mechanism of opening political space for civil society actors by the donors has been transnationalization. The donors have helped civil society organizations *jump* (geographical) *scales*, that is, transcend national borders through the networking of civic actors with European, US and other Latin American non-state organizations. In order to influence domestic policy formulation, Honduran NGOs are now able to contact their counterparts in Washington, Brussels and other European capitals, and ask them to lobby their respective donor organizations (bilaterals or multilaterals) which then may exercise pressure on the Honduran government through G-15 or individually.

Donor support for civil society organizations has also had a differentiating effect on Honduran civil society actors. Those that have been most able to benefit from donor support are a specific kind of organization, the NGOs. In fact, it is donor support that has created NGOs as a distinct category of civic organization in the first place, and in Honduras the very definition of a non-governmental organization is that it receives foreign funding.

The dynamics of civic activism in Honduras

Introduction When talking about civic activism, sooner or later one comes to the question of civil society. The strength (or weakness) of civil society in Honduras depends on the definition one gives to the term. The basic notion of civil society as consisting of intermediate organizations between the private and public spheres may be too wide because, as such, it does not define the nature of the interaction between these two spheres. One could argue that the existence of civil society implies some kind of society–state interaction, at least potentially.

In the widest sense of the term, civil society in Honduras is very large. According to a mapping of 'organized civil society' carried out on behalf of IDB, there are over 8,000 civil society organizations in Honduras (interview: FONAC). These include a variety of associations whose organizational structures and functions differ considerably. It is obvious that football clubs and fraternities of patron saints do not have the same role in public policy formulation, even at the local level, as a trade union, neighbourhood committee, chamber of commerce or a development-oriented NGO.

It is not easy to make sense of this nebulous entity formed by organized civil society. In this section I will defend the thesis that any of these 8,000 informal or formal associations may potentially come to play a role in public policy formulation in one way or another. This evolution is not automatic, however. It necessitates (and at the same time makes possible) the development of a certain form of civic consciousness, a political subjectivity that deviates from the dominant, traditional one in Honduras. This said, I will argue that this is precisely what is going on in the country. This premise suggests an understanding of civil society that emphasizes the capacity of organized citizens to react and respond to political stimuli from the state,[15] and it is precisely this *capacidad de respuesta* that has grown enormously in Honduras after Mitch.

Urbanization, the (slowly but surely) rising levels of education, and the expansion of communications and information technologies have no doubt played an important role in this development. But the changing structures of political opportunity related to hurricane Mitch, its aftermath and the PRS formulation process have been the real catalyst. It is possible to make sense of slow, sometimes invisible deep structural changes in civic activism by using the notion of political opportunity.[16] In this way the evolution of civic activism in Honduras presents three clearly distinct phases: the 'old' civil society that still is there, the 'new' civil society formed immediately after Mitch, and the most recent period during which an institutionalization of civic participation in public policy formulation has materialized. Furthermore, there are signs of a fourth phase, an autonomous, 'non-tutored' bottom-up civic activism – increasing levels of public response to state politics.

Traditional civil society: domestic opportunities dominate Traditional civil society in Honduras is formed by professional associations, trade unions (including peasants' organizations) and organizations related to culture in the narrow sense of the word – youth associations (often sports-related), fraternities of patron saints, artists' leagues and the like. There is also the Federation of Women's Associations, a descendant of the fighters for universal suffrage in the 1940s and 1950s. Of these, two categories have actively participated in policy formulation in the public sphere: trade unions and professional associations (after universal suffrage was achieved). This part of civil society was largely absent from the PRS process.

Business associations such as local chambers of commerce would be a separate case; they have certainly influenced policies deeply. Here I exclude them because of their close sociological and economic ties with political power. In Honduras, the public and private sectors are not as separate as liberal economic (and political) theory suggests (interview: Ministry of Finance).

Trade unions in Honduras date from the period of the concessional state; they were formed on banana plantations and in mines that were given as concessions to foreign capital (Argüeta 1992). During the populist reformist state, peasant associations proliferated, thanks to the cooperative land reform movement. In spite of many processes that tend to diminish the political weight of class-interest-based organizations (privatization, the 'flexibilization' of labour legislation, the distribution of plantations to individual farmers, the separation of trade union elite from the grassroots, etc.), trade unions still play a role in public policy formulation. What is more, Bloque Popular, really a political formation in Honduras today, is the most active of all. It constitutes a confederation of trade unions, waging a fierce battle against privatization, globalization and so on. Teachers' unions are also active but their demands relate more directly, although not entirely, to practical trade-union matters (salaries, working conditions).

Another element of traditional civil society in Honduras that has always played a role in public policy formulation is the professional associations (*colegios profesionales*). Of these, the two most important ones are the National Bar Association (Colegio de abogados) and the Economists' Association (Colegio de economistas). The first has a privileged position because of the role lawyers play as guardians of legality and state institutionality. The second provides the state with qualified technocrats (and NGOs with professional managers, as we shall see).

The main characteristic of traditional civil society in Honduras is that the structure of political opportunity resides in the domestic sphere with very little, if any, jumping of scales. The other characteristic is that, with the exception of trade unions and peasant organizations, it corresponds to the urban, educated middle classes.

New civil society: the transnationalization of political opportunity All through the 1990s private development funding increased in Honduras. Some transnational private development organizations (INGOs), mostly of religious orientation, had worked there from the 1970s. On the eve of hurricane Mitch there were thirteen INGOs working in the country. Increasing foreign funding for non-state actors[17] had also prompted the creation of Honduran associations working in the field of development, the so-called non-governmental organizations, NGOs. It is useful to reiterate that NGOs as a certain formal associational structure (which includes their *personería jurídica*) are private development organizations founded in order to attract and channel foreign (and in some cases, domestic) funding.[18] The boom in NGOs corresponds to the liberalization of the economy and the state. Earlier the state had been able to absorb university graduates as cadres. After state downsizing (that decreased the role that clientelism was able to play in civil servant recruitment), outsourcing and privatization, there were ever fewer employment opportunities in the public sector. Founding an NGO became a rational choice for many competent persons because of competitive remuneration rates compared with the public sector. The dominant political culture also played a role. Some NGOs were used for clientelist purposes. A politician could tell a follower that there were no jobs available in the public sector, but that there were funds to be channelled to NGOs. The clientelist system of spoils in some cases extended to resources available for private development organizations.

The increasing organizational density of private development organizations in Honduras did not automatically constitute a civil society as such, but it was a necessary precondition for the birth of one. The catalyst that profoundly changed political opportunity structures was, again, a natural phenomenon: Mitch. (Let it not be forgotten that in the case of Honduras there is a direct causality: Mitch → HIPC → PRSP.) The transnationalization of funding was not enough to bring about a change; what was needed was the political opportunity provided by Mitch, with international development cooperation in its wake. It is also worth noting that there are other 'new' arenas of civic activism in Honduras that frame advocacy for public policies, not only the development-oriented ones analysed here. Human rights organizations and democracy associations have played an important role in public debate, and some of them even participated in PRS formulation. But because of their lesser prominence in the PRSP process and their greater emphasis on other issues, they are not included in this narrative.

Special attention will be given here to the history of Interforos, the most ambitious civic coalition formation in Honduran civil society. The story of Interforos reveals many aspects of the recent upsurge of civil society participation in public policy formulation in Honduras. As it happens, it was possible for the fieldwork team to observe directly the dynamics of civic activism at Interforos. (Officially it is called Espacio Interforos, a space of debate between civic activism arenas.)

After the first HIPC initiative in 1995, a group of young economists at the National Association of Economists became interested in foreign debt and possible debt alleviation for Honduras. They organized workshops in which some economists working in state administration also participated. They played with statistical definitions of poverty in order to find ways in which the country could meet the entrance criteria of HIPC I. This working group of the Association of Economists grew into a civic association called FOSDEH (Foro social de la deuda externa de Honduras, Social Forum for Foreign Debt). In its founding meeting, it was agreed that FOSDEH was not going to be a legalized association with administrative structures and funding from abroad (i.e. an NGO), but should instead remain an arena for public debate and consciousness-raising on questions of foreign debt and poverty.

The prospect of external funding was too much of a temptation, however, and even before Mitch a part of the original group decided to formalize FOSDEH's organizational structure into a full-blown NGO, a decision which made some original members withdraw from the organization. With Mitch, FOSDEH became the most vocal and technically most competent policy advocacy group in Honduras – and, consequently, an irritation to the political establishment. Hurricane Mitch provided a window of political opportunity that FOSDEH was able to take full advantage of. The leading figures of FOSDEH became part of every public debate and committee where the presence of 'civil society' was required. The representatives of FOSDEH played an important role in the good-will Honduras was able to attract from the international development community at the CG meeting in Stockholm in May 1999. It could even be said that without FOSDEH Honduras would never have reached the HIPC II Decision Point. With the moral and economic support of sister organizations in Washington (e.g. WOLA, Washington Office for Latin America), Brussels (Eurodad) and others (e.g. Kepa in Helsinki), FOSDEH lobbied donor organizations in nine European capitals for the inclusion of Honduras in HIPC. By advocating internally within Honduras, it was able to get the message through to the public sphere about the importance of debt alleviation for Honduran development.

The attitude of high-level Honduran decision-makers towards this sudden civic activism concerning public policy formulation was directly and openly hostile, as perceived by the non-state actors themselves (interviews, FOSDEH; Trocaire) and by non-participant observers (Torres Calderón et al. 2002). On the other hand, civil servants whose personal conviction was progressive (that is, in this context, committed to poverty reduction) and who worked in ministries in charge of PRSP, saw the picture from a more national perspective. According to them, there was no contradiction between civic advocacy on behalf of HIPC and poverty reduction, and Honduras's national interest or the interests of the government (interviews: Ministry of Finance; UNDP). This may be an optimistic assessment of the government's capacity for knowing its own interests, but as an argument about Honduras's 'national interest' it sounds convincing. It is indeed possible that without the intervention of FOSDEH and other civic actors around the CG of Stockholm, Honduras would not have convinced the international development community of its commitment to the cause of national reconstruction and transformation, and later, of its commitment to poverty reduction. FOSDEH and other NGOs were instrumental in Honduras's entrance into HIPC, and in its acceptance by the international development community as a recipient country.

Parallel to the 'metamorphosis' of FOSDEH into an NGO, the density of civic organizations in the Honduran provinces also increased. Prompted in some cases by the presence of development NGOs and in others by religious organizations, several kinds of grassroots associations shot up in Honduran towns and villages.[19] For these organizations, widely dispersed and with little, if any, contact with one another, hurricane Mitch was also a political opportunity. Mitch increased civic consciousness as it revealed profound deficiencies in state organization and in the government's capacity to organize emergency aid and prevention measures. Locally, Mitch brought together many associations and organizations in emergency aid and reconstruction (women especially took a leading role in reconstruction). Nationally, Mitch brought FOSDEH and other Tegucigalpa-based NGOs in touch with the provinces. The main catalyst was the national Master Plan for Reconstruction and Transformation (Plan maestro de reconstrucción y transformación, PMRT) that President Flores set out to formulate. The PMRT was the first national plan for which some forms of consultation were used, and it later served as a basis for the formulation of the PRSP which was, according to official sources, to become a part of PMRT. According to external observers, however, no civil society participation took place in the preparation of the PMRT (Torres Calderón et al. 2002).

The origins of Interforos derive from the political opportunity of the PMRT. It was a rational marriage. For the Tegucigalpa-based advocacy NGOs their new contacts with the provincial 'grassroots' were a condition *sine qua non* that allowed them to present themselves as bona fide representatives of civil society. For the grassroots organizations, FOSDEH and other technically competent advocacy groups with transnational networks amplified their voice and impact in the public sphere and in public policy formulation.

This 'marriage' of local, often informal, diverse and fragile service-based community organizations with little, if any, funding, and capital-city-based, middle-class, technocratic advocacy NGOs with international funding also proved expedient during the formulation of the PRS. Leading NGO figures could present themselves as representatives of Interforos in order to contest dismissive remarks at the negotiation tables according to which they 'did not represent anybody except themselves' (practically all interviewees repeated this remark). When the voice of 'civil society' was not listened to or taken into account in the formulation of the PRSP to the extent that the representatives of Interforos would have liked, Interforos decided to step out of the process and formulate its own poverty reduction strategy. This further strengthened Interforos, as its independent participatory poverty reduction strategy formulation served as a capacity-building exercise for the local organizations that coalesced in Interforos.

Thanks to the existence of Interforos, key persons within FOSDEH were able to establish themselves as part of the Honduran policy elite. A small anecdote is revealing of the transnational political space that these highly qualified NGO activists were able to occupy. It also reveals a lot about the transnationalization of 'civil society', and about the difficulties of changing de facto policy priorities of a massive organization like the World Bank. When the resident staff of the WB and IMF wrote their joint staff assessment report on the Honduran PRSP without mentioning that Interforos had stepped out of the process and formulated its own poverty reduction strategy, the leading figure in FOSDEH threatened to call the president of the WB (James Wolfenson) and tell him about this omission. This could have severely hindered the career opportunities of the concerned staff member. As a result, the staff member revised his report to include Interforos's absence from the PRSP formulation. (This anecdote also indicates that the staff member knew perfectly well that he was not following the official WB policy of openness and participation promoted by the headquarters of his organization.)

One might propose a hypothesis about the difference between Honduras and Nicaragua in the PRS process. In Nicaragua civil society organizations decided to stick to the PRS process in spite of very similar experiences of hostility and feelings of not being listened to by state actors (Bertelsen and Jensen 2002). It could be argued that this difference is due to the position that leading figures of civil society organizations were able to occupy in relation, first, to the state and, second, to the rest of civil society. In other words, the distance taken by Interforos from the official PRS formulation may have been motivated more by the personal ambitions of the key persons of the civic coalition than by popular unease with the consultations. In the last instance, then, the difference between these two countries would be due to the respective natures of the NGO sectors in relation to the state and the general population. In this comparison, Honduran NGOs seem to be more rigid and class-conscious. In Nicaragua, on the contrary, the NGO sector is populated by ex-Sandinista militants, sacked from the state administration after 1990.

With the incursion of key NGO leaders into national public policy formulation, 'civil society' has become synonymous with NGOs. This tendency to omit the traditional Honduran civil society organizations from the definition of the term is particularly pronounced among the NGO elite. They consider *themselves* to be 'civil society', excluding trade unions and peasant organizations which would have much to do with poverty reduction strategies. Within the state administration, however, civil servants have a larger view, and trade unions, peasants and others are represented on most occasions when 'civil society' is needed in decision-making.

After the PRSP formulation, new political space has been opened to non-state actors. There were 'civil society' representatives in the appointment committees for Supreme Court judges and for the Court of Auditors. The same applies to other fora; for instance, there is also a civil society representative on the advisory board of the poverty reduction fund. It is no exaggeration to say that the civic occupation of political space has become institutionalized in public policy formulation in Honduras. A further expression of this is the inclusion of a press release of civil society organizations among the main documents for the Consultative Group of June 2004 on the web pages of the presidency.[20] Institutionalizing the occupation of political space by non-state actors has changed the structure of political opportunity in Honduras. The latest actors to take advantage of the new political opportunities are the political parties. For example, a new 'forum' of civil society was convened in August 2002 (Foro permanente de sociedad civil) in order that a political party could coopt a place reserved for civil society representation on the appointment committee of the Court of Auditors (several interviews).

Later developments at Interforos The capacity-building effect that the participatory PRS formulation in 2000 had on the organizations of Interforos was later to mark the evolution of the civic coalition. The provinces felt that Interforos should have activities beyond merely one or two persons sitting at negotiation tables with the government, and felt confident of their capacity to assume more responsibilities as an umbrella organization. This was felt by many insiders to be a 'historic necessity' for the future of Honduran civil society. In the annual convention of 2001 an important decision was made; Interforos's organizational structure was to be decentralized. The leaders of Tegucigalpa-based NGOs, controlling the technical unit and the leadership of the organization, were opposed to the decision, but they were in the minority.

Interforos's new organizational chart consists of regional (departmental) chapters with a rotating presidency (responsible for 'coordination', the primus inter pares being the *coordinador*) and 'thematic networks'. The latter were mainly populated by the technically qualified, educated urbanites (e.g. FOSDEH in economic policy). The discrepancy, then unresolved, concerned the position of these thematic networks. The majority wanted the thematic networks (advocacy NGOs) to function under the leadership of Interforos's regional chapters, whereas the minority insisted on the national scope and role of their advocacy.

For the year 2001–02 the coordination of Interforos had gone to a province of Western Honduras, with the consequent loss of visibility of Interforos in the capital. The NGO workers remained in their positions as representatives of civil society on decision-making committees, but something was lost: FOSDEH was now supposed to be just the departmental thematic network on economic policy for the Department Francisco Morazán, and not *the* advocacy organization that represented national Interforos. The representative of FOSDEH, which at that time was still a member of Interforos, lamented the loss of visibility due to the decentralization, and complained about the inability of the provincial/departmental activists to 'distinguish the wood from the trees' (interview: FOSDEH).

The problem revolved around the following dilemma: given insurmountable human resource constraints, how could the Interforos leadership attend to building up organizational capacity at the grassroots, while still maintaining an ability to respond quickly, in the language of state administration, to policy proposals in the capital? In the next Interforos annual convention in August 2002, the participants tried to find a solution to this dilemma by reworking the organizational chart, still sticking to the principle that thematic networks had to work under the regional chapters of Interforos. At the beginning of the event, however, something happened. The representatives of FOSDEH and ASONOG (Association of Non-governmental Organizations) performed a spectacular walk-out after having announced that they were going to leave Interforos for good, arguing that the organization had become 'exclusive' and anti-democratic. In a letter to the convention, distributed to the participants the next day, the separatist NGOs regretted the impossibility of finding a common understanding about the thematic networks, and justified their sudden, unexpected exit by citing the predominance of a religious organization and a political party in Interforos. Whereas it was clear to everybody that the Catholic Church, through Caritas, was a firm institutional support locally for many of the organizations present in Interforos, nobody at the convention was ready to accept talk of a dominant political party.

An interpretation of the split within Interforos must take several issues into account. First of all, there is no doubt that the separatists took a personal decision on behalf of their NGOs. A member of one of the associations affiliated to ASONOG said that leaving Interforos had not been discussed in ASONOG, and there were several persons from member organizations of ASONOG among the participants who stayed on at the convention. Why did they take this issue so personally? One is tempted to suggest that this was because the intransigence of Interforos on the thematic networks ultimately threatened their recent elevation to membership in the Honduran policy elite – and perhaps this is precisely the reason why Interforos's grassroots majority was so intransigent on this issue of thematic networks.

As such, Interforos's split should not have come as a surprise. In a highly stratified and anti-egalitarian society there is no reason to suppose that civil society organizations would escape stratification and vertical relations. The contradiction between the two objectives of Interforos – advocacy, requiring rapid reaction and full-time monitoring of policy developments, and the slow and invisible strengthening of capacities and civic consciousness at the grassroots – is difficult to bridge in any circumstances. But there is no way of avoiding the conclusion that, in the last instance, the separatist NGO sector of Interforos opted to try and maintain their position as members of the policy elite instead of pursuing longer-term work for grassroots civil society building in collaboration with the provinces.

At the root of the split was a question of clashing social classes.[21] The resentment felt against the 'dispositif' of a 'low cultural level' was loudly and clearly expressed in speeches at the annual convention and in personal communication with the participants. The members of Interforos felt looked down upon by civil society members who had acceded to the transnational policy elite, and discredited as full citizens by their middle-class partners – hence the intransigence on the issue of thematic networks. According to them, they were 'fed up' with these representatives of Interforos who 'publicly despise [them] and claim that technical policy matters cannot be discussed with "the people" because the people do not understand economic policies'. They resented the lack of reciprocity in the attitudes expressed by the separatists. According to the speeches at the meeting, the FOSDEH activists did not inform the other parts of Interforos about their activities while still using Interforos's name ('they usurp the name of Interforos'). In the words of one participant, the middle-class minority was seen to be 'fight[ing] for more political space although they are the technical unit and policy formulation of Interforos is the matter for the membership in its totality' (speeches at the annual convention, Interforos 22–24 August 2002). Their words were an expression of resentment and, once uttered, such words constitute an act of emancipation from being looked down upon – with sad results for the organization. But this conclusion also suggests that it was not only the NGO figures who walked out; they were actively pushed out of the organization by the intransigence of the grassroots activists from the provinces.

Political implications of the Honduran PRS process

Objective The objective of this final section is to summarize the shorter- and longer-term political consequences that the 'participatory' formulation of a PRS has had on the formation of the Honduran state. Because of the close causal relation between Mitch, HIPC and PRSP, in the case of Honduras the analysis must take into consideration the whole process from the end of 1998 through mid-2004 when some certainty has emerged about reaching the HIPC Completion Point in early 2005. The stress is on changes in the relations within the 'iron triangle' of policy formulation comprising the state, donors and non-state actors. Which actors and ideas have been advantaged by the process in each of these three poles of the triangle, and have been able to occupy space in policy-making? Correspondingly, which actors and discourses have been marginalized in the course of the process?

The state The headquarters of the unit responsible for the technical elaboration of the PRSP were located within a dependency of the Ministry of the Presidency (Secretaría del Estado de Despacho Presidencial) called UNAT (Unidad de Apoyo Técnico). UNAT had been created in 1996 via the Law on Public Administration, and its function is to offer technical assistance to the government and the state administration on economic reforms.

Different reasons have been given for why UNAT and the Ministry of the Presidency were in charge of the logistics and elaboration of PRSP. It seems that the minister of the presidency was the trusted man in the Flores government. He is a dynamic businessman whose strong personality had an impact on the PRS process and on the end result, the PRSP. There may have also been other contingent factors. The fact that the Ministry of the Presidency is located across the street from the Presidential House could have played a role (the Ministry of Finance has its premises in the old centre of Tegucigalpa); but another possible explanation given was that the minister of finance was a woman.

The minister of the presidency personally participated in the sixteen consultations carried out in the capital and departmental capitals (perhaps except for one – interview: Ministry of Finance). According to FOSDEH (interview: FOSDEH), it was FOSDEH that had suggested the organization of PRS consultations in all departmental capitals. This came after the original consultation organized in Tegucigalpa during the early, optimistic phases of the process, when civil society actors were still confident about 'real' participation (consensus-making).[22] There was a certain 'quota' (interview: Sida) of participation (information and consultation) for the population, but the process was not allowed to go too far. In the last instance, an important part of the PRSP (the macro-economic framework copied from PRGF) was left out of consultations completely, and not even made public before the submission of the strategy to the Bretton Woods institutions. The consultations and the expectations that they raised empowered certain segments of civil society, but there was a good dose of disciplining, too. The mechanisms of discipline consisted of two interrelated processes, technocratization and depoliticization, that together set certain limits to the extent and quality of popular participation in the formulation of PRS.

The way that the PRS process was configured in Honduras implied, first, a technocratization of policy formulation. Practically all (professional) employees at UNAT were economists. According to an ex-employee of the World Bank (interview: World Learning), this was evident in the quality of participation and in the final PRSP in Honduras.[23] The creation of UNAT in 1996 (and its precursor in 1993) was intended to increase technical expertise, which implies – and this is the second point – a depoliticization of policy formulation. Depoliticization is used here in two meanings that have to be separated in the case of Honduras. The creation of UNAT and new regulations on civil servants tended to decrease the space that political parties – and, in Honduras, 'political' is normally understood as having to deal with political parties – are able to occupy for rewarding followers. In the second sense of the word, depoliticization also means that matters such as economic policies are considered technical issues, subject to expert knowledge, not subordinated to democratic scrutiny.

Certain characteristics of the Honduran social formation make the country especially prone to the technocratization and depoliticization of policy formulation. There is a very small and uniform 'epistemic community' of economists who all know each other. They have gone to the same one or two schools, studied at the same faculty and, very significantly, work at all three poles of the triangle of policy formulation. They are in state administration, in civil society (NGOs) as well as functioning as local staff at resident donors' offices. It seems that there is a rather fluid exchange of economists between these three poles. The flow from the NGO pole towards the state administration has become increasingly difficult, however, due to two processes: first, because of decreasing employment opportunities due to state downsizing and shrinking space for clientelism; and second, due to the consolidation of the NGO sector as an independent and comparatively well remunerated source of employment.

A slight division might be seen within the epistemic community of economists. Deducing from interviews, the dividing line follows the theoretical orientation in economics as a discipline. The more orthodox, (neo-)liberal economists tend to flock to state administration and IFIs between which there is a constant and fluid exchange of personnel,[24] while the more heterodox, or perhaps Keynesian, economists are more likely to be found in the NGO sector and working for the 'softer' donors such as UNDP and the bilaterals. Because of the negative connotations that the word 'political' has in Honduras, none of these segments really contests the technocratization of policy formulation. They were empowered by the PRS process by virtue of their positions and/or their ability to occupy political space. Because of the Honduras socio-political set-up, they are drawn to technocratization and depoliticization independent of their personal ideological positions.

When asked about which state actors or institutions had been favoured by the PRSP process, interviewees were divided. It seems that there are few clear 'winners', but one clear 'loser', the Parliament (Congreso nacional). The leading role of the minister of the presidency in the process fortified his own political position and that of his ministry. Perhaps, and this is just a hypothesis, the leading position of the Ministry of the Presidency in the PRS process strengthened the presidentialist nature of the Honduran political system, in which the day-to-day exercise of power is far more concentrated in the executive than the constitution actually stipulates.[25] The Social Cabinet, an intra-governmental committee on social affairs, was mentioned in several interviews as a benefactor. This could mean that the line Ministries of Health and Education have a stronger position now than before PRSP. But it seems that within the aggregate, institutional victory of the Social Cabinet there are differences. The Ministries of the Presidency and Finance were clearly favoured, whereas line ministries have benefited only marginally, and did not participate – or were not invited to participate – to the same extent as the more predominant ministries

(Presidency and Finance) of the Social Cabinet. The present tendency of development cooperation towards general budget support does not change this pattern as it reinforces the role of the Ministry of Finance over line ministries.

It has already been mentioned that Parliament was by and large marginal to the formulation of the PRSP. During the preparation phase of the interim PRSP, a hired consultant (of Brazilian nationality) gave a two-hour powerpoint presentation to Parliament about poverty diagnostic in Honduras. And at the end of the presentation, the PRSP was briefly debated and approved by Parliament. Some parliamentarians did, however, participate in consultations as elected representatives of their electoral districts. According to NGO actors, even this small participation by Parliament was due to a press campaign carried out by civil society actors. It is a known tendency that national parliaments were marginalized from PRS processes worldwide (Ojanen 2003). In Central America this lack of involvement has been noticed by donors and several have initiated or implemented projects concerning the political parties and/or the role of parliaments in poverty reduction.

The purpose of the participatory formulation of the PRSP was to raise consciousness about poverty and to bring about the 'ownership' and commitment of national political actors towards the importance of poverty reduction. By now it is possible to assess tendencies in the commitment of the political establishment towards poverty reduction.

In Honduras there is a clear change to be observed in this respect. The term poverty appears with a certain regularity in newspaper headlines, a clear change from the situation in 2002. The government, new in office in 2002, has started using poverty-related phraseology in speeches, and the ERP (the Honduran PRSP) has little by little acquired the status of national development policy. It is as if the administration of President Maduro has learned to play by the rules of the international development community in stressing poverty reduction, conforming to what is considered appropriate behaviour from a recipient country. It is difficult to see that HICP debt alleviation would be strong enough a motivation for this change. The cancelled debt will amount to $960 million over fifteen years. I would suggest that more important than debt alleviation in itself is the image that HIPC casts upon the government in the public eye, and, on the other hand, the collateral grants and loans that the HICP initiative is channelling, and has already channelled, to Honduras.

But the expectations of the donor community for commitment and ownership have still not been fulfilled and the problem has shifted to another level. The debate is actually about what is meant by poverty reduction: is economic growth enough? The Maduro administration stresses the creation of wealth as the means to fight poverty, but there is little progress in redistribution (taxation is still almost as regressive as it was some years ago),[26] land titling to poor peasants, job creation and so on. In the Consultative Group of June 2004 this was expressed in a lively debate between the government presenting sectoral plans for economic growth, and the donors (including IFIs) expressing their concern about unequal distribution of wealth, and feeble investment in health and education as impediments to poverty reduction.

Donors In Honduras, as elsewhere, the Bretton Woods institutions emerge as the main architects and patrons of the PRS process. It is obvious that the PRS process has strengthened their position within the G-15. Some donors were not as enthusiastic about these developments. UNDP perhaps felt (at the headquarters' level) that PRSP was a rival to its Agenda 21 (interview: World Learning). The Inter-American Development Bank (IDB), a large lender to Honduras, may not have been happy about the HIPC initiative to start with. In any event, there have been differences between multilateral donors related to the emphasis and financial support given to civic participation, and one could interpret the relatively strong financial support to civil society by UNDP and IDB as attempts to secure their position in relation to WB/IMF in the development policy arena.

On the whole, the relative weight of IFIs as the largest donors has been strengthened in relation to bilateral donors. There is also another tendency. As the Central American Free Trade Agreement with the United States is poised for approval or rejection by national parliaments, there is a danger that bilateral donors will see their role reduced to one of subsidiary actors who can, at most, try to mend the adverse social consequences of hard-core modernization and trade liberalization.[27]

Honduran interviewees were virtually unanimous in their view that the WB/IMF and the IFIs more generally have strengthened their role in policy formulation. Moreover, it was considered that the donor group G-15 as a whole has been able to consolidate its position in Honduras, implying that subsequent donors entering the country will have less space than the members of the G-15 (the 'early bird' phenomenon). But in terms of the political sociology of state formation, the role of some other donors may have been even more important. The role of UNDP and bilateral donors has been essential in opening and consolidating political space for NGO sectors in policy formulation through networking (the transnationalization of civic activism) and the financing of capacity building.[28] This is precisely the long-term political consequence that seems to have had a permanent impact on the policy regime in Honduras.

Non-state actors The final angle of the policy formulation triangle, the non-state actors, is the one where the impact of the PRS process can be seen most clearly, and most interviewees agreed on the inclusions and exclusions caused by the process. Generally speaking, it can be said that the political space occupied by non-state actors is larger than ever in Honduran history. But the question here is: who are the non-state actors with a voice in public policy formulation – and whom do they represent?

Traditional civil society was almost totally absent from participation in PRS policy formulation in spite of occasional appearances at the consultation meetings. The professional associations were not active in the formulation of PRSP. The trade unions and peasant organizations, and their demands, were totally absent. There are reasons for this.

In the case of one of the peasant unions (interview: ANACH), their representatives had participated in some of the departmental consultations but felt frustrated. The problem relates to ideology and rhetoric. Their demand is land reform, which from the very beginning was not considered by the apparatus in charge of the logistics and elaboration of the PRSP (Ministry of the Presidency, UNAT) to be an issue that should be touched upon in the formulation of the PRSP. The diplomatic way in which this refusal was expressed in the document itself is that land reform and some other issues, such as income redistribution and electoral reform, were considered so politically complex that no consensus could have been achieved within the timeframe for the elaboration of the PRSP (PRSP 2001a: 6). In some other cases, the problem with peasant organizations and trade unions was the lack of communication between the confederation based in Tegucigalpa, the departmental federations and the local associations. Letters of invitation often never reached those who could have participated at the local level. The interviewed representatives of this peasant organization preferred to participate in the poverty reduction strategy formulation of Interforos where their views were better attended to. On the other hand, they spontaneously expressed a good deal of reserve towards NGOs who are 'self-appointed' representatives of civil society in the name of which they negotiate even when 'nobody has given them the right to represent us' (interview: ANACH).

Trade unions are more complicated because there are more national, competing federations. In general it could be observed that trade unions were the most absent segment of civil society in the formulation of PRSP, but in many cases this was a voluntary choice. This is precisely the case of Bloque Popular, the combative coalition of trade unions. They received a letter of invitation to the first consultation in Tegucigalpa but because of their opposition to the convenor (the minister of the presidency) they did not participate. In their words, they 'did not want anything to do with an enemy of the people' (interview: Bloque Popular). The business background of the person in charge of the PRS process contributed to the self-marginalization of a part of the trade union movement for ideological, class-based reasons.

When speaking specifically about the PRSP document, some observers underlined the absence of a gender perspective (interviews: FOSDEH; Trocaire). In the interpretation offered by FOSDEH, the technocratic position prevailed. According to FOSDEH, women could not get through a gender perspective because they 'could not present *propuestas*', that is, concrete policy proposals designed in the technocratic language of state administration. The INGO representative (interview: Trocaire), on the other hand, referred to the position of the PRSP in the political advocacy of feminists and the women's movement in Honduras. The Honduran women are far too occupied with defending their basic gender rights, it is claimed, thus a poverty reduction strategy does not enter into the picture as a policy priority. One could add that the feminist and women's movement is divided. On one hand there is a militant feminist 'sexual rights' movement with transnational contacts (e.g. funding from Sweden), and a nationally-oriented, more traditional women's movement (descendants of the suffragettes), that was, interestingly, more involved with direct poverty-related issues than the former.

The story of Interforos as described above is a good example of the most important inclusion–exclusion mechanism that the PRS process produced. Through transnationalization and technocratization, the PRS process opened and consolidated an important piece of political space for a certain segment of non-state actors, the NGOs. As the case of Interforos shows, this did not necessarily mean that the voices of the poor would have been heard in the formulation of the PRS. Because of an instinctive frame of mind, the 'dispositif' of categorization of persons according to their class and formal education and the dismissal of voices that do not speak the technical language of the epistemic community of economists (a 'capacity to present policy proposals'), the PRS process in Honduras excluded the poor (and women and ethnic minorities) from policy formulation – on the part of both the NGO elite and state actors, all university-educated urbanites. The formulation of PRSP helped to consolidate a small non-state policy elite with its technocratic habitus and international connections, creating at the same time a fracture along class, religious and geographical lines within nascent 'civil society'. But there is no doubt an empowering element to be seen here, too. The split within Interforos was a rebellion by 'the people' against the technocratic NGO policy elite. Their refusal to be dismissed as uneducated expressed in speeches at the convention of Interforos can be seen as an emancipatory awakening, an indicator of a slow but deep change in political subjectivity at the Honduran grassroots.

5 | Conclusion: the politics of consultation

JEREMY GOULD

Deprivation, both relative and absolute, is a scourge affecting the majority of humankind. Inadequate land to produce food; too little money for seed, fuel, medicine or school fees; insufficient means of leveraging the haves and the have-mores into effecting a more equitable distribution of resources and power – this is the daily reality of billions of people. It would seem common sense to applaud any initiative dedicated to the alleviation of deprivation, especially one allegedly designed to oblige the ruling elites of poor countries to give their citizens a fairer deal. The new conditionalities of aid, revolving as they do round poverty reduction, would appear to be driven by a fundamentally human sense of justice.

Why, then, the decidedly reserved tone of this volume concerning Poverty Reduction Strategies? Certainly everyone appreciates that poverty reduction, like Mr Bush's war in Iraq, is 'hard work'. Is it not unreasonable, even a bit disloyal, to demand complicated things like accountability, public debate about macro-economic policy options, and respect for fledgling democratic structures, when the task at hand – delivering billions of people from destitution – is so immense? Are not the criticisms of policy processes lodged in these analyses – grumblings about 'depoliticization', 'technocratization' and the growing 'hegemony of a transnational policy elite' – somewhat disingenuous, given the aid community's unequivocal reaffirmations of its commitment to openness, dialogue and partnership?

How one responds to such questions depends, above all, on how important a role one assigns to political action in dismantling authoritarian orders and entrenched social hierarchies. Thinking about the emerging pro-poor partnerships politically raises questions like: are 'the poor' ever treated equitably before they organize themselves into an irrepressible political force? Do genuinely 'pro-poor' policies ever get carried out without effective political demands for social justice on the part of the assigned beneficiaries? The best-documented experiences of poverty reduction (i.e. the United States, Western Europe, Russia, South Africa) all suggest that the answer is no: the haves share their wealth and influence only when the have-nots can force them to do so.

New conditionalities and state formation

The three case studies presented above give credibility to the claim, advanced in the introductory chapter, that the new modalities of aid are having a transformative impact on the character of post-colonial states and their political domains. One might provisionally term the emerging phase of state formation 'post-developmentalist', although this label tells more about what ended in the wake of the Cold War than about the new processes and relations that are germinating. The emergence of post-developmental states was spearheaded by the structural adjustment programmes (SAPs) of the 1980s and early 1990s. As has been discussed at great length elsewhere,[1] neo-liberal SAPs sought to dismantle regulationist regimes which were seen to constrain the progressive agency of entrepreneurialism and market forces in post-colonial economies.

Setting strict neo-liberal policy conditions on the availability of development financing – in effect, dismantling state control over key economic mechanisms – was the primary lever employed by the creditors to promote the neo-liberal agenda. In theory, deregulation was instrumental to the primary aim of stimulating growth. Two decades of structural adjustment – of selling off public assets and deregulating trade and currency buffers – undermined the (already fragile) capacity of post-colonial governments to manage their economic environments. At the same time, the policies imposed via SAPs led to the large-scale retrenchment of state and parastatal employees, exacerbating unemployment, while weakening domestic purchasing power and the state's revenue base.

By the latter part of the 1990s, the major actors in the international development community were obliged to admit that structural adjustment had catalysed disastrous social consequences for many countries; what's more, privatization, fiscal austerity and market liberalization failed to deliver growth. Caught in the crossfire of aid fatigue among Northern taxpayers, and public outcry by humanitarian advocacy groups over the growth of poverty throughout the 1990s, the aid community regrouped mid-decade to reconsider its strategic options.

Rather than admit to a systemic error in their policy prescriptions, the multilateral development finance agencies and their bilateral allies – that loose consortium of players that Easterly (2002) has aptly termed the 'aid cartel' – opted to blame the victim. 'Weak state capacity' and 'poor governance' were identified as the main causes of poor policy performance (World Bank 1997). Instead of revising lending conditions to allow for greater state control of the economy, the development finance community opted for a stick-and-carrot approach that retained the basic, anti-regulationist elements of structural adjustment.

The carrot came in the form of the Heavily Indebted Poor Countries (HIPC) debt relief initiative (thus garnering support from the transnational humanitarian lobby); the stick was making the incremental HIPC relief conditional upon far-reaching programmes of state reform in accordance with principles of the 'new public management' (e.g. Bangura 2000). Neither stick nor carrot provided the impetus for governments to introduce regulatory measures to protect fledgling industries or improve productivity. On the contrary, privatization has widely deprived government coffers of significant revenues, especially in the form of short-term liquidity, forcing leaders to intensify taxation of the small, already beleaguered class of wage-earners and formal sector businessfolk.

The essence of 'post-developmentalism', then, is its retreat from a nationalist programme of industrial-based accumulation. Structural adjustment programmes (SAPs) were developmentalist in their rhetorical emphasis on growth and productivity, and often, when domestic industries collapsed under the onslaught of cheap, liberalized imports brought about by SAP conditionalities, the Bank and the IMF met a nationalist political reaction. The post-SAP, post-developmentalist policy regime, based on a state–donor 'partnership', no longer has a focus on productivity and growth and, in practice, places no premium on domestic accumulation and industrialization. Inasmuch as post-colonial client governments buy into partnership with the international donor community (and many, due to their irreprievable indebtedness, appear to have little choice), one can justifiably term them post-developmental states.

Aid as politics The new aid modalities are not only in themselves a form of politics, they also impinge on wider political processes. PRS processes take place in a context – the post-Cold War era of neo-liberal globalization – characterized by the pluralization of politics (as single-party regimes disappear), the diversification of the social relations of governance (as new actors gain access to state power), and the fragmentation of political authority (as liberalization and privatization undermine the regulatory powers of the state). Poverty Reduction Strategies, the epitome of the new process conditionalities, are a response to this new order, but they also contribute to the reconfiguration of the political landscape along these lines. This contribution is evident, first, in the way PRS processes promote the centralization and unilateralization of a certain (transnational, technocratic) mode of power related to external financing and public resource management. Second, PRS processes predicate two parallel disjunctures in the political domain: (a) between policy 'formulation' (at the 'centre') and 'implementation' (at the 'grassroots'); and (b) between 'policy' (a technocratic domain of transnational professionals) and 'politics' (an entrepreneurial arena of domestic brokers and elected representatives).

The thread of continuity between the developmentalism of the late twentieth century and the post-developmentalism of the new millennium is the patronizing attitude of creditor agencies towards their clients. The belief, so widespread among international financial institutions, that social justice can be imposed via conditions on external financing is both arrogant and naïve in a way uncannily similar to the claim that democracy can be imposed via military occupation.

This is not to suggest that the Millennium Development Goals and the push for global development partnerships are driven by precisely the same interests that prompted the US-led 'coalition of the willing' to invade Iraq. Rather, the point is that when politicians and economists resort to outlandishly unreasonable justifications for their actions, one needs to be on the alert for concealed or unacknowledged interests. Just as the invasion of Iraq in 2003 conveniently secured access for American and British corporations to a good 10 per cent of the world's known petroleum reserves, new aid modalities auspiciously guarantee, among other things, that major transnational credit institutions are advantageously positioned to issue an expanding stream of new loans to Southern states. In both instances, for all their many differences, strategic interests in institutional survival, career advancement and personal gain are shrouded in pronouncements of virtuous intent.

If there was credible evidence that the wave of lending catalysed by the new conditionalities was making a significant impact on the predicament of the world's marginalized masses, one could no doubt be more generous about procedural issues and short-term political outcomes. This, though, is clearly not the case. For all of the planet's poorest countries, population increase continues to outpace economic growth; despite five years of debt relief under the HIPC initiative, debt servitude continues to compromise the sovereignty of Southern governments, as well as their accountability to their own citizenry. Under new post-developmental partnerships, it will continue to do so for generations to come.

Strategic incentives in aid relations

The view of Poverty Reduction Strategy formulation as a form of transnational politics invokes a relational analysis of the policy arena as a game-like configuration, with multiple ways of both 'winning' and 'losing'. Such a view underscores the importance of understanding how and why different sets of actors act and interact the way they do. Above all, it calls for close attention to the diverse range of interests informing strategic choices different players make in the course of their dealings with one another.

One important conclusion to be drawn from these case analyses concerns the central role that strategic incentives play in driving interactions in the policy arena. Incentives work on at least two levels, that of the individual and that of the organization. Development agencies – both public and private – are obliged to defend an often tenuous niche in the turbulent terrain of the beleaguered aid industry. Major multilateral financial institutions, such as the World Bank and the International Monetary Fund, must maintain profitable portfolios (necessitating consistently high volumes of lending), while also assuaging the critical and vocal political constituencies of their member governments. Bilateral agencies must continually demonstrate the 'value-added' of their particular investments to taxpayers back home, while private aid organizations compete aggressively with one another and against apathy and cynicism for dwindling philanthropic donations.

These imperatives for organizational survival – the bottom line that defines the strategic interests of creditor agencies – translate into incentive structures within which individual staff operate. Portfolio managers within creditor agencies are rewarded for high lending volumes. Field staff of private development organizations who secure lucrative subcontracting assignments from upstream public agencies (i.e. for building 'capacity' in local organizations) are more likely to rise up the career ladder. Through state–donor partnerships, technocrats within borrower governments become subject, directly or indirectly, to these same pressures to perform in accordance with the demands driving their individual and organizational partners. Understanding this helps one to see why partnerships grounded in the promise of debt relief between creditors and public sector financial managers consistently generate ever higher mountains of unsustainable debt.

It would be overly simplistic, however, to insist that the rules of the game governing interactions within the policy arena among donors, governments and (increasingly) non-state actors are determined solely by base creditor interests, as important as these are. The three case narratives above provide ample illustration of the capacity of different actors to manipulate rules of engagement to their own advantage, depending on the structure of political opportunity available to them. The compellingness of moral ideas – the pervasive rhetoric of justice, equity and mutuality with which the aid domain resounds – cannot be ignored. The aid 'game' and its diverse roster of participants is caught up in a persistent tension between the virtuous rhetoric through which aid relations are legitimized, and the consistently disappointing quality of its outcomes for recipient economies. This tension is the source of the recurrent cycles of critique and reform that have characterized the aid domain since its origins.

Quite obviously, the structure of opportunity is extremely context-sensitive. Much the same brood of transnational private agencies are involved in PRS processes in numerous countries, yet their influence and visibility differ enormously from site to site. To cite another example from the case studies, the relationship of two pivotal characters, the World Bank and UNDP, would seem to depend as much upon the political context in which they are operating as on the specific aims of their institutional strategies.

It is, in any event, important to note that the imperatives and incentives driving the operations and behaviour of development agencies, and the modalities they adopt, are not merely *compatible* with the populist neo-liberal rhetoric of consultation, partnership, ownership and poverty reduction; under prevailing conditions of growing cynicism and aid fatigue, they *demand* it.

Crosscutting trends in post-developmental politics

Public policy processes are embedded in the long-term evolution of aid relationships. The dynamics of the aid relationship determines the extent to which a PRS process has effected shifts in the social relations of governance and changes in the structure of political opportunity. The study suggests several general trends. Foremost, the rhetoric of 'local ownership' notwithstanding, PRS processes perpetuate and, indeed, deepen the external patronage of state reform. External agencies, above all the BWIs, define and assess the criteria and benchmarks of 'good government' or, to put it another way, the substance and direction of state formation. This is not new; indeed, conditionalities on structural adjustment lending also aimed at renovating the inner workings of the state apparatus. What is perhaps new under the present aid regime is the intimate involvement of both public and private global actors in domestic policy processes under the rubric of 'local ownership'. At the same time, the subordination of far-reaching policy platforms to the dictates of external agencies promotes the legitimation of technocratic (relative to electoral) authority over domestic policy management. Under the politics of consultation, 'the people' are primarily involved in major policy decisions affecting their everyday lives (and those of their children and grandchildren) not through the ballot or referendum but, if at all, via ad hoc and discretionary modes of donor-sponsored 'workshopping'.

There are significant variations in the scope and depth of these features in the different countries. Only in Tanzania can one speak of these shifts in political practice as clear 'trends'. In Vietnam, by way of contrast, the strong premium afforded to national sovereignty, and the strong roots in society of an uncompromisingly nationalist leadership, provide a buffer against external encroachment in domestic political affairs. Still, there is no question that, even without the HIPC carrot, the PRS process in Vietnam catalysed the leverage of the BWIs within influential policy circles, especially the currency of their rhetoric, analytical predilections and conceptual apparatus. One outcome of this is the continued growth of Vietnam's indebtedness to the BWIs.

The consolidation of BWI-driven policy notions within the iron triangle of policy formulation has occurred across the board, not only or primarily in Vietnam. One indication of this is the growing acceptance of 'poverty' as the central socio-political problem facing all the countries studied. Poverty is a grave social dilemma, but its current status as a policy-orienting concept is deeply problematic. For one thing, when 'stakeholders' debate poverty reduction, they don't discuss substantive, contextualized policy issues. The terms of the debate require that one accepts the poverty reduction framework (defined by generic elements of coordination, ownership, partnership, consultation, social sector primacy, etc.); the focus is on whether one is for or against a certain bundle of specific instruments.

Within the prevailing framework, poverty is posited as a technical problem for which there must be a domestic, budgetary fix. By delinking poverty from its roots in the external economy (terms of trade and debt servitude), and from fundamental economic mechanisms (productivity of labour, degree of industrialization, and patterns of accumulation), the thrust of most Poverty Reduction Strategies is limited to increasing the scope of public spending on primary healthcare and basic education. As important as these social amenities are, their impact on eliminating poverty is marginal at best, unless coupled with vigorous measures to stimulate employment and productivity. PRSs have by and large failed to address these fundamental issues.

A parallel, and closely related, consequence of the new conditionalities for policy-think is the creation of 'civil society' as an organized form of social agency linked to donor operations, and its legitimation as a party to the formulation of public policy. While broadening participation in public policy debates is a hallmark of greater democracy, the cooption of 'civil society' within the new state–donor partnerships does not automatically strengthen democratic institutions. On the contrary, the instrumentalization of civil society via creditor interests can undermine the consolidation of social forces dedicated to greater equity and accountability. As the Honduran and Tanzanian studies clearly attest, the 'consultative imperative' built into HIPC/PRS conditionalities can and does generate complex and divisive struggles among local activists and organizations over the right to be heard. In the case of Tanzania, transnational private agencies found themselves brokering and, to some extent, supplanting local civil society representation in policy consultations.

The empirical studies also provide rich insights into how PRS processes both reorganize and rationalize the social relations of aid management. Across the board, the BWIs have further consolidated their stewardship of the aid cartel, ultimately supplanting the UN team (captained by UNDP) as the nominal coordinator of the aid community. Bilateral agencies, including newcomers like Japan and a virtual multilateral like the European Union, have been increasingly obliged to adapt their procedures and policy statements to templates laid down by the BWIs. Processes of 'unilateralization through harmonization' are not watertight, however; there is a strong undercurrent of resistance to the over-coordination of aid on the part of many bilaterals. Yet, with many major transnational private agencies (Oxfam, World Vision, ActionAid) joining hands with the BWIs in the poverty reduction campaign, it would seem reasonable to chalk up this round to the Washington-based agencies.

This means, in essence, that the multilateral creditors now exercise relatively direct control over core politico-administrative functions in many post-developmental states. The most important of these are the management of the budgetary process and of related government policy. Conditionalities built into development financing continue to provide the leverage by which donor agencies influence budgetary processes. But as external agencies become increasingly present in governmental policy-making bodies, the power to define the tempo, sequencing of events and the agendas of stakeholder consultations are key instruments for controlling initiative and access to the core policy processes (see Gould 2005). These logistical elements of the policy process are, again, largely determined by the Bretton Woods institutions by virtue of their numerically superior manpower on the ground, and through their command of the conceptual framework within which policy-speak is exercised.

The PRS represents a standardized global strategy for the reform of aid relations. The case analyses reveal that the strategy has had differential success in different contexts. Some erosion of the state's policy sovereignty has been a uniform outcome in all cases. Yet there is also significant variation in the extent and depth of this erosion. This indicates that domestic governments can exercise significant degrees of freedom for manoeuvre concerning policy content vis-à-vis donor dictates. The extent of leeway appears to depend on a number of factors.

The most evident are the economic footprint of the country (implying an ability to invoke Western commercial interests in order to extract concessions on the terms of development financing); the extent of the public economy's dependency on aid; the legacy of nationalist ideology within the political elite; the structures of political opportunity available to particular actors; as well as their opportunities to form alliances in order to wield political leverage.

Of these factors, only the level of debt and aid dependency is conducive to quantitative description. Levels of aid as a percentage of a country's Gross National Income (GNI), and the levels of aid per capita can be taken as a proxy indicator of aid dependency.

TABLE 5.1 Indicators of aid dependence for Honduras, Tanzania and Vietnam

	Aid per capita ($)		Aid as % of GNI	
	1997[1]	2002	1997[1]	2002
Honduras	50	64	6.6	6.8
Tanzania	30	35	12.5	13.2
Vietnam[2]	13	16	3.8	3.6

Source: World Development Indicators (2004: Table 6.10), <www.worldbank.org/data/wdi2004/pdfs/Table6_10.pdf>

Notes 1. 1997 figures represent the situation two years before PRSs were introduced by the BWIs. The figures demonstrate the consistent growth of volumes of aid in all three countries. 2. The drop in aid as a share of the GNI in Vietnam reflects the strong growth of the economy over the period in question thus, in the view of the government and its donor advisers, justifying increased levels of lending.

Relating the empirical findings to the figures in Table 5.1, it is evident that the extent of donor control over budgetary processes is directly proportional to the depth of aid dependence. In this respect, both Vietnam and Honduras exhibit significantly greater degrees of policy sovereignty than does Tanzania.

PRS processes also have a direct impact on domestic politics. The country studies have argued that participation in donor–state partnerships have, to varying degrees, weakened domestic accountability mechanisms, that is, the ability of citizens to hold their elected leaders responsible for their actions. Here again, the negative impact of partnerships on democratic process has been variable. This is natural considering the highly variable nature of the political systems in question as well as the different kinds and degrees of democracy found in these three countries, encompassing Vietnam's Communist Party monopoly, Tanzania's de facto one-party regime, and Honduras's dual-party pluralism. The findings indicate that where there has been significant momentum in democratizing political structures (Honduras and to some extent Vietnam), some domestic social forces have been able to take advantage of the rhetoric of consultation and participation to advance their agendas. Where democratic process is intrinsically weak (as in Tanzania), the centralizing features of the PRS process have promoted unbridled technocratization and allowed for the 'crowding out' of domestic social movements.

The consultative imperative built into the HIPC/PRS conditionality implies the empowerment of stakeholders previously excluded from policy debates. It is evident from the case studies that policy processes have in fact become somewhat more inclusive. The question is, who have been empowered, and in what ways? The findings of the country studies differ in this respect, and the small size of the 'sample' cautions against making sweeping statements. That said, two general rules seem to apply. The first is that the opening up of consultative space, both in the form of one-off workshops and of membership in ad hoc policy bodies, has empowered those who are already well versed in the rhetoric and aesthetic of the new aid partnerships. As one Tanzanian colleague put it, the main beneficiaries are those who can 'walk the walk and talk the talk' of poverty reduction. The second rule is that the opening of new consultative space tends to empower those capable of 'jumping scale', that is, actors with simultaneous access to information, contacts and other strategic resources at various 'levels' of the aid industry, from the scale of the community or district civic organization to that of transnational agency headquarters in a cosmopolitan capital city.

How these rules pan out in practice varies a bit from context to context. Governments and donor agencies have a history of dealings with individuals and organizations that also affect the mechanisms of inclusion and exclusion at work under the consultative imperative. Domestic civic groups are better organized, and better versed in the requisite walk and talk, in some places than in others. Similarly, 'global civil society' is thicker on the ground, and more aggressively self-promoting, at different sites (Tanzania and Vietnam) and at different times (Honduras 2001 and 2004). Under no circumstances, however, has the need to consult led to much involvement by domestic business communities or by grassroots groups. Businesspeople don't have the time, or the inclination, for time-consuming series of meetings, especially when consultation agendas skirt their primary concerns (labour law, interest rates, taxation, tariffs, etc.). 'The poor' generally lack the means, as well as the conceptual and the organizational resources, to take part in debates on poverty reduction. Better off, better organized and more articulate actors are usually available to speak on their behalf.

Political implications of the new conditionality

What might one conclude about the new conditionality regime and the emergent political configurations – transnational partnerships – that it legitimizes? While these processes are complex and rife with contradictory elements, three basic premises suggest themselves.

First, it is obvious that there is something fundamentally amiss in the way that the intermeshed systems of international development finance and national policy formulation are constituted. Witness the failure of two decades of stringently conditional aid to engender substantial levels of economic growth; the severe aid dependency resulting from dealings with the aid cartel; the consolidation of hegemonic and unaccountable power wielded by the aid agencies over national policy processes; the persistence of corruption and abuse of office among governments bankrolled by development aid; and the continuation, despite vows to the contrary, of high levels of unsustainable lending to non-productive sectors. Despite HIPC and the PRS there is no indication that most recipient countries will be in any better a position to repay their debts (or be any less aid dependent) forty years down the line when the current wave of IDA loans are due (Saussier 2002: 5–6).[2]

This suggests the need to attend to the nature of *creditor interests* as the key factor affecting the outcomes of aid relationships. Do the new aid modalities, the new rhetoric of partnership, ownership and consultation, and the professed prioritization of poverty eradication reflect a shift in these interests? Has the financial market context within which creditor institutions perform been subjected to democratic regulation? Have the structures of incentives and opportunities which determine individual and organizational success and survival in the domain of international credit undergone significant changes? Have mechanisms of accountability been sharpened to ensure that instances of bad and unsustainable debt can be avoided and redressed? It is difficult to answer affirmatively to any of these questions. Why, then, should one assume that a shift in legitimizing rhetoric is anything more or less than just that?

It seems worth considering that a systemic lack of accountability within processes of development resource allocation (from taxpayer to donor agency; from donor to recipient via various mediating agencies; and from national governments to downstream recipients) reduces the pursuit of efficacious development policies to a game-like process dominated by considerations of power and prestige, prevalence and survival, benefit and advancement, and that these affect (to a greater or lesser degree) the actions of both individuals and organizations.[3] The main point, for these purposes, is not whether populist neo-liberal partnership is a good or bad thing, or whether or not the PRS genuinely reflects the needs and priorities of 'the poor'; rather, one must ask whether the introduction of pro-poor policy regimes empowers actors whose immediate, primary and over-riding interests are enhanced growth, productivity, employment and local accumulation. Any other outcome will fail to break the bonds of dependency and debt servitude, and will tend to perpetuate the subordination of indebted countries to the interests of rich creditor economies.

Second, at an ideological level, the convergence of neo-liberal and populist tendencies is fraught with contradictions. Three political fault-lines are immediately apparent. One is the tension between 'domestic' and 'external' interests. These interests are portrayed in the rhetoric of poverty reduction policies as coterminous, implying that creditor and recipient interests are identical. This identity of interests may well apply to aid managers sitting on either side of the donor–state negotiating table, but the everyday experience of ordinary citizens suggests otherwise. A second tension exists between the liberal rhetoric of democratization and good governance, and the lack of institutional mechanisms for holding the policy elite (and especially its powerful external actors) accountable for the consequences of its dictates. A third fault-line runs between the hegemonic consensus presumed to underscore the poverty reduction partnership, and the pluralism upon which the liberal agenda of democratization is predicated. In brief, then, the consolidation of a neo-liberal state–donor partnership based on populist precepts raises countless alarms concerning the political implications of the alliances emerging at the core of post-colonial states. One should ask, above all, (a) to what extent is a policy regime grounded in populist neo-liberalism commensurate with growth in productivity and job creation; and b) what forms of (democratic) politics are compatible with populist neo-liberalism?

Third, the most dire and long-term threat of the partnerships forged through the HIPC and concomitant PRSP exercises is psychological. The middle classes – the main source of innovative ideas and entrepreneurial energies – display a political imagination that conceives of aid dependence and debt servitude as inevitable. Members of the professions learn to esteem and cultivate skills and disciplines that are rational only within a post-developmental domain. One such (self-)discipline is not to question the moral and intellectual rationale of economic and intellectual subordination. It is not common in post-developmental political society to challenge the basic assumptions upon which aid dependency and the erosion of policy sovereignty are based, i.e. the interpenetration of domestic and foreign technocratic elites and the substitution of foreign lending for taxation.

This psychological subordination is bolstered by a steady flow of material rewards and other incentives to comply with creditor interests. Such rewards make the insular, self-referential vocation of aid management attractive to the well-educated and ambitious sons and daughters of the middle classes. Seduced by access to the dollar economy, they prioritize acquiring skills for, and channelling their energies into, tasks related to building the capacity of client organizations to conform to the procedural and aesthetic requirements of the aid cartel. They labour to create ever new needs for aid within the public and private economies. This occurs at the expense of contributing to the development of domestic manufacturing and processing industries that would generate actual wealth within the national economy. This complex of incentives draws individuals as well as entire organizations into its orbit.

As Jai Sen (2002) among others has argued, one needs to take the narrow (middle-)class nature of the emerging political society into account when assessing the orientation and strategic alliances of its members. This applies to delocalized public sector technocrats in aid agencies and local client institutions, as well as, and perhaps most significantly, to the rapidly swelling ranks of private actors oriented towards employment opportunities within the realm of 'global civil society'. The growing incorporation of Southern professional classes within the ranks of global civil society (see UNDP 2002a and 2002b) expands the political leverage of a transnationally homogenous middle class. Rather than promoting 'globalization from below', this process represents 'globalization from the middle'. Genuinely grassroots, or shall we say nationally grounded, 'processes, identities and cultures' are subordinated to an exclusive dialogue among '"those who fit" in terms of class, lifestyle and language' (Sen 2002: 13, 15). Worse things can occur than the dissemination of a middle-class aesthetic and liberal values to countries shackled by instability and civil strife. Yet the empowerment of the middle classes cannot be an end in itself. The final normative test of state formation is in the extent to which 'progressive' classes succeed in extending the scope to their emanicipatory project beyond their own limited interests to society as a whole.

In order to break the bonds of aid dependency and debt servitude, the intellectual and entrepreneurial classes must choose between a self-referential and parasitic post-developmentalism, and national(ist) development projects – enhancing domestic savings and productive investment, improving the productivity of land and labour, building the revenue base of the public economy, fortifying political accountability mechanisms, etc. These are not new challenges; they comprise the basic themes of classical liberal development theory, but have fallen by the wayside of aid modalities based on 'partnership'. Poverty reduction is an inevitable, albeit mid-term, outcome of these latter processes. The perpetuation of aid dependence and debt servitude, by contrast, leads not to growth, equity or better governance but only to more of the same and, inevitably, to the resentment and frustration that perpetual subordination engenders. This threat is most acute for Africa. The examples of Honduras and Vietnam suggest that it can be resisted, but also that the aid cartel never stops creating ever more sophisticated means of generating indebtedness.

A glimmer of sanity?

There are those who think that 'development' is a self-conscious conspiracy to subjugate the South to Northern dictates. This is perhaps the prevailing view in the bars and bus stops of Dar es Salaam or Lusaka. The aid-as-conspiracy thesis, however, is not what we are arguing here. While we claim that the aid industry functions in a self-perpetuating fashion, and that state–donor 'partnerships' tend to exacerbate already unmanageable debt burdens, we do not suggest that indebtedness and erosion of sovereignty are the explicit aims of actors within the aid industry. Inasmuch as they reflect on the broader picture, aid professionals go to work to reduce poverty, build capacity and empower the vulnerable, not to perpetuate debt bondage.

But even if the actual outcomes of aid are not conspiratorial, there is an element of duplicity or, better, of self-delusion, involved. One of the most curious, and baffling, features of the aid industry is the disjuncture between the virtuous self-portrayal of the vocation, and the self-serving character of the incentive structures prevailing within the domain. Not all aid workers receive lavish rewards for their services but, on the average, expatriate development professionals (and increasingly, domestic aid brokers and consultants) are among the highest-paid public sector functionaries around. Remuneration standards in private agencies, to which poverty reduction work is increasingly farmed out, are similarly very 'competitive'.

To spell out the basic thesis that emerges from this study as bluntly as possible, the new conditionalities perpetuate debt servitude because aid agencies need to move money in order to survive. Creditor agency staff strategize tirelessly to guarantee consistently high volumes of loans because their careers and benefits depend on it. As the dominant creditor agencies, the BWIs have attained stewardship over the entire aid industry (an outcome to which the PRSP/HIPC processes have greatly contributed). Functionaries in bilateral, largely grant-giving bodies also find themselves contributing to debt accumulation by channelling their grants into activities and mechanisms (such as sectoral funding baskets and direct budget support) that improve the recipient's capacity to 'absorb' new credits.

One must ask, finally, is there no awareness of these issues within the development mainstream? It is hard to say with any certainty what the strategic managers of the large creditor institutions are thinking – how they reconcile the imperatives of financial markets and their political patrons with the rhetoric of partnership and poverty reduction. But clearly, as the hegemony of the BWIs grows, leaders of major bilateral agencies are becoming uncomfortable with the more blatant contradictions inherent in the theory and practice of 'partnership'. Indeed, the persistent disjunction between the intents and outcomes of development aid breeds not only the cynicism and disillusionment of the bars and bus stops, but also disquiet and introspection among professionals who take the rhetoric seriously. As the BWIs push for greater harmonization and coordination under their intellectual leadership, they are encountering subtle resistance.

At the annual meetings of the World Bank and International Monetary Fund in October 2004, for instance, UK Secretary of State for International Development, Hilary Benn, called for more open debate on the World Bank's approach to aid conditionality. Mr Benn is reported as having said:

> There needs to be a much greater emphasis on increasing countries' independence in policy-making. There has been too much emphasis in the past on 'one size fits all' answers to economic reform issues like privatisation and trade liberalisation. Sometimes these reforms work for the poor. But sometimes they don't; so the final decision on whether to undertake them must rest on the evidence and with developing countries themselves.[4]

Mr Benn also expressed his concern over the political implications of the new process conditionalities. He argued that donors 'have a fine line to tread in using conditions that strengthen the participation of poor people in decision-making, but [must also] make sure we do not interfere with national political processes. We are determined to get the balance right.'

There is much to do before current patterns of aid relationships can be transformed into genuine partnerships. Given the prevailing scope of global asymmetry, this is unlikely to happen soon. But even without a revolution in the social relations of transnational governance, steps can be taken both to restore the sovereignty of aid recipients and to repoliticize critical development policy choices. This is the first, indispensable, move towards creating political space within which 'the poor', and whatever social forces choose to join them, can struggle for effective means of holding their elected leaders accountable for their actions. Recognition of the complicity of aid in undermining such struggles is an important first step in this process.

Notes

1 | Poverty, politics and states of partnership

1 For an introduction to the long-running debate about post-colonial state formation see Corrigan and Sayers (1985), Joseph and Nugent (1994), Steinmetz (1999), Hansen and Stepputat (2001).

2 The term refers to the signing of their founding charters at Bretton Woods, New Hampshire, in 1944.

3 From 18 per cent of the Bank's policy-based lending in FY80–88 to 45 per cent in FY98–01, and to 80 per cent of all PRSC loans for FY01–03 (World Bank 2002a).

4 The fifty-four completed PRSPs are distributed by regions as follows: Africa 29; East Asia and the Pacific 4; Eastern and Central Europe 10; Latin America 5; Middle East and North Africa 2; and South Asia 4 (World Bank PovertyNet website: <www.worldbank.org/>).

5 Iron triangles are conceptually related to notions such as epistemic community, policy network and so on which emphasize the socio-political dynamics of policy-making. Thus, where coalitions obstruct policy reform, research in this vein has paid attention to the conditions by which triangular cartels can be 'broken', allowing for the formation of a more loosely bound policy network in which it may be possible for a reform coalition to prevail (e.g. Peterson 1993).

6 Extract from *Oxford English Dictionary*, 2nd edn, 1989, <http://dictionary.oed.com>

7 Perhaps it would be more accurate to speak of the *inter*penetration of the state and transnational actors, since one feature of the post-developmental partnership is the 'reciprocal assimilation' (Bayart 1993) of domestic and international elites.

8 Of specific relevance to this study, Thomas Callaghy (2001) has applied these concepts to his study of public policy processes in Uganda to illustrate the interplay of domestic and transnational forces in the negotiation of Uganda's debt relief programme.

9 In social sector lending, policy conditionality has increased from 3 per cent in the 1980s to 21 per cent at the turn of the millennium, on average in all regions (World Bank 2002a: 6).

2 | Tanzania: merging in the circle

1 A full collection of five reports by Helleiner on Tanzania's aid relationship over the period 1995–2001 is to be published by the Economic and Social Research Foundation (ESRF). ESRF has recently been awarded a contract to facilitate 'Helleiner 3', the institutionalization of an independent monitoring group to pre-empt future ruptures between government and donors.

2 Vision 2025 was the first official affi
'socialist' (*ujamaa*) policy regime initiated b
outlines a general set of principles intended
policy. While considered 'home-grown' in conc
both documents was supported by donor agenci
PRSP, both the Vision and NPES documents were
organs.

3 It has been noted that the Tanzanian public ser
duces 2,400 quarterly reports a year for external donors
donor 'missions' (Kelsall 2001: 4, quoting James Wolfen

4 The DAC is a loosely constituted inter-governmental
been instrumental in articulating the emerging multilateral ... on aid
modalities.

5 Agenda for DAC harmonization meetings, 7 and 20 February 2002, Agenda Item 2: identification of transaction costs and suggested solutions (mimeo), emphasis in original.

6 In the rapid rotation career of aid executives, 'long-term' interests refer to issues that are likely to follow them to their subsequent postings. The range of such issues is broader the higher up one is in the management hierarchy.

7 We use the term 'non-state actors' here to refer to those *specific* private organizations that have competed to capture the political space engendered through various mechanisms of consultation, participation and partnership associated with the Tanzania PRS. While hardly a rigorous concept (the vast majority of non-state actors, including the conventional business community, falls outside its scope), it is preferable to the misleading and ambiguous notions of 'non-governmental' or 'civil society' organization. The use of these established terms must be limited in this connection due to their pivotal role in the legitimation of political privileges in the public policy arena – the very phenomenon which the current study seeks to problematize.

8 The notion of epistemic communities as participants in public policy formulation has been elaborated by Peter Haas (1992); Thomas Callaghy (2001) has recently applied this perspective to the global debt reduction policy regime.

9 TCDD is a coalition of national advocacy groups concerned with debt established in 1998 with the strong 'facilitation' of Oxfam/Tanzania (interview: Oxfam).

10 The favourable view of local business may be attributed, in part, to the membership of the Tanzania Chambers of Commerce and Industry in the TCDD/PRSP 'Macro' Working Group.

11 As far as we can ascertain, the only TCDD/PRSP recommendation adopted in the government's PRSP is that the goal for the percentage of under two-year-old children immunized against measles and DPT be increased from 75 to 85 per cent.

12 The top five priority issues identified by zonal workshop participants were, predictably: education, agriculture (extension, inputs and pricing), health, infrastructure (roads, transportation and electricity) and water.

IPC does not make any new funds available. What HIPC money' refers to the resources Tanzania is not ote to debt servicing.

nors were also closely involved in sectoral working groups which ulated sectoral programmes and in the zonal and national workshops on PRSP, to an extent that the whole PRSP process can be seen as donor-driven. Wangwe (2001: 10) notes: 'GoT makes deliberate effort to regain ownership over the reform process but at the same time it is expected that donors will adjust aid policies and delivery mechanisms.'

15 'Civil society' is less of an idea than a fetish for scholarly and pragmatic discourse on contemporary politics. No attempt is made here to summarize the voluminous literature on the concept and reality of 'civil society' in Africa.

16 *The Poverty and Human Development Report* represents a unique merging of a governmental policy monitoring activity under the PMS with UNDP's established practice of producing national HDRs, a concrete manifestation of the interpenetration of the state and a multilateral aid agency.

17 The other two technical working groups, one on census and surveys, and another on administrative data, include donor representatives but no non-state actors. These two groups are responsible for ensuring that routine and periodic data collected by the government agencies are incorporated in the Poverty Monitoring System.

18 Consortium website (TZon-line).

19 This assessment is based on interviews with members of the R & A TWG, including ESRF as lead agency in the PPA Consortium, and the UNDP (as a major 'backstopping agency') in March/April 2002.

20 Draft Strategic Plan for Civil Society Organizations engaged in Policy Processes (March 2002, mimeo).

21 The discussants are Godfrey Tweve [GT] of Concern Worldwide – a transnational private aid agency with roots in Ireland (see below) – and Joachim Njoki [JN] of Concern for Development Initiatives in Africa (FORDIA), a Tanzanian NGO. The interview was conducted by Jeremy Gould [JG] in Mtwara on 27 March 2002.

22 From 1998/9, USAID and DfID, among others, began systematically to subcontract with select TPAAs (CARE, ActionAid, Save the Children, Oxfam, Concern International, etc.) to 'build civil society capacity'. Support to advocacy skills and activities was a central component of these programmes.

23 For example, Tacosode, a government-sponsored umbrella organization established in 1965, and the independent Tango, set up in 1989 in the wake of associational liberalization.

24 In Masasi, these central government grants are often supplemented by substantial amounts of local revenue accruing from the cashewnut trade – a major source of rent-seeking for local elites, particularly through the collection of development levies from farmers (interview: Office of the Auditor; see also Chachage and Nyoni 2001).

25 It is, however, noteworthy that the Tanzanian constitution maintains that the 'National Assembly may deliberate upon and authorise any long or

short term plan which is intended to be implemented in the United Republic and enact a law to regulate the implementation of the plan' (United Republic of Tanzania 1998: art. 63, 3c).

26 The task of budgetary oversight is effectively performed through the Public Expenditure Review (PER) exercise, introduced in 1998 and coordinated by the World Bank. The major policy tool is the Medium-term Expenditure Framework (MTEF), introduced in 1997 and managed by the Ministry of Finance in close cooperation with the World Bank. The MTEF defines the limits of sector-specific expenditure in the medium term.

27 This relates to the fact that forecasts on the availability of funds (the 'resource envelope') tend to be over-optimistic as regards both revenues and development aid. According to a recent study, Tanzania's aggregate budget outturn as a percentage of the required sum for 1999/00 was only 54 per cent overall and as low as 37 per cent in education (Evans and Ngalwea 2001: 18).

28 The first multiparty elections were held in 1995, and the second in 2000. Both times, the CCM had a landslide victory.

29 Compared with the heyday of donor-run projects in the 1980s, direct donor implementation has decreased dramatically in recent years. Increasingly, donors channel resources into 'basket funds' and direct budget support, or subcontract project management to a private development agency. While donor involvement is still not negligible, the radical reduction of technical aid at the point of implementation seriously limits donor engagement in the complex patrimonial politics of the grassroots.

30 According to a number of estimates made by the MPs and observers interviewed, as many as 70–80 per cent of MPs have their 'own' NGO/trust fund or act as the major patron of a local association.

31 <http://www.worldbank.org/poverty/strategies/review/ danish4.pdf>

3 | Vietnam: dealing with donors

1 The Japanese development agencies, JICA and JBIC, are newcomers to the alliance but exercise increasing influence because of the huge volume of aid and loans channelled into Vietnam.

2 *Statistical Yearbook 2002* (2003: 373); *Vietnam Development Report 2004* (2003: 55).

3 Most sources refer to commitment of FDI and ODA, but the actual distributed amount is usually considerably lower, and ODA funding not spent will usually not remain in the budget. Information from GTZ representative, Hanoi.

4 CIEM (2003: 21).

5 The percentage of disbursement of donor funds has increased in 2002–03 to about 65 per cent ('Making ODA Pay', *Vietnam Investment Review*, 1–7 December 2003, pp. 12–13).

6 Another important source of income was the SOEs, but they were also weighted on the expense side with state loans for the companies.

7 The analysis was based on 4,800 household interviews across the country.

8 This analysis was based on 91,732 households.

9 The basic ideas derive from longer studies including Jerve et al. (2002); Wolff et al. (2002); *Civil Society Participation in Poverty Reduction Strategy Papers (PRSPs)*, 2000.

10 All three documents are to found in Communist Party of Vietnam (2001).

11 It is not explained why the data from the first Vietnam Living Standard Survey (VLSS) in 1993 of 51 per cent living in poverty and 20 per cent in food-poverty had increased to 58 and 25 respectively, when referred to in *Attacking Poverty*. Several donors produced different poverty assessments based on the same data from 1993; they were now pooled and the various organizations collaborated in the 1998 survey. No doubt such surveys are in danger of many types of problems both in the collection of information and the analyses (*Attacking Poverty* 1999: 152, 157).

12 In recent years a vigorous discussion has taken place about the nature and role of the LNGO in Vietnam, both among the INGOs and the NGOs, and in government circles. It is basically agreed that the character of the NGOs is not those of most other countries, and alternative terms such as 'civil organizations' (Wischermann and Nguyen 2003) or 'popular organisations' (Vasavakul 2003) have been suggested. One opinion is to exclude mass organizations from the NGO classification, because they are not non-governmental. Others find that they should be included because they fulfil a new role like NGOs funded by non-governmental organizations (Care International 2002; Nørlund et al. 2004).

13 For further reference to participation, see UNDP (2003), Wolff et al. (2002) and Shanks and Turk (2002).

14 UNDP has come up with a more positive interpretation: 'PRSP is being mainstreamed into the annual plans of the line ministries and provinces and implemented through the existing development planning instruments and processes' (UNDP 2003: 154).

4 | Honduras: transforming the concessional state?

1 Also referred to as a 'banana republic'.

2 The two historically important power groups in Latin America are the landed elite (*hacendados*), owners of large estates, dependent on primary commodity exports (including extraction as in mining) for their political power, and the 'comprador' bourgeoisie, dependent upon imports of industrial goods (consumer goods and, in the times of import substitution industrialization, capital goods). The landed elite has traditionally been descended from the old colonial aristocracy: rural, conservative and connected to the military; whereas the comprador bourgeoisie has been urban, middle class and, at least to some degree, a meritocracy. With the exception of Getulio Vargas's Brazil and Juán Perón's Argentina, Latin American military dictatorships (including Pinochet's Chile) have in general favoured natural-resource-based commodity exports to the detriment of national industrial development. On the many shortcomings of resource-based commodity

production as a model of economic development in Latin America, see Green (1991); Gwynne and Kay (1999); Franko (1999).

3 Modernization understood here as abolition of patrimonial privileges, emancipation from paternalism, the rule of law and so on.

4 There are no reliable statistics on actual delinquency and crime in Honduras, but according to media coverage, there are several murders a day, and several kidnappings were reported (more than one a week) during the fieldwork period. There are almost one million unregistered weapons in circulation, and the carrying of rifles openly is part of the everyday urban streetscape. A more complicated problem is the youth gangs (*maras*), consisting of youngsters, armed to the teeth, formed explicitly according to the model of US youth gangs and originally started by young criminals expelled from the USA to their countries of origin. There are about 35,000 persons involved in about 300 *maras*, with the number of 'hangers-on' members around 75,000. This means that there are about 100,000 youngsters in the country whose socialization happens through exposure to very aggressive violence. It is obvious that repression is not sufficient to resolve the problem of *maras* in Honduras. For the moment the Honduran government is on the defensive against international human rights pressure, because of 'social cleansing', presumably carried out by the police. In December 2002 alone, sixty-four youths were murdered in Honduras, and the rate shows no signs of going down.

5 There may have been a slight change in this respect over the two years since the fieldwork was carried out in 2002.

6 In Peru the dichotomy of the 'dispositif' is about clean and dirty (Nugent 1992). In the absence of clear physical distinctions between social classes, cleanliness or dirtiness is used to classify people (irrespective of whether or not they really are clean or dirty). In Peru as in Honduras, the specificity of this classification is that it points 'downwards': its function is not to regulate social mobility but rather to keep the 'dirty' down, prevent people from rising socially. To be concrete: in Honduras an NGO representative from the capital would typically ask his/her interlocutor from the provinces 'What is your educational level?' as an acknowledgement that the rural citizen would have said something intelligent.

It is probable that similar mechanisms are to be found in most cultures in the world. In Finland, the distinction made between Finnish and foreigner (*suomalainen–ulkomaalainen*) plays a similar kind of role in social classifications as the Peruvian variant, 'clean–dirty', and the Honduran variant 'educated–uneducated', and is as unconscious and effective in (re)producing social hierarchies as the latter.

7 According to Bourdieu, anybody who can afford to purchase the brand products that make 'the distinction' has an access to 'better circles'.

8 But most of them 'fortunately' left the country for Kosovo shortly thereafter according to the same interviewee; the present number of INGOs in Honduras is twenty-one.

9 It has to be pointed out that one important donor is not present at G-15, Taiwan (in Central America it is mainly known as the Republic of China). Central American countries are among the few countries in the world who

recognize Taiwan as a legitimate state in the international arenas (the UN, for instance), in exchange for massive aid that is not counted in the official DAC figures. According to *Tiempos del Mundo* (31 October 2002, p. 14), Taiwan is the fifth largest donor to Honduras, with a donation of at least US $30 million per annum. The relative political weight of the Republic of China in Honduras can be seen in the fact that President Maduro made his first official state visit to the Asian island in late October 2002 – combining it with his honeymoon!

10 In 2003, the GNP of Honduras was US $6.93 billion, and the population was 6.5 million.

11 A rotating presidency every six months in which only the (almost) original six members participate; after the Japanese presidency (end of 2002), all fifteen members can propose their presidency for which an unanimous decision is needed, based on an assessment of physical presence in the country, human and financial resources to run the group and commitment.

12 Both the donor side and civil society representatives expressed doubts about the new system of sectoral committees. Their number reduced from fifteen to seven, the topic in each was too wide and participants too numerous to hold a real debate on important issues (Interviews: Oxfam, G-15).

13 In Nicaragua the situation was to the contrary, according to the same source. It seems that there is much variation between the different representations of IFIs in the degree to which the official policies of the headquarters are integrated into action 'in the field', and that this variation may be partially due to the people occupying the leading posts at the field offices.

14 Julia Ojanen comments on this subject: 'The debate about whether or not the macro-economic framework reflecting the "Washington consensus" should be included in the PRSP misses the point in the sense that the PRSP is closely related to debt relief under the Highly Indebted Poor Country (HIPC) initiative. This debt relief is in turn conditioned upon a track record of structural adjustment; HIPC triggers and PRGF benchmarks reflect stringent macro-economic policies as a condition for debt relief. So any debate about the macro-economic content of the PRSP is in effect technically pre-empted.'

15 Here I use the term civil society in a totally neutral way, without a priori positive connotations. Thus, the youth gangs (*maras*) are a well organized part of civil society in Honduras and definitely are able to (and do) respond to the government's actions.

16 On the concept of political opportunity, see the discussion in Chapter 1 of this volume.

17 The increase was largely due to ideological reasons. The (neo-)liberal ideology about the limited role of the state, and the parallel, theoretically connected ideal of 'civil society' prompted donors to channel an increasing part of their funds through civic associations, both domestic and international.

18 With this I am not calling into question the motivations and leading ideas of these organizations; all are well-intentioned and most certainly do a good job. The point here is the 'structural nature' of NGOs. Their organizational structure (*personería jurídica* with its requirements) is to a large part imposed by external funding. Inherent in the concept of the NGO is the direction of accountability: whereas in a civic association or a popular

organization, the leadership is accountable to the 'bases', in an NGO (or INGO), the leadership is in the first place accountable to donors, to the source of funding.

19 A nice description of some of the related processes is offered in Torres and Calderón et al. (2002).

20 <http://www.sdp.gob.hn/grupoconsultivo>

21 To reiterate: it was a multiple clash in terms of *distinction*: the two parties of Interforos that parted ways differed in social class, education, urban–rural, capital city–provinces and, sociologically interestingly, by religion. As it happens, some key persons in the NGOs are Protestant whereas the majority of Interforos's members are Catholic, as are most Hondurans (Interview: HCCI).

22 Different degrees of participation can be situated on a continuum (from lower to higher) information sharing → consultation → consensus → joint decision-making.

23 As contrary to other countries, namely in Africa, where the process was led and carried out by anthropologists.

24 Some Honduran economists jokingly claim that the Ministry of Finance is a subsidiary office of the IMF. It is also said with empirical evidence that in Honduras there is a regular movement between those two: when the other party wins elections, it takes all local staff from the IMF to the ministry – and the former staff is hired as local staff by the IFI. And in the next elections the movement is reversed.

25 'The principal loser was the President' (because of the predominant role of his minister) (Interview: Trocaire).

26 A study by SIDA (ASDI) and IDB from 2003 indicated that the Honduran lowest income quintile pays 79 per cent more tax in relation to income than the highest quintile (SIDA-IDB 2003).

27 Among other issues negotiated in CAFTA, the question of staples (beans, maize, rice) will directly affect poverty levels. The USA demands free trade for its (subsidized) production of beans, maize and rice, which would severely increase hunger in the landless peasant or small-farm-dominated Central American countryside. In the case of the poorest countries – Nicaragua and Honduras – it is suggested that the poorest, who are net consumers, will draw benefit from lower prices, and the most affected ones will be the small-scale landowners stable enough to be net producers. These producers are the segment of peasantry with which development cooperation is mostly working.

28 UNDP gave US $70,000 to civil society organizations in order to support the participatory PRSP formulation. This aid was a substantial contribution to the capacity building of civic activism.

5 | Conclusion: the politics of consultation

1 Jenkins (2003) gives a succinct summary.

2 It has been estimated, for example, that Tanzania's total debt in 2010 will be about three times as large as it was prior to the HIPC debt relief in

2000 (Danielson 2001: 18), due to new loans contracted mainly from the multilateral financial institutions (World Bank and African Development Bank).

3 For a fascinating if exceedingly formalized application of game-theoretical precepts to the analysis of aid relations see Ostrom et al. (2001).

4 'UK Government calls on World Bank to review its conditions on aid' at <http://www.dfid.gov.uk/news/files/pressreleases/pr-conditionality-full.asp> (accessed 7 October 2004).

About the contributors

Jeremy Gould has a PhD in Social Anthropology from the University of Helsinki and is a Fellow of the Academy of Finland and Associate Professor of Development Studies at the University of Helsinki. He is currently working on an ethnography of the legal domain in Zambia. His main publications include *Localizing Modernity. Actors, Interests and Association in Rural Zambia* (1997) and (with H. S. Marcussen) *Ethnographies of Aid. Exploring Development Texts and Encounters* (2004).

Nguyen Dinh Tuyen has a PhD in Economics from the Academy of Science in Moscow. He worked as a researcher at the Institute of Science Management, Hanoi, specializing in technology transfer and the renovation of science and technology. He is the general director of B & H Consulting Corporation in Hanoi.

Irene Nørlund has a PhD in History and a BA in Social Anthropology from the University of Copenhagen. She has worked as a senior researcher at the Nordic Institute of Asian Studies and as Associate Professor of International Development Studies at Roskilde University. She is currently a consultant based in Hanoi dealing with development cooperation, participatory approaches and social change. Her main publications include *Asian Values and Vietnam's Development* (1999) and *Vietnam in a Changing World* (1996).

Julia Ojanen has an MA in Political Science from the University of Helsinki and an MA from the College of Europe. Her work has focused upon the politics of aid in Africa and on issues of aid subcontracting in the European Union. She is currently based in Vientiane, Laos.

Maaria Seppänen has a PhD in Geography from the University of Helsinki. After a decade of research and teaching at the Institute of Development Studies, University of Helsinki, she is currently working for Finnish Development Co-operation in Central America. Her publications include *Global Scale, Local Place? The Making of the Historic Centre of Lima into a World Heritage Site* (1999).

Tran Ngoc Ca has a PhD in Economics from the University of Edinburgh and an MSc from the Research Policy Institute, University of Lund. He is currently Deputy Director of the National Institute of Science and Technology Policy and Strategy Studies in Hanoi. His main publications include 'Reforming the Science, Technology, Education and Training System in a Transitional Economy: The Case of Vietnam', in C. Brundenius and B. Göransson (eds), *Reconstruction or Destruction? Science and Technology at Stake in Transitional Economies* (1999) and *Learning and Technological Capability in Firms. Vietnamese Industries in Transition* (1999).

Bibliography

Abrahamsen, R. (2001) *Disciplining Democracy: Development Discourse and Good Governance in Africa* (New York: Zed Books)

Argüeta, M. R. (1992) *Historia de los sin historia* (Tegucigalpa: Editorial Guaymuras)

Arkadie, B. Van and R. Mallon (2003) *Vietnam. A Transitional Tiger?* (Australian National University: Asian Pacific Press)

Attacking Poverty (1999) Joint Report of the Government–Donor–NGO Working Group, Consultative Group Meeting for Vietnam, 14–15 December 1999

Bagić, A. (2004) 'Talking about "Donors". Women's Organizing in Post-Yugoslav Countries', in J. Gould and H. S. Marcussen (eds), *Ethnographies of Aid. Exploring Development Texts and Encounters* (Roskilde: Department of International Development Studies)

Bangura, Y. (2000) *Public Sector Restructuring: The Institutional and Social Effects of Fiscal, Managerial and Capacity-Building Reforms* (Geneva: UNRISD)

Bayart, J.-F. (1993) *The State in Africa. The Politics of the Belly* (London: Longman)

Bertelsen, M. and S. Jensen (2002) *Poverty Reduction Strategies – A Possibility for Participatory Economic Policymaking? The Central American Experience.* Unpublished MA thesis, University of Roskilde and Eurodad

Bigsten, A. and A. Danielson (2001), *Tanzania: Is the Ugly Duckling Finally Growing Up? A Report for the OECD Project 'Emerging Africa'*, Research Report no. 120 (Uppsala: Nordiska Afrikainstitutet)

Blom Hansen, T. and F. Stepputat (eds) (2001) *States of Imagination. Ethnographic Explorations of the Post-colonial State* (Durham, NC: Duke University Press)

Booth, D. (2001) *PRSP Institutionalization Study. Final Report* (London: Overseas Development Institute)

Bourdieu, P. (1984) *Distinction: A Social Critique of the Judgement of Taste*, trans. Richard Nice (Cambridge, MA: Harvard University Press)

Brett, E. A. (1993) 'Voluntary Agencies as Development Organizations: Theorizing the Problem of Efficiency and Accountability', *Development and Change*, 24: 269–303

Brock, K., R. McGee and S. Sewakiriyanga (2002) *Poverty Knowledge and Policy Processes: A Case Study of Ugandan National Poverty Reduction Policy* Research Report no. 53 (Sussex: Institute of Development Studies)

Buch-Hansen, M. (2003) *Aligning the PRSP Process with Environment and Sustainable Development in the Case of Vietnam*, Paper (Roskilde: Department for International Development Studies, Roskilde University)

Callaghy, T. (1990) 'Lost Between State and Market: The Politics of Economic

Adjustment in Ghana, Zambia, and Nigeria', in J. Nelson (ed.), *Economic Crisis and Policy Choice: The Politics of Adjustment in the Third World* (Princeton, NJ: Princeton University Press)

— (2001) 'Networks and Governance in Africa: Innovation in the Debt Regime', in T. Callaghy, R. Kassimir and R. Latham (eds), *Intervention and Transnationalism in Africa. Global–Local Networks of Power* (Cambridge: Cambridge University Press)

Care International (2002) *Civil Society in Vietnam*, Background Paper (Hanoi: Care International)

Cerny, P. (2000) 'Political Agency in a Globalizing World: Toward a Structurational Approach', *European Journal of International Relations*, 6(4): 435–63

— (2001) 'From "Iron Triangles" to "Golden Pentangles"? Globalizing the Policy Process', *Global Governance*, 7(4): 397–413

Chachage, C. S. L. and J. Nyoni (2001) 'Economic Restructuring and the Cashewnut Industry in Tanzania' (Dar es Salaam: Tanzania Agriculture Situation Analysis)

CIEM (2003) *Vietnam's Economy in 2002* (Hanoi: National Political Publishers)

Civil Society Participation in Poverty Reduction Strategy Papers (PRSPs), Report to the Department for International Development (DfID), Vol. III, Vietnam Case Study, June 2000

Communist Party of Vietnam (1996) *8th National Congress Documents* (Hanoi: Gioi Publishers)

— (2001) *9th National Congress Documents* (Hanoi: Gioi Publishers)

Concern Worldwide (2001a) *Annual Report 2001*. <http://www.concern.ie/news/annual.htm>

— (2001b) *Financial Statement 2001*. <http://www.concern.ie/news/annual.htm>

Corrigan, P. and D. Sayers (1985) *The Great Arch. English State Formation as Cultural Revolution* (Oxford: Basil Blackwell)

Cruikshank, B. (1999) *The Will to Empower. Democratic Citizens and Other Subjects* (Ithaca, NY: Cornell University Press)

Dang Ngoc Quang and Nghiem Hong Son (2001a) *Mapping the Government–NGO and the World Bank Relationship. A Case Study of Vietnam* (Hanoi: Rural Development Services Centre)

— (2001b) *Rapid Assessment of the PRSP Formulation Process. A Case Study of Vietnam* (Hanoi: Rural Development Services Centre)

Dang Phong and M. Beresford (1998) *Authority Relations and Economic Decision-making in Vietnam. An Historical Perspective* (Copenhagen: NIAS)

DANIDA (2001) *Review of the PRS Processes in Tanzania. A Contribution to the International Review of the PRSP Process*, Final Draft Review Report. <http://www.worldbank.org/poverty/strategies/review/danish4.pdf>

Danielson, A. (2001) *Can HIPC Reduce Poverty in Tanzania?* Paper presented at the WIDER Conference on Debt Relief, Helsinki, 17–18 August 2001 <http://swopec.hhs.se/lunewp/papers/lunewp2001_014.pdf>

d'Ans, A.-M. (2002) *Honduras. Difícil emergencia de una nación, de un Estado,* trans. from French by Albert Depienne (Tegucigalpa: Renal Video Producción)

Delany, J. (2003), 'Hepr-vn-list, Hunger Eradication and Poverty Reduction List', *People Army Newspaper*, 18 November 2003

Directory of Vietnamese Non-government Organizations Working for Hunger Eradication, Poverty Reduction and Community Development in Vietnam (Hanoi: VUFO-NGO Resource Centre, 2002)

Easterly, W. (2002) 'The Cartel of Good Intentions: Bureaucracy versus Markets in Foreign Aid', *Foreign Policy*, July/August: 40–9

Eberlei, W. (2001) *Institutionalised Participation in Processes Beyond PRSP. Study Commissioned by the Deutsche Gesellschaft für Technische Zusammenarbeit (GTZ) GmbH* (Duisburg: Gerhard-Mercator-University)

Economic and Social Research Foundation (ESRF) (1999) *Multilateral Debt Fund. Analysis and Monitoring of the Debt Issue*, Report prepared for DANIDA

Edwards, M. and D. Hulme (1996) 'Too Close for Comfort? The Impact of Official Aid on Nongovernmental Organizations', *World Development*, 24: 961–73

El concepto de transformación (n.d.) *El concepto de transformación y la organización del G-15*, Presidencia pro tempore del Grupo de Seguimiento a la Declaración de Estocolmo 5–15, República Federal de Alemania (Tegucigalpa: Embassy of the Federal Republic of Germany)

Eurodad (2001a) *Many Dollars, Any Change?* <http://www.worldbank.org/poverty/strategies/review/eurodad1sum.pdf>

— (2001b) *Putting Poverty Reduction First. Why a Poverty Reduction Approach Must be Adopted.* <http://www.worldbank.org/poverty/ strategies/review/eurodad2sum.pdf>

Evaluation (2004) *Evaluation of the National Targeted Program on Hunger Eradication and Poverty Reduction (NTP on HEPR) and Program 135* (Hanoi: UNDP VIE/02/001)

Evans, A. and E. Ngalwea (2001) 'Institutionalising the PRSP Approach in Tanzania', in D. Booth (ed.), *Overview of PRSP Processes and Monitoring* (London: Overseas Development Institute)

Evans, A. and A. van Diesen (2002) *Tanzania's Poverty Monitoring System. A Review of Early Experiences and Current Challenges* (mimeo)

Ewald, J. (2001) 'The Interface between Democracy and Economic Change – The Case of Structural Adjustment and Democracy in Tanzania', in A. Närman and J. Ewald (eds), *Göteborg University in Africa* (Göteborg University: Centre for Africa Studies)

— (2002) *Economic Reforms and Democratisation in Tanzania: The Case of the Election 2000 and the Need to Go Beyond Electionalism*, Paper presented to the Conference on Democratization and Conflict Management in East Africa, February–March 2002

Ferguson, J. (1990) *The Anti-Politics Machine: 'Development', Depoliticization, and Bureaucratic Power in Lesotho* (Minneapolis: University of Minnesota Press)

Feza Lwaitama, A. (2002) *Nyerereism in the 21st century in East and Central Africa. A Theoretical Appraisal of Pan-Africanist Sensibilities under Globalisation*, Paper presented at the 3rd International AmFiTan Development Ethics Conference, University of Helsinki, 12–15 August 2002

Fisher, W. F. (1997) 'Doing Good? The Politics and Antipolitics of NGO Practices', *Annual Review of Anthropology*, 26: 439–64

Franko, P. (1999) *The Puzzle of Latin American Economic Development* (Lanham, MD: Rowman and Littlefield)

Gibbon, P. (1998) *Limping Towards a Ditch without a Crutch: The Brave New World of Tanzanian Cotton Marketing Cooperatives*, CDR Working Paper Subseries on Globalization and Economic Restructuring in Africa, no. 3 (Copenhagen: Centre for Development Research)

— (2001) 'Civil Society, Locality and Globalisation in Rural Tanzania: A Forty-Year Perspective', *Development and Change*, 32: 819–44

Gould, J. (2001) 'Aid Modalities and the Arts of Government', Paper presented to a workshop, 'The Impact of Aid', Centre for Development Research, Copenhagen

— (2005) 'Timing, Scale and Style: Capacity as Governmentality in Tanzania', in D. Mosse and D. Lewis (eds), *Anthropology Upstream: The Ethnography of Aid Donors and Neoliberal Reform* (London: Pluto Press).

Gould, J. and J. Ojanen (2003) *Merging in a Circle. The Politics of Tanzania's Poverty Reduction Strategy*, Policy Papers 2/2003, (Helsinki: Institute of Development Studies, University of Helsinki)

Government of Vietnam (1998) *Decree no. 29/1998/ND-CP. Regulation on the Exercise of Democracy in Communes*

— (2001) *Decree no. 17/2001/ND-CP of May 4, 2001. Issuing the Regulation on the Management and Use of Official Development Aid*

— (2001) *Interim Poverty Reduction Strategy Paper (I-PRSP)*, Hanoi, <www.vdci.org.vn>

— (2001) *Strategy for Public Administration Reform for the Period 2001–2010*, March 2001

— (2002) *Vietnam. The Drive to Partnership*, Informal Report for the Consultative Group Meeting for Vietnam, December 2002

— (2003) *A Review of the Three-year Implementation of the Five-year Socio-economic Development Tasks (2001–2005)*, Government Report presented to the CG Meeting, Hanoi, 1–2 December 2003

Green, D. (1991) *Faces of Latin America* (London: Latin American Bureau)

Gwynne, R. and C. Kay (1999) *Latin America Transformed: Modernization and Globalization* (London: Arnold)

Haas, P. M. (1992), 'Introduction: Epistemic Communities and International Policy Coordination', *International Organization*, 46(1): 1–35

Habermas, J. (1992), *The Structural Transformation of the Public Sphere. An Inquiry into a Category of Bourgeois Society*, trans. T. Burger (Cambridge: Polity Press [1962])

HakiKazi Catalyst (2001) *Tanzania without Poverty. A Plain Language Guide to*

Tanzania's Poverty Reduction Strategy (Arusha: HakiKazi Catalyst)

Hansen, T. B. and F. Stepputat (eds) (2001) *States of Imagination: Ethnographic Explorations of the Postcolonial State* (Durham, NC: Duke University Press)

Harrison, G. (2001), 'Post-conditionality Politics and Administrative Reform: Reflections on the Cases of Uganda and Tanzania', *Development and Change*, 23: 657–79

Helleiner, G. (2002) 'Emerging Relationships between Poor Countries and External Sources of Finance: The Case of Tanzania', *International Journal*, LVIII (2) (Spring)

Helleiner, G., T. Killick, N. Lipumba, B. Ndulu and K. E. Svendsen (1995) *Report of the Group of Independent Advisers on Development Cooperation Issues Between Tanzania and Its Aid Donors* (Copenhagen: Royal Danish Ministy of Foreign Affairs)

Hudock, A. (2002) *Laying Foundations for Sustainable Development: Good Governance and the Poverty Reduction Strategy Paper* (Washington, DC: World Learning)

International Monetary Fund (2004) *Report on the Evaluation of Poverty Reduction Strategy Papers (PRSPs) and the Poverty Reduction Growth Facility (PRGF)*, Independent Evaluation Office, <http://www.imf.org/External/NP/ieo/2004/prspprgf/eng/index.htm>

IMF and IDA (2002) *Joint Staff Assessment of the Poverty Reduction Strategy, Vietnam*, June–July 2002

Input for the PRSP Review; Poverty Reduction and Participation (Copenhagen: North/South Coalition and Ibis)

Interim Poverty Reduction Strategy Paper, Honduras (Tegucigalpa: Government of the Republic of Honduras, 3 January 2000)

Jackson, R. and C. Rosberg (1982) 'Why Africa's Weak States Persist: The Empirical and the Juridical in Statehood', *World Politics*, 35(1): 1–24

Japan's Development Cooperation in Vietnam – Supporting Broad-based Growth with Poverty Reduction, GRIPS Development Forum, Tokyo, May 2002

Jenkins, R. (2003), 'International Development Institutions and National Economic Contexts: Neo-liberalism Encounters India's Indigenous Political Traditions', *Economy and Society*, 32(4): 584–610

Jerve, A. M. et al. (2002) *Evaluation of the Comprehensive Development Framework, Viet Nam Country Study*, Draft Final Report, 7 July 2002, Prepared with support from the World Bank, Ministry for Foreign Affairs, Japan, and Asian Development Bank

Joseph, G. M. and D. Nugent (eds) (1994) *Everyday Forms of State Formation. Revolution and the Negotiation of Rule In Modern Mexico* (Durham, NC: Duke University Press)

Jubilee Plus (2001) *Tanzania Reaches Completion Point – but Her Debt Remains Unsustainable* <http://www.jubilee2000uk.org/worldnews/africa/tanzania_completion.htm> (accessed 23 November 2001)

Keck, M. and K. Sikkink (1998) *Activists Beyond Borders. Advocacy Networks in International Politics* (Ithaca, NY: Cornell University Press)

Kelsall, T. (2000) 'Governance, Local Politics and Districtization in Tanzania: The 1998 Arumeru Tax Revolt', *African Affairs*, 99: 533–51

— (2001) 'Shop Windows and Smoke-Filled Rooms: Governance and the Re-Politicization of Tanzania', *Modern African Studies*, 40(4): 1–23

Kiondo, A. (1994) 'The New Politics of Local Development in Tanzania', in P. Gibbon (ed.), *The New Local Level Politics in East Africa. Studies on Uganda, Tanzania and Kenya*, Research Report no. 95 (Uppsala: Nordiska Afrikainstitutet), pp. 38–65

KK Consulting Associates (2001) *An Assessment of the Depth of Understanding of the PRSP in the Government*, Report commissioned by DFIDEA (T) (Dar es Salaam: DFIDEA)

Latham, R. (2001) 'Identifying the Contours of Transboundary Political Life', in T. Callaghy, R. Kassimir and R. Latham (eds), *Intervention and Transnationalism in Africa. Global–Local Networks of Power* (Cambridge: Cambridge University Press)

Lineamiento (2002) *Lineamiento de Trabajo para el Grupo de Seguimiento a la Declaración de Estocolmo. Período abril 1, 2002–septiembre 30, 2002*, Presidencia pro tempore del Grupo de Seguimiento a la Declaración de Estocolmo 5–15 (Tegucigalpa: Embassy of Japan)

Long, N. and A. Long (eds) (1992) *Battlefields of Knowledge. The Interlocking of Theory and Practice in Social Research And Development* (London: Routledge)

McAdam, D. et al. (eds) (1996) *Comparative Perspectives on Social Movements. Political Opportunities, Mobilizing Structures and Cultural Framings* (Cambridge: Cambridge University Press)

McCarthy, A. (2002) *The Policy-Making Process in Vietnam,* Public Administration Reform Study (Hanoi: Mekong Economics paper)

McGee, R. et al. (2002) *Assessing Participation in Poverty Reduction Strategy Papers: A Desk-based Synthesis of Experience in Sub-Saharan Africa* (Sussex: Institute of Development Studies)

MacIntyre, A. (1994) 'The Theses on Feuerbach: A Road not Taken', in C. Gould and R. Cohen (eds), *Artifacts, Representations and Social Practice* (Dordrecht: Kluwer Academic Publishers)

Madon, S. (1999) 'International NGOs: Networking, Information Flows and Learning', *Journal of Strategic Information Systems*, 8: 251–61

Making ODA Pay, Interview with Resident Representative of UNDP and documentary, *Vietnam Investment Review*, 1–7 December 2003, pp. 12–13

Malaluan, J. J. C. and S. Guttal (2002) *Structural Adjustment in the Name of the Poor. The PRSP Experience in Lao PDR, Cambodia and Vietnam* (Bangkok: Focus on the Global South)

Mbembe, A. (2001) *On the Postcolony* (Berkeley: University of California Press).

Mbilinyi, M. (2001) *Budgets, Debt Relief and Globalisation* (Accra: Third World Network Africa)

Mercer, C. (1999) 'Reconceptualising State–Society Relations in Tanzania: Are NGOs Making a Difference?', *Area Journal*, 31(3): 247–58

Ministry of Labour, Invalids and Social Affairs (2001) *Poverty Alleviation Strategy, 2001–2010* (Hanoi: MOLISA)

Mjema, G. (2000) *Strategic Long Term Planning and Policy Management: Some Reflections from Tanzania*, DPMN Bulletin, VII(2)

Mkapa, B. W. (1999) 'Tanzania's Vision Regarding Partnership-based Cooperation', Speech at the workshop on 'Making Partnerships Work on the Ground', Ulvsunda Slott, Stockholm (Dar es Salaam: Government Printer)

— (2000) Speech to the Consultative Group, Dar es Salaam, September

Mmuya, M. (1998) *Tanzania. Political Reform in Eclipse. Crises and Cleavages in Political Parties* (Dar es Salaam: Friedrich Ebert Stiftung)

Moore, S. F. (2001) 'The International Production of Authoritative Knowledge; The Case of Drought-stricken West Africa', *Ethnography*, 2(2): 161–89

Moving Beyond Good and Bad Performance. Why the Emphasis on 'Selectivity' Could Undermine the Current Focus on Ownership, Participation and Poverty Reduction (Brussels: Eurodad, June 2002)

Msekwa, P. (2000) *Reflections on Tanzania's First Multi-Party Parliament: 1995–2000* (Dar es Salaam: DUP)

Mushi, C. (n.d.) Training module on 'Policy Analysis' for Tanzanian NGOs (UNDP: Dar es Salaam)

National Human Development Report 2001 (2001) *Doi Moi and Human Development in Vietnam* (Hanoi: Political Publishing House)

NGO Policy Forum (2002) *Draft Strategic Plan for Civil Society Organizations Engaged in Policy Processes* (mimeo)

Nguyen Thang and J. Weeks (2003) *Evaluation of UNDP's Role in the PRSP Process. Vietnam Country Pape*r (London: Centre for Development Policy and Research, School of Oriental and African Studies)

Nørlund, I., Tran Ngoc Ca and Nguyen Dinh Tuyen (2004) *Dealing with the Donors. The Politics of Vietnam's Comprehensive Poverty Reduction and Growth Strategy*, Policy Papers 4/2003 (Helsinki: Institute of Development Studies, University of Helsinki)

Nugent, G. (1992) *El laberinto de la choledad* (Lima: Friedrich Ebert Stiftung)

Ojanen, J. (2003) *National Politics of Policy-Making and the Global Development Aid Consensus. The Case of Poverty Reduction Policies and the Parliament in Tanzania and Uganda*, Unpublished MA thesis, University of Helsinki

Ostrom, E. et al. (2001) *Aid, Incentives and Sustainability. An Institutional Analysis of Development Co-operation* (Stockholm: Sida Studies in Evaluation)

Oxfam (2002) 'Influencing Poverty Reduction Strategies: A Guide' <www.oxfam.org.uk/policy/papers/prsguide/prsguide.html>

Painter, M. (2003) *Marketisation, Integration and State Restructuring in Vietnam: The Case of State Owned Enterprise Reform*, SEARC Working Paper Series, no. 39 (City University of Hong Kong)

Pasha, M. P. and D. L. Blaney (1998) 'Elusive Paradise: The Promise and Peril of Global Civil Society', *Alternatives* (23): 417–50

Peterson, M. A. (1993) 'Political Influence in the 1990s – from Iron Triangles to Policy Networks', *Journal of Health Politics, Policy and Law*, 18(2): 395–438

Phong, D. and M. Beresford (1998) *Authority Relations and Economic Decision-Making in Vietnam. A Historical Perspective* (Copenhagen: Nordic Institute of Asian Studies)

Piron, L.-H. with A. Evans (2004) *Politics and the PRSP Approach – Synthesis Paper*, Working Paper no. 237 (London: Overseas Development Institute)

Ponte, S. (2002) *Farmers and Markets in Tanzania* (Oxford: James Currey)

PRSP (2001a) *Poverty Reduction Strategy Paper, Honduras* (Tegucigalpa: Secretaría del Estado de Despacho Presidencial, August 2001)

— (2001b) *Poverty Reduction Strategy Paper. Joint Staff Assessment* (International Monetary Fund and the International Development Association, September 2001)

Riles, A. (2000) *The Network Inside Out* (Ann Arbor: University of Michigan Press)

Samji, S. S. and A. Albee 'Selected Studies of Civil Society in Tanzania: Policy, Social Capital Networks and the Vulnerable', <http://www.tzonline.org/pdf/selectedstudiesofcivilsociety.pdf>

Saussier, J. (2002), 'Feedback on the User's Guide to Poverty and Social Impact Analysis (PSIA)' (Washington: World Learning) <http://poverty.worldbank.org/files/13048_worldlearningfeedback.pdf>

Sen, J. (2002), 'Civilising Globalisation? Globalising Civilisation? Some Reflections Towards Civil Governance and a Conscious, Critical Globalization', Paper presented to the Helsinki Conference 2002 on Searching for Global Partnerships <http://www.helsinkiconference.fi/netcomm/news>

Seppälä, P. (2000) *Towards Local Partnerships. The Social Interfaces of Aid in Rural Tanzania* (Helsinki: Ministry of Foreign Affairs)

Shanks, E. and C. Turk (2002) *Policy Recommendations from the Poor*, vol. II (Hanoi: World Bank)

Shivji, I. (1998) *Not Yet Democracy: Reforming Land Tenure in Tanzania* (Dar es Salaam: IIED/HAKIARDHI)

— (1976) *Class Struggles in Tanzania* (London: Heinemann)

SIDA-IDB (2003) *Honduras: hacia un sistema tributario más transparente y diversificado* (Guatemala: Embassy of Sweden), published as a supplement in Honduran newspapers.

Sobhan, R. (1996) *Aid Dependence and Donor Policy. The Case of Tanzania. With Lessons from Bangladesh's Experience* (Dhaka: Centre for Policy Dialogue, University Press)

Socialist Republic of Vietnam (2002a) *High and Sustainable Development to Reduce Poverty*, Government Report to the Consultative Group Meeting, Hanoi, 10–11 December 2002

— (2002b) *The Comprehensive Poverty Reduction and Growth Strategy*, Hanoi, May 2002

— (2003a) *A Review of the Three-year Implementation of the Five-year Socio-economic Development Task (2001–03)*, CG Meeting, 2–3 December 2003

— (2003b) *Decree no. 88/2003/ND-CP Providing of the Organization, Operation and Management of Associations*, Cong Bao, Official Gazette, no. 10, August 2003

Statistical Yearbook (Nien Giam Thong Ke) 2001 (Hanoi: Statistical Publishing House, 2002)

— (2002) (Hanoi: Statistical Publishing House, 2003)

Steinmetz, G. (ed.) (1999) *State/Culture: State-formation After the Cultural Turn* (Ithaca, NY: Cornell University Press)

Swartz, M. (1968) *Local-level Politics: Social and Cultural Perspectives* (Chicago, IL: Aldine)

Taking Stock (2003a) *An Update on Vietnam's Economic Developments and Reforms*, Progress and Donor Support, Mid-year Consultative Group Meeting, Sapa, 19–21 June 2003

— (2003b) *An Update on Vietnam's Economic Developments and Reforms*, Consultative Group Meeting for Vietnam, Hanoi, 2–3 December 2003

Tango (n.d.) *TANGO Involvement in PRSP and Its Impact in Poverty Eradication Initiatives* (mimeo)

Tanzania Coalition for Debt and Development (TCDD) (2000) *Poverty Reduction Strategy Paper: Input from Civil Society Organizations*, Draft paper prepared by the TCDD/PRSP Drafting Committee on the basis of Reports by Working Groups on Food Security, Health, Education and Poverty Analysis, 11 March 2000

Tanzania Development Assistance Committee (2002) 'Principles for Promoting Harmonisation and Aid Effectiveness', March 2002

TASOET (2000) 'Civil Societies Work on PRSP in Tanzania'

Tendler, J. (2000) 'Why Social Policy is Condemned to a Residual Category of Safety Nets, and What to Do About It: Thoughts on a Research Agenda for UNRISD', Comments for UNRISD meeting, Stockholm, 23–24 September 2000

Thérien, J.-P. (2002) 'Multilateral Institutions and the Poverty Debate', *International Journal*: 234–52

Therkildsen, O. (1998) *Local Government and Households in Primary Education in Tanzania: Some Lessons for Reform,* CDR Working Paper no. 98.6, June (Copenhagen: Centre for Development Research)

Torres Calderón, M. et al. (2002) *Deciphering Honduras. Four Views of Post-Mitch Political Reality* (Cambridge, MA: Hemisphere Initiatives)

Turk, C. (2001) *Linking Participatory Poverty Assessments to Policy and Policy Making. Experiences from Vietnam* (Hanoi: Hanoi Country Office, World Bank)

Tvedt, T. (1998) *Angels of Mercy or Development Diplomats: NGOs and Foreign Aid* (Oxford: James Currey; Trenton, NJ: Africa World Press)

UNDP (2002a) *Development Cooperation Vietnam* (Hanoi: UNDP)

— (2002b) *Overview of Official Development Assistance in Vietnam* (Hanoi: UNDP)

— (2003) *Evaluation of UNDP's Role in the PRSP Process*, Vol. II: Country Reports (New York: UNDP)

— (2004) *ODA flow to Vietnam*, <www.undp.org.vn/undp/fact/ODAflow.pdf> (accessed 14 January 2004)

UNDP and MPI (1997) *Vietnam's Development Partners. Profiles of Cooperation Programmes* (Hanoi: UNDP)

United Republic of Tanzania (1998) *Constitution* <http://www.tanzania.go.tz>

— (2000) *Poverty Reduction Strategy Paper (PRSP)* (Dar es Salaam: Government Printer)

— (2001a) *Report on the PRSP National Consultative Workshop* (Dar es Salaam)

— (2001b) *Poverty Monitoring Master Plan* (Dar es Salaam: Government Printer)

Vasavakul, T. (2003) 'From Fence-Breaking to Networking: Interests, Popular Organizations, and Policy Influence in Post-Socialist Vietnam', in B. J. Tria Kerkvliet, R. H. K. Heng and D. W. H. Koh (eds), *Getting Organized in Vietnam. Moving in and Around the Socialist State* (Singapore: ISEAS)

Vasavakul, T. et al. (2003) *Decentralisation in Vietnam – Working Effectively at Provincial and Local Government Level* (Hanoi: Adam Fforde and Associates, <www.aduki.com.au>

Vietnam Development Report 2001. Vietnam 2010. Entering the 21st Century. Partnerships for Development, produced by Government–Donor–NGO Partnership Groups, prepared for Consultative Group Meeting for Vietnam, 14–15 December 2000

Vietnam Development Report 2003. Vietnam: Delivering on Its Promise, World Bank in collaboration with the ADB, Consultative Group Meeting for Vietnam, December 2002

Vietnam Development Report 2004. Poverty, Joint Donor Report to Vietnam Consultative Group, Hanoi, 2–3 December 2003

Vietnam. INGO Directory 2002–2003 (Hanoi: NGO Resource Centre, 2002)

Voipio, T. (2001) *Final Report and Handing Over Notes* (Mtwara: Rural Integrated Project Support, RIPS)

Vu Manh Loi, Tran Thi Van Anh and Tran Thi Que (2003) *The Comprehensive Poverty Reduction and Growth Strategy (CPRGS): A Gender Analysis*, Report supported by the Royal Netherlands Embassy, Hanoi, June 2003

Walther, M. (n.d.) *Lessons from the Analysis of the First Five Full PRSPs* (mimeo)

Wangwe, S. M. (2001) *Poverty Reduction Strategy Paper: Experiences and Lessons from Tanzania*, Paper prepared for the Meeting of the ECA-Sponsored PRSP Learning Group from African Countries, Addis Ababa, 5–6 November

Weyland, K. (1999) 'Neoliberal Populism in Latin America and Eastern Europe,' *Comparative Politics*, 31(4): 379–401

Wischermann and Nguyen Quang Vinh (2003) 'The Relationship Between Civic and Governmental Organizations in Vietnam: Selected Findings', in B. J. Tria Kerkvliet, R. H. K. Heng and D. W. H. Koh (eds), *Getting Organized in Vietnam. Moving in and Around the Socialist State* (Singapore: ISEAS)

Wolff, P. et al. (2002) *The Comprehensive Poverty Reduction and Growth Strategy in Vietnam. Process, Donor Contribution, and Prospects for Its Implementation* (Bonn: German Development Institute)

World Bank (1995) *Viet Nam. Poverty Assessment and Strategy* (Washington, DC: World Bank)

— (1997) *World Development Report 1997: The State in a Changing World* (Washington, DC: World Bank)

— (2001) *Vietnam Country Assistance Evaluation* (Washington, DC: World Bank) 21 November 2001, <www.vcdi.org.vn/eng/cprgs/pov_strat001.htm>

— (2002a) *Participation in Poverty Reduction Strategy Papers. A Retrospective Study*, Participation and Civic Engagement Group, Social Development Department, <http://www.worldbank.org/participation>

— (2002b) *Participation in Poverty Reduction Strategy Papers. A Retrospective Study* (Washington, DC: World Bank)

— (2002c) *Poverty Reduction Support Credits*

— (2003) *Poverty, Vietnam Development Report 2004*, Joint Donor Report to the Vietnam Consultative Group Meeting, December 2003 (Hanoi)

— (n.d.) *Group Discussion Summary, Theme I-B: Parliaments and Civil Society*, 2nd African Forum on Poverty Reduction Strategies <http://www.worldbank.org/wbi/attackingpoverty/activities/dakargd2summ.html>

World Bank Institute (2002) *The Elimination of User Fees for Primary Education in Tanzania. A Case Study on the Political Economy of Pro-Poor Policies* (Dar es Salaam) <http://www.worldbank.org/wbi/attackingpoverty/events/Tanz_0602/casestudy_tanz.doc>

World Bank Institute and Parliamentary Centre (2002) *Handbook on Parliamentarians and Policies to Reduce Poverty.* <http://www.parlcent.ca/publications/pdf/handbook.pdf>

Index

accountability, 21, 52, 60, 103, 135, 144, 146, 147
ActionAid, 49, 87, 90, 143
Adjusted Millennium Goals, 97
aesthetic discipline, 47–9
aid, 112; as conspiracy, 150; as percentage of Gross National Income, 144; as politics, 137–9; changes in procedures and modalities of, 1; role in perpetuation of inequality, 16; transaction costs of, 19
aid cartel, 137, 146, 148; generation of indebtedness, 149; self-perpetuation of, 150
aid dependency, 144, 146, 149; assumptions of, 148
aid fatigue, 136, 140
aid organizations, competition between, 139
aid-rent extraction, 48
Aleman, Arnoldo, 111
Asian Development Bank (ADB), 76, 94, 98
Asian financial crisis, 70, 76
Asian tiger economies, 69
Asian-Pacific Economic Cooperation (APEC), 84
Association of Non-governmental Organizations (ASONOG) (Honduras), 125
Association of Southeast Asian Nations (ASEAN), 84
autonomy, as element of ownership, 65

battlefields of knowledge, 62
Benn, Hilary, 151
Bertelsen, M., 114
bilateral donors, 105, 111, 131, 132, 143, 151
Bloque Popular (Honduras), 118, 133
Bourdieu, Pierre, 'distinction', 108
Bretton Woods institutions, 2–4, 10, 17, 25, 29, 88, 150; as main architects of PRS process, 131; growing hegemony of, 150
bureaucratic bourgeoisie, 15

Cambodia, 69
Canada, 111, 113
Cao Viet Sinh, 66
capacity building, 23, 45–7, 52, 61
Care organization, 49
Caritas organization, 125
cashew nut marketing in Tanzana, deregulation of, 58–9
Catholic Church, support for Interforos, 125
Central American Bank of Economic Integration (CABEI), 111
Central American Free Trade Agreement, 131
centralization, 78
Centre for Legal Research and Services (LERES) (Vietnam), 93
Cerny, Philip, 11
Chama Cha Mapinduzi (CCM) party (Tanzania), 8, 53–4, 57, 59
China, 69, 71, 83
Ciluba, F., 61
citizenship, technologies of, 46
civic activism, in Honduras, 116–26
civil society, 7, 12, 24, 25, 26, 38–52, 99, 105, 120, 145; advancement of, 115; creation and cooption of, 142; depoliticizing of, 49–51; donor support for organizations of, 116; global, 149; old, 123 (absent from PRS formulation, 132); old and new, 117; participation of, 28, 32, 33, 35, 40, 112; privatization of, 52; relation to state, 46; representation of, 122; surrogate, 50; synonymous with NGOs, 123; use of term, 116
civil society organizations (CSOs), 35, 36, 37, 42

clientelism, 15
Communist Party of Vietnam, 68, 71, 77, 79, 81, 86, 145
Comprehensive Poverty Reduction and Growth Strategy (Vietnam), 66–103; debate about, 99; presentation of, 96–103; context of, 73–84; creditor interests: compliance with, 148; examination of, 146
Concern organization: Civil Society Development Program, 41–2; in Tanzania, 40–5
conditionalities, 24, 25, 70, 135, 145, 151; new, 136–9 (failure of, 146; perpetuate debt servitude, 150; political implications of, 146–9); reduction of, 10
conditions, portrayed as partnerships, 1
consultation: abuse of, 63; politics of, 135–62
corruption, 17, 22, 146
Country Assistance Strategy (CAS), 19
crowding out, problem of, 63

Dar es Salaam, National Consultative Workshop, 29
debt, 23, 82–4, 144; generated by aid cartel, 149; unsustainable, 146, 147, 150
debt relief, 2, 112, 130, 139, 140; in Honduras, 120; in Tanzania, 25, 29, 55; in Uganda, 9
debt servitude, 149; perceived inevitability of, 148
delinquency, related to poverty, 108
democracy, 37, 78, 102, 112, 135, 142; constitutional, hostility to, 8; fast-track, 51; negative effect of aid partnerships on, 144–5; representative, 52–60
democratic politics, and poverty reduction, 60–5
democratization, 104, 105, 146, 147; from below, 46
Department for International Development (DfID) (UK), 42, 49, 61, 94, 95
depoliticization: of civil society, 49–51; of policy formation, 8, 31, 50, 115, 128, 135
development, as conspiracy, 149
development agencies, niche creation by, 139
disbursement anxiety, 22
disciplinary power, 45–7
disjuncture between policy and politics, 52–5
documentary hygiene, 50
doi moi, 69, 70, 71, 77
donors, as part of the state, 9

Eco-Eco organization, 93
Economists' Association (Honduras), 118
education: access to, 26; related to productivity, 107
efficiency of aid management, 24
employment, promotion of, 29
empowerment, 38–52, 61, 63; of middle classes, 149; of previously excluded stakeholders, 145
'epistemic community' of economists, 128–9
equitization, 79–80
ESRF company, 49
Eurodad organization, 120
European Commission, 112
European Union (EU), 42, 111, 143
external actors, installed within domestic political space, 9

Farmers' Union (Vietnam), 92
Fatherland Front (Vietnam), 78, 92
Federation of Trade Unions (Vietnam), 100
Federation of Women's Associations (Honduras), 117
feminist movement, in Honduras, 133
Flores, R., 121, 127
food, access to, 26, 87
Food and Agriculuture Organization (FAO), 94
Foucault, Michel, 45

G-5 group, 110–11
G-15 donor group, 131–2, 113
gender, 91, 112

Germany, 111; donor to Honduras, 111
golden pentangle, 11
good governance, 26, 111, 112, 147; obsession with, 22
Gould, Jeremy, 36–7
governance, 45, 47; poor, 137; problems of, 23; reforms of, 58 *see also* good governance
Grassroots Democracy Decree (1998) (Vietnam), 94, 99
grassroots partnerships, creation of, 43
growth, 66; in Vietnam, 72–3
Gesellschaft für Technische Zusammenarbeit (GTZ), 94, 112

harmonization, 65, 143, 151; as site of power struggle, 22–4; politics of, 18–22
Harrison, Graham, 9
health care, access to, 26
Helleinder, Gerald, 17
Helleinder Report, *Development Cooperation Issues Between Tanzania and its Aid Donors*, 17, 19, 24
Highly Indebted Poor Countries initiative (HIPC), 2, 8, 18, 23, 25, 29, 55, 68, 83, 105, 109, 110, 112, 115, 119, 120, 121, 127, 130, 131, 137, 139, 141, 145, 146, 148, 150
Ho Chi Minh, 69
Honduras, 13–16, 142, 144, 145, 149; transition of concessional state, 104–34; US low intensity war in, 109
horizontal coordination of policies, 85
Hunger Eradication and Poverty Reduction (HEPR) (Vietnam), 81, 88
Hurricance Mitch, 14; as political opportunity, 121; damage caused by, 110; socio-political effects of, 104, 115, 117, 119, 120, 127; emergency aid, 110

indigenization of policy functions, 35, 49
Inter-American Development Bank (IDB), 111, 113, 131
Interforos coalition, 114, 119 134; decentralization of, 124; developments in, 124–6; formulates own poverty reduction strategy, 122–3, 133; origins of, 121–2
Interim Poverty Reduction Strategy Papers (I-PRSP), 25–6; Honduras, 114; Tanzania, 27, 30; Vietnam, 88–9
International Monetary Fund (IMF), 2, 3, 11, 17, 19, 24, 64, 70, 79, 82, 94, 98, 111, 114, 137, 139, 151; Enhanced Structural Adjustment Facility, 3; poverty reduction agenda, 49; Poverty Reduction and Growth Facility (PRGF), 3, 25, 89, 102; Poverty Reduction Support Credit, 103; report on Honduran PRSP, 122
International NGOs (INGOs), 66, 67, 73, 88; as donors, 103; complementing role of NGOs, 94; critical of NGOs, 93; Forum, in Vietnam, 91–2; presence of, in Vietnam, 89–92; religiously oriented, 118
Iraq, invasion of, 138
Irish Aid, 42
iron triangle of policy formulation, 5–6, 7, 9, 11, 23, 54, 141
Italy, 111

Japan, 76, 113, 143; donor to Honduras, 111; largest bilateral donor in Vietnam, 95
Japan Bank for International Cooperation (JBIC), 94
Japan International Co-operation Agency (JICA), 94, 112
Jensen, S., 114
Joint Staff Assessments (JSA) of World Bank, 10
Jubilee 2000, 39, 113
jumping scale, actors capable of, 145

Kepa organization (Helsinki), 120
Keynesianism, 129

Korea, South, 70

land reform, 131; in Vietnam, 71, 72
Latham, Robert, 9–10
Law on the Poverty Reduction Fund (2002) (Honduras), 112
local NGOs (LNGOs), 73, 92
local ownership of projects, 39, 85
localized modes of politics, 56

Maduro, R., 130–1
market integration, 22
market liberalization, 58
Marxism-Leninism, 77
Masasi Non-Governmental Organization Network (Mangonet) (Tanzania), 40–5
Master Plan for Reconstruction and Transformation (PMRT), 121–2 (Honduras)
Medium-Term Expenditure Framework (MTEF), 2–3
methodology of analysis, 4–8
micro-ization, tendency to, 50
middle class: aid dependence of, 148; empowerment of, 149; trans-nationally homogeneous, 149
Millennium Development Goals, 91, 94, 98, 100, 138 *see also* Adjusted Millennium Goals
Ministry of Labour, Invalids and Social Affairs (MoLISA) (Vietnam), 81, 88, 96
Ministry for Plannng and Investment (MPI) (Vietnam), 86, 88, 89, 96, 97, 98
Ministry of the Presidency (Honduras), 127, 129
Mkapa, Benjamin, 8, 18, 54
Morazán, Francisco, 124
multilateralization, paradoxes of, 22–4
mutual interest of state and donor actors, 6
Mwinyi, A.J., 17

National Association of Economists (Honduras), 119–20
National Bar Association (Honduras), 118
National Committee for the Advancement of Women (Vietnam), 93
National Poverty Monitoring Steering Committee (Tanzania), 31
National Poverty Eradication Strategy (Tanzania), 18, 26
Ndulu, Benno, 18
neo-liberalism, 104; convergence with populism, 7, 147–8
Netherlands, 111
New Forum of Civil Society (Honduras), 124
new public management, 137
ngo-ization, tendency to, 50
Nicaragua, 111; PRS process in, 123
Njoki, Joachim, 36
non-governmental organizations (NGOs), 36, 40–5, 59, 66, 88, 116; in Honduras, 105; in Nicaragua, 123; in Vietnam, character of, 92; policy elites, rebellion against, 134
non-state actors, 7; in Honduras, 132–4; participation of, 25–31; political opportunities, 24–5
Nyerere, Julius, 17, 27

OECD Development Asssistance Committee (DAC), 'Working Checklist for Strengthening Development Partnership', 19
opportunity structure concept, 12
'ownership' of policy, 2, 65, 146
Oxfam, 26, 49, 87, 90, 91, 143

parliament, 37; and policy formation, in Tanzania, 55–6; attitude of World Bank to, 53–5; marginal-ized from PRS process, 130
participation, 26, 36, 85, 114
Participatory Poverty Assessment Implementing Consortium (Tanzania), 32–4, 35, 36, 38
Participatory Poverty Assessments (PPA) (Vietnam), 87
partnership, 1, 2, 146, 150, 151; conceptualization of, 6–8; localization of, 3
party-state, 71
peasant organizations, 117, 123, 132

People's Aid Coordinating Committee (PACCOM) (Vietnam), 90
Phan Van Khai, 66
planning, improved, 98
pluralism in policy arena, 137; importance of, 65
Pol Pot, 69
policy coalitions, 9
Policy Forum for NGOs (Tanzania), 34
policy implementation, politics of, 56–7
poor people: amorphous notion of, 7; differing needs of, 32; lack of media voice, 108; voices of, 37, 38
population growth, 139
'post-conditionality' policy, 9, 10
post-developmentalism, 136, 137, 138, 148, 149; cross-cutting trends in, 14, 141
post-Washington consensus, 84–5
poverty: acceptance of, as central socio-political problem, 141–2; causes of, 31; related to low education, 107; seen as technical problem, 142; substituting for 'development', 97; use of terminology of, 97, 130 *see also* food poverty
Poverty Monitoring System (Tanzania), 25, 31–8, 42
poverty reduction, 67, 68, 72, 80–2, 84, 85, 87, 96, 98, 108, 113, 121, 142, 149, 150; and democratic politics, 60–5; consensus, 1–4; learning the language of, 145
Poverty Reduction Budget Support (PRBS), 23
Poverty Reduction Strategy (PRS), 3, 4, 11, 12, 21, 24, 51, 52, 57, 139, 145, 146; as standardized global strategy, 143; role of village institutions in, 60; processes of, 48, 104, 105, 106, 109, 110, 138, 140, 141, 142, 147 (as empowerment, 129; in Honduras, 123 (political implications of, 127–34); in Nicaragua, 123; reservations about, 135)
Poverty Reduction Strategy Papers (PRSP), 2, 3, 28, 29–31, 34, 35, 53, 54, 96, 107, 128, 148; processes, 103, 108, 114, 119, 150 (as rival to Agenda 21, 131; in Tanzania, 30, 62; in Vietnam, 66–103; Parliament's relation to, 130; understanding of, 55)
Poverty Task Force (PTF) (Vietnam), 86, 89, 90, 91, 93, 95
Poverty Working Group (PWG) (Vietnam), 86, 88, 90, 91, 93
private government, emergence of, 52
privatization, 58, 79, 118, 137; becomes equitization, 80
privatized modes of politics, 56
professional, connotations of term, 106
professional associations, Honduras, 118, 132
professionalization of development advocacy, 39
professionals in development, remuneration of, 150
pro-poor growth, euphemism, 50
pro-poor policy, 8–13, 40, 62, 135, 147; scepticism about, 60
Pro-Poverty Partnerships, 3
Pubic Expenditure Review (PER), 3
Public Administration Reform) (PAR) (Vietnam), 78–9
public consultation, demands for, 11
public policy process, 5–6
public/private discussion, redefinition of, 107

remuneration levels of professionals, 150
Repoa company, 49
Riles, Annalise, 47–8
Rodríguez, Cardinal, 112
Russia, 82

Save the Children organization, 49, 87, 90
self-reliance, grassroots, 27
Sen, J., 148
service sector, 73
Sida organization, 82, 90, 112
social cleansing, in Honduras, 107

Social Forum for Foreign Debt (FOSDEH) (Honduras), 120–2, 124–6, 127, 133
social sector spending, 7
socialism, 79
sovereignty, 16, 141; of policy making, 143 (eroded, 148, 150)
Spain, donor to Honduras, 111
state: concessional, transformation of, in Honduras, 104–34; employment, reduction of, 28; reform agenda, 2; relation to civil society, 46
state formation, 136–9
state of law, 112
stateness, redefinition of, 1
Steer, Andrew, 85, 96
Stockhom Declaration, 112; Follow-up Group, 111
strategic incentives in aid relations, 139–40
Structural Adjustment Programmes (SAP), 3, 8, 10, 46, 136, 137, as source of instability, 21
Sweden, 111, 113; donor to Honduras, 111; donor to Vietnam, 95

Tanzania, 8, 9, 13–16, 17–65, 141, 142, 144, 145; breakdown of relations with aid donors, 17; creation of, 14; debt relief of, 25, 29, 55; Local Government Reform Programme, 57–8; National Poverty Eradication Strategy, 26; Tanzanianization policy, 34–5
Tanzania Assistance Strategy, 18
Tanzanian Coalition on Debt and Development (TCDD), 26–8, 34, 40
taxation, 131, 137; substituted by foreign lending, 148
Technical Follow-up Group, 112
technocratization of policy formulation, 128–9, 134, 135
Thailand, 70
trade unions, in Honduras, 117–18, 123, 132, 133
transnational actors and local politics, 51–2
transnational policy elite, 135
transnational private aid agencies (TPAA), 34, 37, 38, 48, 49, 51, 52; as political actors, 39–45; as surrogate civil society, 50; in Tanzania, 38–9
transnationalization of political space, 8, 134
transparency, 52, 102, 111
Tweve, Godfrey, 35–7
two track policy process, 98

Uganda, 64; debt relief in, 9
Unidad de Apoyo Técnico (UNAT) (Honduras), 127–8
unilateralization through harmonization, 143
Union of Soviet Socialist Republics (USSR), 69
United Kingdom (UK), 111
United Nations Development Programme (UNDP), 40, 49, 82, 88, 94, 99, 100, 111, 114, 129, 131, 132, 140, 143; Foro de Fortalecimiento de la Democracia (FFD), 112
United Nations Research Institute for Social Development (UNRISD), 7
United States of America (USA), 111, 113; largest bilateral donor to Honduras, 111; Vietnamese exports to, 83
urbanization, 117
USAID, 49

Veterans' Union (Vietnam), 92
Vietnam, 2, 14, 66–103, 141, 144, 145, 149; agricultural production, 72; American blockade of, 69; American War, 68–9; application for WTO entry, 84; as HIPC, 76, 82; commitment to poverty reduction, 101; Comprehensive Development Framework (CDF), 84–5; exports to USA, 83; foreign direct investment in, 73, 76, 84; Living Standard Survey, 81–2, 86, 102–3; net exporter of rice, 72; three-sector approach, 73; ways of governing, 77–80
Vietnam Chamber of Commerce and Industries, 73

Vietnam Union of Science Technology Associations, 93
Vietnam: Attacking Poverty, 86
village institutions, role of, in PRS, 60

Washington Office for Latin America, 120
water, access to, 26
Weyland, K., 8
Wolfenson, James, 18, 122
women's movement, in Honduras, 133
women's organizations, ethnography of, 47
Women's Union (Vietnam), 90, 92, 93
World Bank, 2, 3, 10, 11, 17, 18, 19, 24, 49, 54, 55, 60, 61, 64, 66, 67, 70, 76, 79, 81, 82, 88, 90–1, 93, 94, 95, 98, 99, 111, 113, 137, 139, 140, 151; as lead donor agency in Vietnam, 102; attitude to Parliament, 53–5; Country Assistance Strategy (CAS), for Vietnam, 85–6; poverty reduction agenda, 49; Poverty Reduction Support Credits (PRSC), 3; report on Honduran PRSP, 122
World Trade Organization (WTO), 11; Vietnam's application for entry, 84
World Vision, 143

Zambia, 61